Religion

A Study in Beauty, Truth, and Goodness

KENT RICHTER

College of DuPage

D1451936

New York   Oxford
Oxford University Press

Oxford University Press is a department of the University of Oxford.
It furthers the University's objective of excellence in research,
scholarship, and education by publishing worldwide.

Oxford   New York
Auckland   Cape Town   Dar es Salaam   Hong Kong   Karachi
Kuala Lumpur   Madrid   Melbourne   Mexico City   Nairobi
New Delhi   Shanghai   Taipei   Toronto

With offices in
Argentina   Austria   Brazil   Chile   Czech Republic   France   Greece
Guatemala   Hungary   Italy   Japan   Poland   Portugal   Singapore
South Korea   Switzerland   Thailand   Turkey   Ukraine   Vietnam

For titles covered by Section 112 of the US Higher Education
Opportunity Act, please visit www.oup.com/us/he for the
latest information about pricing and alternate formats.

Published by Oxford University Press
198 Madison Avenue, New York, New York 10016
http://www.oup.com

Library of Congress Cataloging-in-Publication Data

Names: Richter, Kent E., author.
Title: Religion : a study in beauty, truth, and goodness / by
    Kent Richter.
Description: New York : Oxford University Press, 2016.
Identifiers: LCCN 2016001934 | ISBN 9780190291198
Subjects: LCSH: Religion.
Classification: LCC BL51 .R432115 2016 | DDC 200--dc23 LC record
available at http://lccn.loc.gov/2016001934

Printing number: 9 8 7 6 5 4 3

Printed in Canada on acid-free paper

TABLE OF CONTENTS

PREFACE

This text, *Religion: A Study in Beauty, Truth, and Goodness*, is the result of many years of trying to teach "Introduction to Religion" to freshman and sophomore students at the university level. I say "try to teach" because this course, from the outset of my teaching career, was difficult to organize, even with the help of texts from well-respected authors and well-established publishers. A course in "World Religions," it seemed, was always easier, so much focused on information organized according to the great religious traditions students, for the most part, recognized as "Hinduism," "Buddhism," "Christianity," and the like. But "Introduction to Religion" does not organize itself in this way; it requires one to step back from the raw data of religions' beliefs and practices and to develop a way to think about religion in general. One needs, apparently, an organizational tool for thinking about religion; it is not just presenting information from the world's religions themselves.

For this text, the solution to organization came in a growing appreciation for the abstract values of beauty, truth, and goodness. A brief paper I wrote on using these concepts as an approach to inter-religious dialog helped me think further about how different religions might work into this pattern without, I hope, sacrificing distinctive ideas and values within the respective faiths and traditions. Thinking about religion in terms of beauty, truth, and goodness also helped me place some value on religion itself, given that these three ideals are surely, both individually and collectively, values we might all hope to find, or at least claim to seek.

No doubt for some people ancient abstract values are no longer living ideals, just as, no doubt, some prefer the outsider's approach to religion over the insider's. In the end, these are choices the instructor must make. One benefit, however, of the approach that features beauty, truth, and goodness was that one can find an organizational approach that makes some sense and does some justice to the deeply interwoven nature of religion itself. That is, if we think of religion having aesthetic, cognitive, and behavior elements—each broadly construed so as to be open to many different religious forms—we can begin to see not only a list of these elements but even how they apply one to another: how ideas inform behaviors and behaviors lead to experiences and experiences change ideas. All this works together, I hope, to help us see religion less as a haphazard collection of ideas and actions and more as a way of life. It helps us see logic and coherence in what some might think is pure irrationality, and perhaps it allows us to see both why religion "works" in people's lives and why they struggle with it. All this, coupled with the basic value we might intuitively find in the ideas of beauty, truth, and goodness, might help us take religion seriously, whether we ourselves are "religious" or not.

At least this is how it worked for me, and my hope, of course, is that it might work similarly for the students and the instructors that use this text. In the end, the internal structure and theoretical ideals used in this text are intended as a useful schema. The text is also intended to be brief and yet to fill the schema with examples sufficient to make sense of the concepts and definitions used. A student, I hope, will find ample information from the world's religions so that his or her interest in the data of religious studies is piqued, and will find definitions and logical structures within the presentation that help him or her to make sense of how those data are lived and felt by real human beings.

My thanks go out to many people who helped me in the work of producing this text. The editors at Oxford University Press were astoundingly positive and encouraging, in spite of my general naivety about the project. Robert Miller and Alyssa Palazzo were wonderful. My colleague Peter Kanetis used the text in draft form, caught errors, and helped me see the text as generally useful. My former student and, now, good friend Jessica Price and my daughter-in-law Sandy Richter helped find pictures. Finally, several reviewers—James Lochtefeld, Thomas Martin, William Barbieri, Deanna Thompson, Linda Schearing, and others—offered both encouragement and very proper critique that helped me fix factual mistakes and find balance in presentation that my own eyes could never have seen. Even where I didn't follow their advice, I was concerned that I should have. As a result, any errors or mistakes in emphasis left in this text are purely my own. I hope that in spite of faults, the text can be a valuable learning tool to any who risk reading it.

Religion

INTRODUCTION

A COURSE CALLED "INTRODUCTION TO RELIGION" is neither a course on World Religions nor a Philosophy of Religion course. That is, we do not study the religions of the world one by one, with chapters on, say, Hinduism and Buddhism, Christianity and Islam; nor do we research and analyze religious concepts for their philosophical defenses, with arguments for the existence of God or discussions about the philosophical possibility of miracles. Rather, Introduction to Religion is the study of religion in a very general way, such that we can apply what we learn to a religion we already know well—perhaps our own—or to a religion we are just beginning to study. This general approach suggests we look at the contents of various religions mostly to understand how the elements fit together, how they function in people's lives, and how the religions present themselves as coherent and reasonable ways of life. At the end of a study like this, we might hope that a student can say, "Oh, that's why Christians call Jesus the savior," or "That's why Buddhists meditate." We might see better why "prayer" for a Christian is a bit different from "prayer" for a Muslim, and why a philosophical Hindu might not want to use the word "God" to describe Ultimate Being, but then again why the word might work after all.

That is not to say that we hope to come out of an Introduction to Religion course knowing everything there is to know about all the religions of the world. Of course, that's impossible. We hope to emerge from this course only with a vocabulary for understanding religion, a way of applying terms and concepts for getting inside what religions do and say, as they go about directing the lives of literally billions of followers all over the globe. The vocabulary developed here, we hope, works like a tool box, giving the curious student of religion a set of tools for studying, naming, comparing, and interrelating the various elements that make up different religions. I am not here trying to prove any particular religion true or false—nor, for that matter, to defend a religious way of life in general—but rather I am trying to help the reader develop a way to talk about religion intelligently.

Admittedly, deciding what it means to talk about religion intelligently is already a matter of some dispute in the study of religion. I have already hinted that this text makes an effort to "get inside" religion, but this language betrays a certain strategic choice in the way the text approaches the topic. Some would prefer to approach the study of religion from the outside, taking as their systematic approach the assumptions of psychological or sociological study and exploring how religion fits into these models. This text, however, is grounded on the assumption that the approach from the inside, an effort to see and feel and understand religion as if I were religious, would be more honest and fair, in some sense, to the material. To make oneself wholly an outsider invites the alleged joke of a music professor who said to a religious studies professor, "If we taught music the way you teach religion, no one would ever play a note."

This text, then, presumes that people will in fact play the notes of religion and that playing the notes is perhaps a good thing. It presumes that we might want to try to get a feel for what religious people actually feel, or understand what they actually believe, even if we ourselves neither feel it nor believe it. This phenomenological approach to religion seems, therefore, a valuable way to introduce the study of the various elements that go into a religion. More about the "phenomenological approach" in Chapter 1.

Reference to "the various elements" that constitute religion may seem unclear, but those elements become evident as the book progresses. They are, in fact, rather evidently listed in this book's table of contents. They are also listed, in a more mysterious way, in the title of the book, where Beauty, Truth, and Goodness are mentioned so prominently. These terms, as the part headings in this text indicate, suggest that there are specific and understandable things that religions tell us to feel, to believe, and to do. And it is one of the themes of this book that these dimensions of religion, like the various elements described in more detail chapter by chapter, are both individually distinct and deeply, intimately interwoven. It is my hope that by the end of the text, the reader will have a sense that, as complicated and messy as religions may seem, there is a kind of cohesiveness within religion, a logical connectedness that makes religion into an ordered and meaningful way of life.

Beauty, Truth, and Goodness are also used here because they are ultimate human ideals. That is, we want to experience beautiful things just because of their Beauty; we want to know truth just because it is Truth; and we want to do good just because it is Goodness. Thus the capital letters. Their order here, starting with Beauty, is partly because it seems religion starts with simply a sense of the wonderful, a feeling of awe perhaps that begins to make us think about the mysteries of life. Yet in this text, I start with "Truth" and end with "Beauty" because, almost inevitably, we must talk about the ideas of religion in order to move on to discuss religious action and, finally, religious experience. We shall see how these dimensions of religion in fact depend on one another, and how religions themselves emphasize different aspects of the religious phenomenon while, perhaps unavoidably, applying all three dimensions in various ways. Religions, I argue, make sense, but they are not simple.

None of this development of vocabulary and dimensions and models of religion should make us think that "all religions are the same." Such a claim is, for some people, a nice thought or even a hope, but it is certainly not a thesis of this book. In many ways we shall find that the claims of the world's religions are simply not reconcilable, their prescribed actions and even their varying religious experiences displaying important differences and contradictory assumptions. At the same time, commonalities and similarities are evident; there is, after all, something that makes the religions of the world "religions." Thus I shall discuss ways in which the unity of religions may seem promising but may also be problematic.

It should also not be assumed that the thematic development of this study of religion and its toolbox of religious terms is the only, or even the best, way to understand religion. For example, in Chapter 3 I talk about the founders of religion as "prophets" and "sages," noting the similarity in the concepts and their important differences. Could other terms be used to describe these ideas? Might there be a better, more illuminating vocabulary for understanding the similarities and differences between, say, Islam and Buddhism that is implied by these terms? Probably so. But the vocabulary of elements and key concepts that is developed here is, I hope, still a useful set of tools; and if the reader finds, upon careful thought and application of these terms to the wide variety of phenomena we see in the world's religions, that different, more nuanced concepts are better tools, that is great. For in the end, the goal is to understand religion, not to memorize a list of terms.

A similar caution should be added here about the overall rubric of this book that describes religion in terms of Beauty, Truth, and Goodness. I have come to appreciate this three-fold exploration of religion for the way it reveals the multifaceted nature of religion while hinting at religion's force and strength. Thinking in terms of these high ideals of human life has helped me appreciate different religions in different ways while avoiding any tendency to lump religions together into an oversimplified mass. As human ideals, these concepts also help me to see the very human face of religion while, as ideals *per se*, helping me look beyond the human, which, is, I think, where religions generally point. Thus the three-fold exploration of religion, I find, is a fruitful and meaningful way of thinking about religion. Again, it may not be the only way or the best way, but it is meant to be a useful, illuminating, and encouraging way to take religion seriously and thoughtfully.

In the end, my hope is that those who study religions as Beauty, Truth, and Goodness find something fascinating and powerful, whether in fact they are attracted to religion themselves or not. At the same time, however fascinating religion might be, this study is also a demanding intellectual effort. We must think and we must work hard in hopes of understanding this fascinating realm of human life. In a way, therefore, studying with this text is itself an endeavor in knowing, doing, and feeling, a miniature effort to mix truth and goodness and beauty. That, at least, is the intention of this text.

CHAPTER 1

DEFINING "RELIGION"

SOMETIMES PEOPLE RESIST DEFINING a word because they think it is more open-minded to leave ideas vague and unspecified. If we were talking about what books we like or our favorite flavor of ice cream, it might indeed seem wise just to admit that everybody has his or her own favorites and it makes no sense to try to define what a "good book" or "good ice cream" is. The problem becomes even more acute if we are talking about what we think a "good person" is, for in the process of trying to define what "good person" means, we might be quite aware that we could insult someone if he or she fails to fit our definition. We can note, however, that the problems here are not really about defining what a book is, or even (though this is more troubling) what a person is. That is, we don't debate whether, say, *The Lord of the Rings* is a book, or whether Julius Caesar was a person; our debate is about "good." And that is because there may seem to be something judgmental about that term, and many of us in the post-modern West think we should not be judgmental.

Similarly, when people try to discuss religion, they might feel that trying to define the word "religion" would put us in danger of being judgmental. This may be because the word "religion" seems to have a kind of judgment built into it. After all, isn't religion about higher truths, the meaning of life, the ultimate source and purpose of our very existence? If Person A is "religious" and Person B is "unreligious," we might automatically get a sense that Person B will be judged (at least by Person A) as wrong or bad. But let us suggest here from the beginning that the problem isn't with the word "religion," but with a kind of interest we might naturally have in what is the true religion, or the right religion. Like with the "good book" or even the "good person," the problem is not with the noun but with the adjective. And for this text, let me say from the outset that I shall not try to decide which religion is true—although that is, I will argue later, an unavoidable conversation—but I shall instead try to talk about what religion is. That might be much simpler.

On the other hand, it might still be quite difficult, because religion is just a hard thing to define. In a way, it is like trying to define some other vague and multifaceted form of human behavior, only worse. Consider, for example, how you might define "party" or "game" to some alien from another planet. Suppose you tell the alien that you went to a party, and the alien asks you what a party is. "Well," you say, "it's when a bunch of people get together and drink and laugh and have fun." The alien might ask if, then, a party has to have a minimum number of people, if it must include "drinks," and if sometimes people actually go to parties and have a horrible time. With such questions you might realize that your definition seemed to be wrong in every part, and yet it wasn't necessarily a bad definition. Notably, if the alien asked you to explain what a party is, and you replied, "It is a child's word for toilet," that would clearly just be wrong. That's "potty," not "party."

The point is, a definition doesn't have to be perfect to be useful, and it is clear that some attempts at definitions might just be mistaken. It might seem impossible to find exactly the right definition of something as vague and general as human religion, but we can certainly try to come up with definitions that are useful for understanding the varied and vague human phenomenon that people generally call "religion." And if we ever were to meet an alien who asked us to explain this human phenomenon, it would seem worth the risk of perhaps making mistakes or leaving some confusion if it helps the alien understand humanity a little more. In the same way, for those earthlings who want to study religion as a human phenomenon, we can take the risk of suggesting definitions, though we admit, even insist, that we will need to question, reconsider, and refine those definitions. But in the end, we hope, we might have a useful definition of this strange phenomenon that will help us understand what we're looking at, how it works, and who practices it.

As a final, opening point, note how many times I used the word "phenomenon" in the preceding paragraph. This word is used because many scholars have suggested that the approach we are taking in this study of religion is **phenomenological**. The "phenomenological study of religion" is an approach to studying religion that intentionally avoids discussions of which religion might be true or valuable and, instead, attempts to pursue simply a description of what the phenomenon is. Someday, perhaps, we must all sit with friends or ponder in the solitude of our hearts/minds and deeply consider whether a particular religion is true, or good, or beautiful. Indeed, that pondering is—as the title of this book suggests—almost unavoidable if we really understand the phenomenon of religion. But for this text, we are only trying to understand how religions themselves consider truth and goodness and beauty. And to do that, we must study religions phenomenologically.

This phenomenological approach should not make us think there are no other ways to approach the study of religion. The careful and academic study of religion in fields like sociology has great value for trying to understand the broad effects of religious belief and practice on social organization and cohesion, economic and political systems, family organization, and similar social structures. You will find such connections throughout this text, perhaps especially in Chapter 9. Similarly, the psychological study of religion helps us consider the effects of religious belief and practice on one's sense of identity or how one considers the value or disvalue of life and relationships. Here, too, various aspects of religious psychology are evident here and there in this book, perhaps notably in parts of Chapters 6 and 10. Inasmuch as sociology and psychology are rigorous academic disciplines, these approaches might involve careful appeals to statistics and experimental analyses that would give the study of religion a more scientific feel than we get from the phenomenological approach. But as the table of contents of this text might suggest, the human phenomenon of religion is much broader than either of these disciplines alone would suggest, and it is possible that these narrower foci would have the tendency to be reductionistic. I shall consider this notion of reductionism later.

For now, then, let us simply agree to use these academic disciplines where they are pertinent and to stay with the phenomenological approach. In this way, we may hope to see the broader picture of religion and perhaps even to get a bit inside the feel and belief of various religions as we endeavor to discover how the wide variety of elements that make up religion fit together into coherent and meaningful ways of life. Of course, to begin such a grandly hopeful study, we still have yet to define our key term: "religion."

TOO BROAD AND TOO NARROW

In the phenomenological study of religion, we must first undertake the problem of defining the object of our study. In taking steps toward defining "religion," let us not forget that we do indeed want to be open-minded and not judgmental. But, as already noted, that doesn't mean we must avoid having a definition of "religion" at all. Rather, it means avoiding the presumption that one religion is right and others are wrong. We may not go so far as to say that we, in fact, know that "nobody's right and nobody's wrong." Ironically, that would itself be a judgment about religious truth and would in fact amount to saying that anyone who does claim his or her religion is "right" would have to be wrong. For example, if a devout Muslim were to quote their scriptures, saying, "The true religion with God is Islam" (Quran 3:19), this would seem to contradict the more "open-minded" statement expressed previously. But as students taking a phenomenological approach to the study of religion, we may only note that Islam can be a somewhat exclusive religion. Other religions, we would find, are less exclusive. But it is not our job to assume that an exclusive religion is wrong and an inclusive religion is right.

So we approach defining "religion" not just by avoiding definition, nor by assuming that inclusive religion is good. But we do want an inclusive definition of "religion." That is, we want a definition of "religion" that somehow includes both Islam and Hinduism, Daoism and Judaism, Wicca and Christianity. We must avoid saying, "Religion is a human phenomenon in which people worship Jesus as savior," since it is clear that there are other religions that do not do so. This means it is indeed possible to make the mistake of defining "religion" by one's own traditions and contents, failing to see that a definition must be broad enough to contain many different phenomenological descriptions. If one were to define "book" as a printed story about Hobbits, one would clearly be mistaking one's specific interest in *The Lord of the Rings* for something much broader. Our definition of "book" must be broad enough to include *LOR* but also the Harry Potter books, not to mention *A Christmas Carol*, *The Cat in the Hat*, and even the textbook you hold in your hand right now (assuming you have a printed version). Certainly *LOR* (and the others mentioned here) are good examples of books, but the details of their contents do not define "book." Similarly, Christianity is a good example of a religion, but its specific contents do not define the category of all the things we call religions.

While it is thus quite possible—and quite common—for people to suggest a definition of "religion" that is **too narrow**, it is also possible to suggest a definition that is **too broad**. For example, suppose someone suggests this definition: "Religion is a set of personal beliefs." We might quickly note that this definition has so little content that it tells us almost nothing about religion. In fact, it is so broad that it seems to include almost anything people think about. Surely we all have personal beliefs about our favorite sports team, about our spouses and loved ones, about political candidates, even about the best way to make money and about the possibility of life on other planets. Yet in general, none of these beliefs constitutes religion.

But wait! Who's to say these are not religions? Why can't my beliefs about political candidates, for example, be religion? To answer that question, imagine this scenario. Imagine a man who is very involved in politics, does hours and hours of volunteer work for his favorite candidate, and badgers everyone he knows to solicit votes on his candidate's behalf. Imagine, too, that our man was raised Catholic, goes to church maybe twice a year (unless his campaign work intrudes), and barely cares at all about the moral and doctrinal teachings of the Church. If you talk to him, our fellow will likely only want to talk about the political situation and his hopes for the election of his favorite candidate. But if you directly ask him what his religion is, he would probably say, "I'm Catholic."

The point is that religious people themselves usually tell us what religion is. That is not to say that all people of all religions would use the term "religion" to define themselves and their practices. In fact, some people actively avoid the term for a variety of reasons, such as those who might prefer to say they are "spiritual" but not "religious." We might, upon examination, find that such a "spiritual" person has some disdain for the specific beliefs, or the organizational structure, or the explicit ethical ideals of the religions he or she knows, and therefore he or she prefers not to identify with any such specifics. But if we could have a slow and peaceful conversation with this person, we might ask if his or her spirituality implies any beliefs at all that can be communicated in order to find ideas shared with others. We might ask if these beliefs in turn have any implications for how like-minded believers interact, or if spirituality suggests any kind of practical responses, moral or ritualistic. In pursuing such a conversation, we might slowly find that our spiritual person does have beliefs and moral behaviors associated with this spirituality, and in this way we shall find ourselves talking about the truth, goodness, and beauty of religion, whether we want to use the word "religion" or not.

At the same time, we might find that our spiritual person just hasn't ever thought about it much. In that regard, we might find that he or she is a lot like our politically minded Catholic. That is, there may be some room in these people's lives for something like religion, but their greater energies and interests are overwhelmingly in something else. Yet these energies and interests do not make religion. Indeed, as we saw in the political Catholic example, one can have a religion and not be very interested in it. Thus we might have to conclude that, whatever "religion" means, we cannot define the term simply by how much it is practiced or understood. In passing, then, we can note that this definition, "Religion is a practice to which one is especially devoted," is probably too broad. People can evidently be quite devoted to things that are not religious and have little or no devotion at all to things that are.

All of this discussion, then, about definitions that are "too broad" or "too narrow," is meant to give us some general direction for what a good definition of "religion" might look like. Perhaps oversimplifying, we might say that a definition of "religion" is too narrow if it specifies contents too much and thus excludes genuine religions, and a definition of "religion" is too broad if it is so vague and unspecific that it would include non-religious phenomena. With that said (and perhaps sounding too much like the Goldilocks story), we should say that a useful definition will be neither too broad nor too narrow, but "just right." But how do we estimate "just right"? Let us look at my previous examples. "Religion is worshiping Jesus as Savior" was too narrow because it focused too much on a single tradition, Christianity, and thus had no place for seeing other religions as religions. At the same time, "Religion is a set of personal beliefs" is too broad because it can include many human phenomena besides religions. So, as simplistic as it sounds, a "just right" definition will be one that positively includes in the definition of "religion" those phenomena we generally recognize as religions, while excluding those that we don't. And if this sounds problematically circular—like defining a cat by it having whiskers and defining whiskers by their attachment to cats—it's because it is. But as I discuss in the next section, this circular way of defining religion by experimentally including and excluding candidates that fit or don't fit the definition is really pretty reasonable.

As a last point about the "too narrow/too broad" idea, consider that there is some quite useful thinking that can come from the application of these criteria. Sometimes a person might meet an atheist who insists he or she is "not religious," and yet someone might be inclined to reply, "But atheism is your religion." On one level it seems presumptuous to tell someone he or she has a religion when they insist otherwise. At the same time, there are interesting historical cases of groups whose practices were not called "religion" until that word, that title, became culturally useful. We can note, for example, the suggestion that the religious practices of some Native American groups were dismissed as "superstition" or "paganism" until the Native Americans themselves were willing to adopt the term "religion" and thus claim a kind of equality (at least under law) with the dominant religions of Christianity.[1] These examples suggest that the tendency to include the atheist was probably due to having a definition of "religion" that was too broad, and the tendency to exclude the Native American traditions was probably based on having one that was too narrow. Thus keeping in mind the dangers of the two opposite errors, defining religion too broadly or too narrowly, we might be able to construct a definition that helps us understand how people understand themselves.

THE DIALECTIC OF DEFINITION AND EXAMPLE

I noted in the previous section that there is a strange circularity in saying that we want a definition of "religion" that includes religions and excludes non-religions. This sounds circular because it seems as though we need to know already what religion is so that we can pick some examples of religions and non-religions that will in turn be used to test our definition. And if this seems like a troubling case of circular logic, that's because it is. Or almost.

In fact, what we see here is what this section title calls "the dialectic of definition and example." A dialectic, in general, is a system of thought or analysis in which two distinct parts work together, each one developing and adjusting the other. On one level, a dialectic can be as simple as a conversation between two people, whose opposing ideas are tried each against the other, until (we might hope) the two can come to some kind of honest agreement. In the dialectic described in this chapter, I merely note that there is a kind of mutual development going on between definitions of words and their application to examples. This is a general fact about definitions and examples. When I started this chapter, I considered defining "party" as a gathering of people that involved drinking and having fun. But it might have quite quickly become clear that there are a lot of parties that don't involve drinking (a 5-year-old's birthday party, for example), and perhaps we all know from experience that there are parties in which people don't have much fun. These examples then move us to reconsider the definition, refine it, and then try it again.

This work of defining a term and then trying it out is the dialectic of definition and example. In religion, there are a number of examples that nobody seems inclined to dispute. For example, Christianity and Islam, probably Hinduism and Buddhism, as well as lesser-known religions, like Jainism or Shinto, probably all qualify. From my earlier example, we might also want to include certain Native American practices or some forms of animism or shamanism or ancestor veneration that appear throughout native cultures all over the world. If we start with this list, we might already have an idea of how to build a definition: we will simply look for their common elements.

Unfortunately, common elements are not easy to find. For example, Christianity and Islam are clearly focused on God, while Jains and some Buddhists would insist they are

Figure 1.1 Though often depicted with a halo, the Buddha is not a god.

"non-theistic" religions. Even though one may readily find images of the Buddha that make him look godlike, Theravada Buddhists would insist he is only a man, though a man with uncommon insights into the meaning of life. Thus, if we try to define "religion" by a focus on God, we will have a definition that is too narrow, precisely because it fails to include Buddhism. That should then help us to broaden our definition, perhaps by accepting a more abstract concept of God or by suggesting that non-theistic religions might have other supernatural elements besides God.

At the same time, as we've seen, one might be tempted to avoid being too narrow, hoping to include Buddhism, by saying, "Religion, then, is a system of beliefs that guide people's behavior." Unfortunately, we now probably have a definition that is too broad. To test the definition, we can try out something generally not considered religion, such as an economic or political ideal. Surely, for example, Marxism qualifies as a system of beliefs that guides behavior, and yet it doesn't seem to be religion. Considering Marxism, then, will force us to be a bit more definite in our efforts to specify religion. In this way the examples—of religions and of non-religions—help us refine our definition in hopes of getting it "just right."

However, we can admit, at this point, that we may never get it just right. We might find that, after having wrestled some with defining "religion" and having a pretty good idea of our concept, there might still be borderline cases, or even examples that fail or fit our definition quite contrary to our intuition. In spite of all we've said here, we might work on a good definition and find in the end that our best effort yields a set of criteria such that, like it or not, atheism really is a religion, however much the atheist might protest. More realistically, what will we finally conclude about, say, Scientology or Confucianism? We might, using our carefully crafted definition, decide that they are religions, or that one is and the other isn't, and we might find Scientologists or Confucians who will protest. But at that point, we, like good scholars, can turn to our definition and turn to the contents of these two philosophies and try to explain to our friends how and why we have used this term. Some Confucians or Scientologists might suggest we have misunderstood their beliefs, or they might suggest that our definition needs further refinement. And if this conversation is peaceful, both points are good for discussion. Indeed, either way that discussion is simply more "dialectic," and it ultimately advances our understanding of religion.

REDUCTIONISM AND FUNCTIONAL EQUIVALENCE

A final clue toward helping us define the term "religion" comes as a kind of expansion on the problem of some definitions being "too broad." When people suggest, for example, that "religion is a set of beliefs or practices to which one is very devoted," they have probably given us a definition that is too broad. We have already seen why. But we might look more closely at why an idea like devotion figures so prominently in such a broad definition. And I will suggest that the reason is because there are many things in life that **function** like a religion but that are not religions. This requires explanation.

When we talk about someone being very devoted to a political party, or being an especially avid sports fan, or perhaps having a deep, deep appreciation for Elvis Presley, we might be tempted to say that these beliefs are like a person's religion. We can even imagine that someone would jokingly say, "Elvis is my god." But the point is that these are jokes. More accurately, they are metaphors. That is, we say someone's dedication to his sports team functions like a religion in his life, even though, ironically, his own religion might not be very important. Similarly, we might speak of someone who exercises daily or is always going to vote Democrat as doing so "religiously." When we use such a metaphor, we are saying that there are some beliefs and behaviors in a person's life that provide that person with the kind of direction and purpose—and, yes, devotion—that we might expect from a religion. Yet these beliefs and behaviors are still not religion. Thus we might say such things are "**functional equivalents**" of religion, or ways of life that function for people like a religion, but which are not religions.

Thinking about functional equivalents of religion can help us refine our definition of "religion" in two ways. First, they can help us avoid a common pitfall that I will call "reductionism." As the term suggests, **reductionism** happens when someone takes a relatively complex concept and reduces it to some simpler, and probably secondary, quality. As an example—perhaps one of questionable taste—if a young, newly married man says he really misses his wife, a humorous or perhaps cynical friend might say, "You just want sex." The friend might in fact be right to a degree; but on the other hand, he might be guilty of "reductionism." That is, he has taken a relatively complex relationship and reduced it to a single **element**. Surely we are not too bold when we suggest that sex is not the central element of the marriage relationship. At least, let us hope, it is not the only element.

I have already hinted that when we speak of reductionism in the study of religion, we commonly find it to occur when people—often scholars and philosophers—reduce religion to certain psychological or social functions. For example, if someone says, "Religion is a projection of a father figure into the heavens," as Sigmund Freud said,[2] he or she may be noticing something true about religion, but it is reductionistic to suggest that this is the full or best description of religion. Freud was confident that religion, so defined, was rooted in our psychological feelings of helplessness, thus the wish for a father figure whom we could count on for safety. Now, like the sex-minded friend in the previous paragraph, Freud might be partly right; certainly there are very important psychological elements to religions we encounter in the world. But Freud's description is certainly not a phenomenological one. That is, he is certainly not de-scribing religion the way people feel and understand it themselves. Rather, he has constructed a psychological theory and used it to interpret the phenomena, reducing (apparently) the whole of religion to this possibly peripheral element. Thus it is reductionism.

A similar form of reductionism occurs with Karl Marx's famous claim that "Religion is the sigh of the oppressed creature; it is the opiate of the masses."[3] For Marx, the very essence of being human lies in our ability to labor, and through our labor to create. Capitalism, he argued, is an economic system that makes one person labor (for example, in a factory) to create products that he does not subsequently own (rather, the factory owner does). Thus capitalistic labor "alienates" the worker from himself and leaves us all "oppressed." And to satisfy our sense of alienation, to give us a drug (the opiate) to calm our disquiet, we invent religion. Or so says Marx. Again, it is not necessary to argue here whether or not Marx has a good point about human economics or even human nature. We only need to note that his definition of "religion" again takes only one element—here religion's socio-economic functions—and makes it central to, even completely definitive of, religion. From a phenomenological perspective, this is once again reductionistic. As before, it is not necessary to say Marx is totally wrong, but we do need to see that his definition fails to describe the deeper, richer phenomenon that we call "religion."

Sometimes people who have a more or less negative attitude toward religion in general—or perhaps just to one religion in particular—are attracted to reductionistic definitions. When a person suggests that religious people are merely afraid of dying, or that they need "a crutch," or that they are just trying to find friends, he or she is dab-bling with reductionism. And such reductionism, I am suggesting, fails to give a full picture of the complex phenomenon that is human religion. It invites, moreover, the further error of easily mistaking functional equivalents for religions, inasmuch as we can find many ways to assuage our fear of dying, many practices that function like a crutch, and many social avenues for finding friends. We might imagine an older gentleman who plays golf "religiously" because staying busy and active helps him avoid thinking about the fact that he is nearing his own death. Thus golf might be for our gentleman a functional equivalent of religion, because it helps him cope with the fear of dying. But religion is much more than coping with this fear; probably so is golf.

So let us beware of functional equivalents of religion and the temptation to reduce religion to its psychological and social elements. At the same time, I have already noted repeatedly that these reductionistic descriptions of religion may not be totally wrong. This leads me to the second way in which speaking of functional equivalence can help us define religion. For what we learn from reductionism is not totally negative. It is a mistake to reduce religion to only these psychological or social elements, but it is not totally wrong to recognize that religion does have these elements. Indeed, the satisfaction of psychological and social needs is perhaps an important part of how religions function. That is why, as I have already noted, Sociology of Religion and Psychology of Religion are important and valuable academic disciplines.

The valuable part of this observation, then, can be found in the repeated use of terms like "function" and, less obviously, "element." Throughout the previous paragraphs, there are numerous uses of these terms, and you might notice that the preceding discussion does not deny that these functions and elements exist. Indeed, you will find in the ensuing chapters of this book useful definitions of the various specifiable contents of religion in general—religion's elements—and similar definitions of what religions do, the effects they have in human life—religion's functions. So we shall see that a focus on any specific element or function of religion is not a bad thing, but we do want to say here that such a focus cannot be sufficient for defining "religion." Consequently, we can actually learn a great deal about religion by asking ourselves how we think religions function and why. What are its elements? What makes religious elements function the way they do? How are religious elements different from similar elements in other, non-religious phenomena? When we start trying to answer such complex and intriguing questions, we will find ourselves advancing definitions of "religion."

GETTING AT LAST TO DEFINITIONS

At this point, the student might want to simply attack the problem of defining religion head on, inventing his or her own definition and trying it out. That is fine. But it is also often a good idea to realize that we are not the first people to try to think carefully about these things, and we can learn a great deal from those who have offered useful definitions of "religion" before us. Looking at others' definitions does not, of course, relieve us of the responsibility of constructing our own thoughtful and defensible definition. Even if we adopt wholesale another scholar's definition, it is still incumbent upon us to defend that definition, clarifying why it is a good definition, better perhaps than alternatives.

For example, anthropologist E. B. Tylor, coming from his nineteenth-century studies of primitive cultures, offered the simple definition that "Religion is belief in spiritual things." We can see right away that this definition distinguishes religion from other kinds of belief and doesn't make the mistake of saying religion is just "strong belief." Religion indeed seems to have something to do with belief, but it is also belief in (or about) a certain kind of thing, a specifiable religious element. We can use this clue later in constructing a longer, perhaps more complete definition. But here, with Tylor's definition, we might want to add that such belief has implications for people far beyond what they believe. Indeed, we might also find, as we work through the dialectical process noted earlier, that some religions emphasize belief more than others. For some, religion might be much more about a kind of behavior; for others it might be much more about a kind of experience or feeling. Indeed, stressing these elements of religion instead of belief might change the definition of "religion" quite a bit.

For another example, consider the ideas of Immanuel Kant. Writing in Germany in the eighteenth century, Kant developed very influential and detailed theories about the nature of human knowledge, objective morality, political theory, and more. In a book written late in his life, rather characteristically and somewhat presumptuously entitled *Religion Within the Limits of Reason Alone*, he suggested religion should be defined as "the recognition of our [moral] duties as divine commands." Notable in this definition is Kant's great focus on the element of morality. Not particularly religious himself, Kant was nevertheless sharply focused on morality and considered our sense of moral law and moral duty to be perhaps the most wonderful aspect of our humanity. Yet if he had simply said religion is devotion to morality, we might well have said his definition was reductionistic. Thus we note that Kant did not define religion merely as being moral. Morality, no doubt, was for Kant a key element of religion, probably its most essential part, and Kant probably was quite confident that one could be entirely moral without being religious (something I discuss again in Chapter 8). But he also realized that religion added something to our devotion to moral law. Religion added some sense that moral law had a connection to a divine being.

Yet another example: Writing in Germany about a generation after Kant, another, perhaps more spiritual philosopher named Friedrich Schleiermacher suggested that "the essence of religion consists in the feeling of absolute dependence." For Schleiermacher, it was not that ethics was unimportant; but he seemed to see that religion carries with it an aesthetic component, a "feeling." It is not clear in this definition what one feels dependent upon, and in one sense Schleiermacher's definition might be in danger of being far too broad. But there is some help in his addition of the word "absolute." For any young boy is probably dependent on his parents, and employees are perhaps dependent on getting paid a salary from work, but no one would say this "feeling of dependence" was religion. No, there is something about the religious feeling that makes it deeper, final, or, to use Schleiermacher's term, absolute. And even if the definition as Schleiermacher gives it seems vague, still too broad perhaps, he seems to realize that he has to point our dependence toward something greater than parents and paychecks.

Clearly, we could multiply trial definitions for several more paragraphs, and all of them could be appeals to some great scholar, anthropologist, or philosopher. The twentieth-century theologian, Paul Tillich, suggested religion is "a state of being grasped by an ultimate concern . . . which itself contains the answer to the meaning of life." In this definition, we might see something like a feeling, similar to Schleiermacher's definition, but we might also see something about belief in his connection of the feeling to finding an answer to what life is all about. Another anthropologist, Anthony Wallace, writing about 100 years later than Taylor, suggested "religion is a set of rituals, rationalized by myth, which mobilizes supernatural powers. . . ." Evidently, he, like Taylor, saw that religion must be connected to spiritual beings, if that is what he meant by "supernatural powers." But notice that his first emphasis is on ritual, a kind of activity, rather than a kind of belief. In that sense, his definition is less like Taylor's and more— perhaps surprisingly—like Kant's. That is, for Wallace, religion is primarily not about what people believe, but about what people do.

In all these definitions—and in many more we could muster—patterns might begin to emerge that will ultimately inform a definition of "religion" used in this book. But before getting to that, we might look at one more source of a definition: the dictionary. It is almost certainly a temptation—or maybe a very reasonable choice— simply to turn to a good dictionary to find a definition of a tough word. That, after all, is what dictionaries are for. So when we look up "religion" in *Webster's New World Dictionary of the American Language*, we can confidently quote this: "Belief in a divine or superhuman power or powers to be obeyed and worshiped as the creator(s) and ruler(s) of the universe." That may be useful, but then we look farther. Definition #2 says religion is "Any specific system of belief, worship, conduct, etc., often involving a code of ethics and a philosophy." Is that the same? Is it better? Worse? We may keep looking. Definition #3 says religion is "the state or way of life of a person in a monastic order." Unless one automatically knows what this means, this definition will be misleading. Finally, a fourth definition says religion is "any object of conscientious regard and pursuit," which is, more or less, a definition we have already considered as clearly too broad. All this is to note that a dictionary might help, but it might not. Quoting a dictionary in order to get a definition of a term as tricky as "religion," like quoting philosophers and anthropologists, is not a bad idea, but the quotation alone is insufficient. We are still going to have to decide what elements the definition is highlighting, whether those elements are truly central to religion, and whether there are still other elements the definition omits. Amazingly, we never quite escape the challenge of having to think for ourselves.

A WORKING DEFINITION OF "RELIGION"

It may seem to be long overdue, but let us at last turn to offering a definition of "religion" that can serve as a work in progress for this text. From all that has gone before, we might see some patterns emerge that can help us focus on the elements that seem most central to religion in general, and then, as we go through the book, we will go into detail in examining these elements and dialectically try our definition against examples. By the end of this section, we shall have a trial definition; by the end of this book, perhaps we will be able to decide if our working definition actually works.

The proposed definition of "religion" to be used in this text might be something like this: "**Religion** is a complex set of beliefs, behaviors, and experiences rooted in some notion of transmundane reality thought of as Ultimate Being." A hint of this definition actually appears in the subtitle of this book: *Beauty, Truth, and Goodness*. Admittedly that title phrase is obscure, perhaps too poetic, but the same basic elements of religion are noted there that appear in the more formal definition. That is, where this working definition speaks of belief, the title inserts the dramatic word "Truth." Similarly, where the more prosaic definition mentions behavior and experiences, the title of the text uses the terms "Goodness" and "Beauty," respectively. Thus Beauty, Truth, and Goodness correspond in the proposed definition to religious experiences, religious beliefs, and religious behaviors. And a "complex set" of these elements is thus the focus of the definition.

We can see these elements in the definitions we examined in the previous section. We noted there how many of the definitions focused on belief, such as in Tylor's "belief in spiritual things." Others, like Kant's, clearly focused on morality, on the "Goodness" aspect of human life. And finally others, like Schleiermacher's and Tillich's, seemed to emphasize some kind of feeling, an inner experience that somehow lies at the center of the phenomenon of human religion. And all of them were right. That is, it might be a benefit of the definition we propose in this section that we try to include all three elements, precisely because each of those elements alone seems insufficient.

But there is more. Our general human desire to know what is true, to do what is good, and to experience what is beautiful is something we find far beyond the realms of religion. Why, after all, should a scientist study the physical makeup of some galaxy where no human will ever go and no practical result may ever give us cleaner energy or better medicine? It seems that much human effort goes into our desire for knowledge just because we desire knowledge. That is, truth seems to be a high and glorious human ideal, whether we see the practical benefits of it or not. Similarly, artists of all kinds echo the famous slogan that encircles the head of the roaring lion we see at the beginning of MGM movies: *"Ars Gratia Artis,"* art for art's sake. Art—and we might add sunsets and blooming roses—does not seem to be about science or about practicality; it is about beauty in and for itself. And finally, when we think of morality or human rights, we might be willing to admit—though there are many philosophical theories about this that are beyond the scope of this book—that perhaps the highest and best motivation for trying to do something morally good is just because it is morally good. Thus truth and beauty and goodness drive us as humans in a wide variety of ways, many of which are not evidently religious.

But this is where the definition of religion goes on. When we want to understand the source and meaning of our lives, or understand the deepest nature of our own selves or the possibility of our eternal destiny, we are seeking some kind of "truth" that is more than—or, at least, different from—what the scientist is doing. Even in Tylor's definition the focus is not just on belief but on belief in "spiritual things." Similarly, while Kant in his own ethical writings may not have had much place for God, his definition of "religion" takes moral duty and necessarily connects it to some sense of the divine. In the same way, a definition that tries to connect belief, behavior, and feelings declares them to be "rooted in some notion of transmundane reality." And this, it can be argued, is what makes religious belief, behavior, and experience into the quest for Truth, Goodness, and Beauty. The capital letters are not just because those words are in a title; the capital letters reflect the sense that religion points us toward Something greater and higher than the world of scientists, moral theorists, and artists. Religion points us toward Something that is beyond our normal world—that is what

Figure 1.2 Using religion-like imagery in its propaganda posters, the communism of Mao Zedong's China may have been a "functional equivalent" of religion. The people hold aloft the Red Book of Mao's sayings.

"**transmundane**" means, after all. Thus the capital letters on Truth, Goodness, and Beauty; thus the capital letter on "Something."

So what is this Something? In definitions we looked at previously it seems to appear, as I just noted, in words like "spiritual" or "divine." In other definitions we may find it hidden in concepts like "absolute" or "ultimate," or hiding in plain sight in Wallace's reference to "supernatural." In the world's religions, against which we must try out any proposed definition, we will encounter our mysterious Something in notions like God, gods, spirits, ancestors, Brahman, Dao, *kami*, and others. We shall also find that the Something does *not* seem to appear in non-religious contexts, such as a strong commitment to a social system, a sports team, or a political candidate. Thus we hope that our definition is neither too narrow nor too broad. One could argue, of course, that some example—ancestors or the Dao—fails to be a properly supernatural Something, or one could argue that Elvis or Mao Zedong should in fact be on the list. And we can be open to these suggestions. In fact, a deeper discussion of the nature of transmundane reality in many religious examples is the focus of Chapter 2.

Meanwhile, here in Chapter 1, I can conclude my offering of a definition of "religion" by noting how the rest of this text unpacks the contents of belief, behavior, and experience. Part I, for example, emphasizes "Truth" and deals, as noted, with religion's various beliefs about the transmundane Something, but also with what various religions teach about their own historical origins, about scriptures and the authority of beliefs, about the nature of creation, and about human life and human destiny. In Part II, various chapters consider "Goodness" in terms of how religions supply the contents of, and the authority behind, morality, social order, and even government. This part also discusses the behavioral aspect of religion that we commonly call ritual. And finally, Part III attempts to deal with religious experiences directly, but also how art and natural beauty apply to religion, and how religion seems ultimately to promise a kind of final fulfillment of all it means to be human. These are grand ideals indeed.

Yet the greatness of these ideals should not surprise us. Even those who would reduce religion to forms of psychological comfort or sociological control recognize the kind of power religion has in offering comfort and meaning on a personal level, as well as organizational structure and moral guidance on a social level. For good or ill, religion is one of the most powerful human phenomena in the world. Those human practices that are functional equivalents of religion seem to function like religions precisely because of the way they help people find direction, learn to understand who they are, where they come from, and where they are going. Thus those human phenomena that are *like* religions find that likeness precisely in their ability to give people beliefs they can hold, ideals they can use to guide behavior, and a variety of feelings that they seem to find meaningful. We might have suspected, therefore, even by looking at examples and definitions that don't quite fit the model of religion, that religion itself would give people explanations of reality that they hope are true, directions for morality and society that they consider good, and experiences of meaning, purpose, and joy that they find beautiful.

KEY TERMS IN CHAPTER 1

elements (of religion) The various specifiable contents of religion in general.

functional equivalents (of religion) Ways of life that function for people like a religion functions, but which are not religions.

functions (of religion) Specifications of what religions do, the effects they have in human life.

phenomenology (as a study of religion) An approach to studying religion that intentionally avoids discussions of which religion might be true or valuable and, instead, attempts to pursue simply a description of what the phenomenon is.

reductionism   The definition or study of a relatively complex concept (like religion) that reduces it to some simpler or secondary quality (such as religion's social functions).

religion (this text's proposed definition)   A complex set of beliefs, behaviors, and experiences rooted in some notion of transmundane reality thought of as Ultimate Being.

too broad   The nature of a definition of "religion" that is so general, specifying so little content, that it includes human behaviors that are not religion.

too narrow   The nature of a definition of "religion" that specifies too much content and so omits some religions.

transmundane   Having the quality of being beyond the normal world.

PART I

TRUTH, OR WHAT RELIGION WOULD HAVE US BELIEVE

THE WORD "TRUTH" IS not a particularly comfortable term. Especially when we talk about religion, it seems that we in the post-modern West may be rather disinclined to discuss religious ideas in terms of truth, preferring perhaps to stick with less challenging words like "belief" or "opinion." For we might think that people can disagree amicably about beliefs and opinions, but if someone is going to claim that his or her religion contains truth, the person almost immediately seems to us closed-minded. At the very least, if I think my beliefs are true, I seem to be saying that someone else's beliefs are false. And we don't like that.

But there are at least two reasons to use the word "truth" anyway. First, recall from Chapter 1 that we are looking in religion for some rather grand ideals; that is why I put a capital letter on "Truth" in the first place. So, to make things even more uncomfortable, we might be talking here not merely about "truth," but about "Truth." And if that makes us uncomfortable, perhaps it should. For religions do make rather significant claims about themselves, about the value of their teachings and their practices, about the fulfillment of life that can be found in these beliefs and practices, and so on. Trying to be so nice that we don't offend others or challenge ourselves rather ignores the importance that religious truth claims have in many religions. So there is something right—speaking again phenomenologically—about letting the Truth of religion challenge us. To insist that we are really only talking about beliefs or opinions is not to study religion phenomenologically; it is to force our twenty-first-century sensitivity onto the entire study of religion.

The second reason to risk using the word "truth"—or even "Truth"—is to avoid another twenty-first-century pitfall: the tendency to think that the only kind of genuine truth in human reason is found in science. Huston Smith, a scholar of world religions with a very interesting pedigree of study, ranging from Christian missionary work in China to hallucinogenic experiments in Chicago, once suggested that we make a mistake if we give science the whole realm of truth, when in fact science is a relatively restricted area of human thought. This is not to say that science is bad; quite the contrary. Science is a powerful tool for the ongoing human effort to understand the world around us and to make it useful to us as technology. But science is an area of human rationality that requires a strict method of repeatable experimentation and a tendency to reduce observations to mathematical formulae. And that is certainly a good thing, except that a great deal of human experience does not yield itself to this kind of rationality. Neither history nor political theory, let alone philosophical studies of morality and, indeed, religion, lends itself to a scientific method. Yet it would be a mistake to abandon these areas of human experience to the irrational. People can and do think logically and carefully about history and politics and ethics and religion, and it is good that we have a noble term like "truth" to reward their efforts. It is also good that we don't, as Smith says, give science a kind of blank check to define in its own terms all that we as human beings think and do and feel.[1]

So there is good reason to risk using the word "Truth" in our study of what religions would have us believe. But it is indeed a risk, and we are not mistaken to use the word with caution. Clearly it is not our purpose in this book to decide which religion—if any—is true, but it is our purpose to take religious truth claims as seriously as religious people themselves do. Even so, we must now admit that how seriously people take their religious truth claims varies from one religion to another. As you will see herein, some religions are much more insistent than others about the exclusiveness of their truth claims. Some religious followers tend, in fact, to avoid stating beliefs in some propositional form, precisely because they would rather emphasize the moral or experiential side of their religion. And when it comes time to consider how these people give weight to their experiences, their morals, and their rituals, we shall have to take those claims seriously, too.

Yet here is a paradox: When we find some religious writers emphasizing religious experience or religious behaviors over religious truth claims, we shall be looking, ironically enough, at what they say. This means, even when someone would rather not emphasize a truth claim and would instead emphasize an experience, he or she will make this emphasis in a number of ways which include making truth claims about the relative importance of experience. Actually, when we discuss the nature of religious language and storytelling in Chapter 5, we will note how some teachers of religion in fact finally prefer to stop talking; instead, they use actions or even just silence as the best way to teach the meaning of their religion. Yet even when we discuss the religious uses of silence, we go on discussing. In the end, this is, after all, a book on religion, and that commits us to using words, even if only to say that some religious teachers would rather we didn't.

Thus we begin this analysis of religion with a discussion of religious truth. In particular, we begin in Chapter 2 with a discussion of what religions mean by that which our working definition calls Ultimate Being. In Chapter 3, I look at what the religions of the world say about their own origins, where and when and through whom we finite humans have been introduced to Ultimate Being, and how dependable our understanding of this great Something can be. We will find, going on to Chapter 4, that the sources of religious beliefs often end up being finalized in written words, in books that become scripture, thus establishing a kind of authority for what is believed—and done and felt—in the human relation to the transmundane reality. The discussion of the origins of religions and of their sacred writings brings us into the realm of discussing history, yet we quickly find that "history" is often more like legend, legend like myth. Consequently, in Chapter 5 we have to consider how to read and understand religious storytelling and instruction, so that, once again, we might be cautioned about how we use a word as powerful as "Truth." And finally, here in Part I, we use Chapter 6 to discuss a variety of religious beliefs that often are more or less finalized in doctrines and teachings about who we are and why we exist. By that time, whether or not we are convinced about the truth of any such religious beliefs, it will be time to reconsider "Truth" and reassess what we've seen before we press on to discuss "Goodness."

CHAPTER 2

CONCEPTS OF
ULTIMATE BEING

RELIGIONS ARE ABOUT RELATING ourselves to a greater Reality, the tremendous Something that we have been calling Ultimate Being or transmundane reality. Yet precisely because this Something is transmundane, it is not very easy to talk about what it is. Indeed, as I have just noted, it might be preferable in some religions not to talk about it at all.

Yet I have just argued that talking about the greater reality is, in some ways, unavoidable. Even those who would tell us that Ultimate Being cannot be explained or described do so by talking to us. Ironically, perhaps, even words like "ineffable" and "indescribable" are descriptions. One famous description of the great Something within religion was offered by Rudolf Otto (1869–1837), who tantalizingly described It as a "*mysterium tremendum et fascinans.*" This Latin phrase translates (rather unmysteriously) as "the tremendous and fascinating mystery," and it was Otto's contention that we recognize in this description something essential to the gods and spirits and powers and forces of religion that seem to lie beyond our ability to understand. There is certainly great mystery here, we shall see, but it is not a mystery we can easily ignore, for it is a wonderful mystery. There is Something "out there" that attracts us (the fascinating, or *fascinans*, part of the concept) and scares us (the terrifying, or *tremendum*, part) at the same time. It may seem strange, but it is utterly common within Biblical language, for example, to speak of both fearing and loving God.

"God" is, of course, one option when we speak of Ultimate Being. It would be a mistake, however, to think that God is the only term, or the best term, for Ultimate Being. As we describe the Ultimate Being in this chapter, therefore, we shall have to use a strategy similar to that adopted in Chapter 1, namely defining a term with an effort to be both broad enough to be inclusive and narrow enough to be helpful. Also, we shall generally adopt the strategy of using examples to test our definition. That which some religions call "God" may be an important example of Ultimate Being, but we cannot narrow Ultimate Being down to that example. By the same token, someone might want to say that others' "ultimate being" can be whatever they feel it is, whatever is "great" to them, but this would be such a broad understanding of Ultimate Being that it would be quite unhelpful. Once again, definitions that are too narrow and those that are too broad should be rejected.

But what options do we have? We know that we are seeking a definition of "Ultimate Being" that is broad enough to include concepts other than God, but at the same time narrow enough to exclude someone's favorite sports team. More philosophically, perhaps, we can begin to recognize abstract qualities in our ideas of Ultimate Being that can help us develop our definition. We see right away, for example, that when we talk about Ultimate Being we are talking about something ultimate. This trivial point is not without value. For when we think of **ultimacy**, we think of a kind of finality, something (or Something) that is at the end of a search, the last and final thing that makes sense of everything else. Others have written of the "logic of the holy" in these terms, noting that for anything we consider holy or sacred (such as a holy book or scripture), we can find a greater power or authority that is the source of its holiness. But ultimately, we must come to find Something (such as God) that just is sacred in itself, a power that "just is."[2] Of course, this is not enough for us to describe all those Beings that the world's religions hold to be ultimate, especially still focused on "God" in this example. To clarify the idea further and more broadly, we simply have to begin looking at the examples that the religions present in their own terms.

We shall see, therefore, that the study of the various religions' cases of Ultimate Being will help us explore and describe the tremendous and fascinating mystery. We shall find similarities between ideas like God and Dao and Brahman, as well as animist spirits and ancestors, that help us to understand the Reality that is at the very core of religion. Then, as we explore their similarities and differences, we will begin to see how they seem to share traits of transcendence and mystery, power and greatness, that make them, for their devotees, the wonderful and fearsome "Somethings" that they are. As we gather this information, we shall be constructing a definition. Naturally, some examples will seem to fit the definition better than others, but in the end, hopefully, we shall have some understanding of this mystery that makes religion religious.

GOD AND GODS

We noted even in our first efforts to define "religion" that some definitions will tend to focus on the worship of God. For those people accustomed to the religious contexts of Judaism and Christianity and Islam—and this accounts for half the world's population—this idea of God is indeed central. It is only one idea of Ultimate Being among several, but it is a very widespread and powerful conception, and that requires us to take some time to explore what people mean when they speak of God.

In the Judaic religions, God—and "Allah" is merely the Arabic word for "God," or technically "the God"—is understood to be the creator of all things, thus somehow before all existence and independent of it. God is said to be powerful enough merely to speak "Be" and things exist. God in the Torah, the scriptures of Judaism (and part of scripture for Christianity), names himself "I AM," a name medieval philosophers thought indicates that God's existence is absolute and independent. As I already noted in the logic of religion, other things depend on the Ultimate Being in order to be considered holy, but the Ultimate Being just is "the holy." Similarly, other things depend on God for their existence, but God "just is."

As God sits outside and before all creation, and as creation is itself dependent on God, we may say that God is **transcendent**. This word primarily means to express God's existence as being beyond and outside of all we think of as time and space. And yet, at the same time—again, according to the Judaic religions—God oversees the history and meaning of his created worlds, interacting, to various extents and at various times, with people to whom he delivers his message and guidance. God concerns himself with human lives and cares about human morality, promising at times rewards or punishments, blessings and curses for human individuals and entire nations. So while God is transcendent, far beyond this paltry, finite existence, God can love or hate, speak and call, command, judge, and forgive.

Generally, we call belief in God or gods "**theism**," from the Greek word *theos*, meaning god. The idea of one single God is "**monotheism**"; belief in multiple gods is "**polytheism**." The distinguishing mark of theism, however, is that this kind of spiritual, transmundane power is personal, or personified. When we describe theism as belief in a personal god, we do not mean to express some individual subjective belief, as if we say, "This is my personal god, but your personal god might be different." Rather, we mean that God has personal traits, the kind of qualities of mind and emotion that we associate with persons, rather than, say, animals or plants. When we speak of the monotheistic idea of Allah, then, to say God is personal is to stress that Allah is like a person, having plans and intentions, interacting with human beings as if through speech. God is, in a way, like a human mind (though infinitely greater), having thoughts and emotions, and so the Jewish and Christian scriptures speak of God's instructions and God's words, along with His anger and love.

Similar descriptions can be found with polytheism. The gods of popular Hinduism interact with human beings rather directly, often in stories of how they manifest among human populations to speak and even physically embrace their worshipers or fight their foes. Vishnu, for example, is said to have descended into physical form numerous times and is especially worshiped as Rama or as Krishna. These "descend-ings" of Vishnu are his **avatars**, a term obviously borrowed in recent times to describe real people's "descent" into online gaming and other forms of participation in the "lower world" of the Internet. In Hinduism, the avatars, gods in human or animal forms, can have wives and children, friends and lovers of various kinds. They fight in battles, have birth legends, and perform magical and heroic deeds. Like the ancient Greek and Roman gods, they can be glorious or apparently flippant or flawed.

All of this may seem to raise problems for the concept of theism, inasmuch as our Ultimate Being is supposed to be transcendent and beyond all worldly limitations, but can seem in polytheism to be all too human. Even in monotheism, to attribute emotions and relationships to God may seem limiting and **anthropomorphic**. This term etymologically means "having human form," and it might seem that anthropo-morphic gods are simply human beings made bigger. It is arguable that this is true in many cases and might be a powerful critique of theism from a philosophical point of view. At the same time, any human-like characteristics, according to the medieval philosophers of Christianity and Islam, are not meant to show that we have created for ourselves a human-like deity, but rather that God has created us to be persons like Himself. God is not anthropomorphic, they would say, but rather we are "theomorphic."[3]

Other examples of gods in the world religions can be examined to show variations on the idea of a personal deity. In indigenous religions, nature itself is thought to be populated with a wide array of spiritual beings that live within the inanimate objects of nature. Indeed, our word "inanimate" literally means having no soul (*anima* = soul), but for many native cultures around the world, nature is very much animate. Trees, rocks, rivers, along with various living creatures like plants and animals, are not inan-imate at all, but are persons with whom the people interact, in order to succeed with hunts and harvests and to avoid disaster. Angry spirits in the water or the wind can kill; happy spirits with whom we retain a good relationship reward us with health and prosperity. This belief in spirits that inhabit nature and interact with people is called **animism.**

Also common in indigenous religions is worship of ancestors, and these spirits, often interwoven with natural objects, are understood simply to be human beings who have died and become spiritual beings. The notion of humans becoming gods is not as strange as we might think, inasmuch as there are multiple cases of perfected and idealized human beings in India and China as well. While the Buddha and Mahavira, the respective founders of Buddhism and Jainism in India, are not gods, we find that in both religions the popular movements of devotion that develop within those religions elevate Buddhas and Tirthankaras to the status of special, all-knowing, transcendent persons, sometimes able to hear our worship and even answer our prayers.

Figure 2.1   A typical pose for Guan Yin, bodhisattva of compassion.

In many of the cases of polytheism or animism or deified humans, the problem of anthropomorphism reappears. Didn't we start this discussion of Ultimate Beings with the emphasis on the absolute creator? Haven't we been noting the logic of how all that is holy and ideal ends in some transcendent reality? So how can God be merely one of many gods or be merely a man? Indeed, these are questions worth pondering. Christianity offers an interesting and singular case of pondering this problem, inasmuch as Christians believe that the human being Jesus of Nazareth was also an incarnation (literally, "in-flesh-ment") of God. Thus, they say, Jesus was a man clearly capable of suffering and in need of food, and yet also the one divine creator God. How can this be?

For Jews and Muslims, the answer is simple: It can't be. Muslims in particular (as we will see in the next chapter) recognize Jesus as a prophet, but would never believe that Allah would become incarnate as a human. For Hindus, the answer is equally simple: there are many, many human-divine beings, and Jesus may be one more. But for Christian monotheists, the problem is a tough one. To solve the problem, Christians debated ardently the idea of Jesus' "two natures." They claimed that he was clearly human, such that he could suffer limitations and even death, yet he was also divine, such that his omnipotence and transcendence remained unchanged. Ultimately, the issue found its resolution in the development of the doctrine of the Trinity, stating that God is three persons in one eternal being, and that Jesus is the incarnation of God the Son, the "second person" of the Trinity. Yet this was emphatically not polytheism, the Christians say, nor was the incarnation of the Son a change in his divinity. Christians debated the relation of the Son to the one triune God, along with the interrelation of Jesus' two natures, for centuries, and arguably the discussion is still not over.

MONISM

Though we have used Hinduism as an example of polytheism, some Hindus would insist that this religion is not polytheistic but monotheistic. In that argument, the person might be claiming that all the gods are really manifestations of one God, Vishnu, for example. Others will push this monotheism further and suggest that the one God that manifests as all the gods is less nameable, more obscure, without a mythology or any divine family or divine-human interaction. This greater abstraction finds its culmination in the concept of Brahman, a Hindu idea that emerged in the last of the early Hindu scriptures and became the foundation for much philosophical Hindu speculation. This idea of Brahman thus becomes for us no longer an example of theism, but of monism.

"**Monism**" refers to belief in an ultimate reality that is single and unique, like God, but not personified. Even in the word, we see the "mono" indicating oneness, but there is no *"theos."* Thus, in an interesting way, even materialistic atheists are monists, inasmuch as they believe that there is only one substance to reality, namely the physical substance we know through our senses and study with our science. But in religion, monism refers to the idea of a single, absolute Ultimate Being, somehow behind or within the world we know, somehow the substance of all creation. We can say It is eternal and absolute, ultimate in the sense we have been considering, but It is not God.

Figure 2.2   The syllable OM, the chanted sound representing Brahman, depicted gloriously, but necessarily without personal qualities.

Going back to the example, we find that for philosophical Hindus, Brahman is thus not a relational person-like deity, but something more like an ultimate substance or energy behind the reality we see and touch in the world around us. Especially with the concept of "Nirguna Brahman"—*nirguna* meaning "without qualities"—Hindus say the ultimate being has no qualities we can name, no aspects of personhood or activity that makes sense to us, and yet still it is somehow the foundation of creation. It is the single Reality behind the plurality we experience; it is the force that holds reality together. Yet Brahman is impersonal, not "He," so much as "It." Thus, instead of thinking of a creator God like an artist painting a picture, we should think of Ultimate Being as the paint or, better yet, the canvas itself, somehow behind and within all things, and yet not with any qualities or characteristics of its own. This is Brahman.

Ultimately, the idea of Nirguna Brahman implies a denial of the relational aspect of Ultimate Being that we saw with God and gods. That is, no one prays to Brahman, nor does Brahman reveal Its will to humanity. Brahman is no more concerned with human morality than is gravity. We shall speak more of these implications in later chapters. For now, we might only note that one implication of this idea of Ultimate Being is that the world of plurality, the world of objects and relationships, can be considered an illusion. All things truly are one, they are all Brahman, and to see the world as a great collection of individual things is "ignorance." This, too, is a point to be considered in later chapters.

In Buddhism (or at least some forms of Buddhism), the concept of Emptiness, or the **Void**, functions as a similar notion of monistic Ultimate Being, but with the important difference that, technically speaking, it is not any "thing" at all. That is, in reaction to the Hindu search for Brahman as a substance within all things, the Buddha declared that, in fact, within all things there is no substance, a "no-thing-ness." Yet the paradox in Buddhist philosophy is that this no-substance can be named, given a kind of ultimate designation, like putting a capital "N" on the word "Nothing." Thus the Buddhists began to speak of ultimate reality as the Void or Emptiness (Sanskrit: *sunyata*). Even so, one should not try to form an image of the Ultimate Being, for to grasp for any substance, even an eternal substance like Brahman or an eternal person like God, is to make the mistake of having desires. Instead, one must seek to peer behind the illusion of plurality, the illusion of self and objects, and find—Nothing. This nothing, this Void or Emptiness, then, is the single greatest reality, the true nature of all things. It is what finally makes all things one.

In China, the concept of **Dao** can also be considered monistically. We shall see in later chapters that, for Confucius and the great sages concerned with human society, the Dao was understood relationally, not, however, as if it were a god that one could pray to or receive revelation from. Rather, the Dao was for Confucius the final pattern and order of nature as exemplified in human relationships: father to son, subject to ruler. In contrast, the Dao to the Daoists was the final pattern and order of nature exemplified by nature itself in the constant change and balance between night and day, summer and winter, males and females. The Dao, then, is in both cases Ultimate Being, inasmuch as the balances and order of things is a kind of final truth, an order of things that is simply given in nature. The Dao just is. At the same time, the Dao is monistic, for, even though it represents balances of two things—whether fathers and sons or night and day—the point we should see is that finally and absolutely these balances represent a wholeness. Thus the famous *yinyang* symbol depicts the black and white teardrop shapes interwoven and mutually defining. *Yin* and *yang* are in balance and symbolically form a single, perfect circle: The Dao is one.

MISCELLANY AND MIXTURES

Theism, to summarize previous points, suggests belief in a person-like Ultimate Being, whether in monotheism or polytheism, while monism suggests belief in a depersonalized power or substance. Yet in both cases these beliefs carry the idea of ultimacy and finality. By and large, we find monotheism in the religious family of Judaism; we find monism in India and China. Yet it is not so simple to divide the world, or religions, into two camps, the theistic and the monistic. As we've seen, Hinduism in particular has a clearly polytheistic side and a monistic philosophy. It even suggests the possibility of a monotheistic understanding of Ultimate Being if we think of all the various gods as *avatars*—descents—of Vishnu. It is not clear if all these ways of viewing Ultimate Being are consistent, but one finds all of these elements in Hinduism nonetheless.

Indigenous religions, too, offer an interesting mix of theistic and monistic notions, as well as polytheism and animism. Many indigenous cultures, for example, emphasize the animistic spirits of nature and ancestor worship, but also will confess belief in a "High God," a creator God that is somehow over and above and before the various spirits of nature and family. In these cases, the High God is often distant and uninvolved in human affairs, not impersonal, but simply too far removed from the world to be as vital to daily life as the spirits of rain and soil. At the same time, one also finds monistic elements in indigenous religions, such as in the tribal Polynesian idea of **mana**. Among Polynesian Islanders, *mana* is the spiritual power that somehow inhabits the objects of nature like a mysterious force. *Mana* thus pervades all reality, an immanent, monistic essence that is the very life and power of things living and non-living, a power that witch-doctors can tap into for spiritual force and that average people touch at their peril.

Buddhism offers an interesting case of the difficulty of specifying Ultimate Being. We have already talked about the concept of Emptiness, and we will see in later chapters how it implies the ideal religious life of renouncing the world, becoming a monk, and finding the ideal state of mind in enlightenment. But for the average Buddhist

Figure 2.3 A sacred tree taken in Japan to be the presence of deity, marked by the *shimenawa* and *shide* (braided rope and jagged folded paper).

layperson who has no intention of becoming a monk, the ideal of Enlightenment and finding the Void may be too abstract. Historically, then, we find that later schools of Buddhism began to emphasize the Buddha himself as a manifestation of a more divine ideal. In fact, other Buddhas and **bodhisattvas**—enlightened persons still living in this or other worlds as teachers and savior figures—appear in different schools of Buddhism and become objects of popular devotion. Thus Buddhism over time develops new scriptures that emphasize worship and prayer to enlightened beings, historical and mythical. Even later, schools of Buddhism like Zen develop and begin to emphasize that all people have a kind of innately pure mind, a Buddha Mind, that is perfect and unchanging, very like—though the Buddhist would emphatically disagree—the Brahman soul that, according to Hindu philosophers, is pure and eternal within all of us. Thus our true **"Buddha Nature,"** the "true self," is a kind of absolute perfection and power within us all, whether we know it or not.

All of this is to confess, to some degree, that the terms we develop to discuss the concept of Ultimate Being are somewhat problematic as we begin to apply them to the religions of the world. As we will see throughout this book, however, the point is to develop and use the vocabulary that allows us to discuss carefully the elements of the religious phenomenon, even if we conclude that the terms we develop don't quite fit. At the very least, we should begin to see that none of these religious "objects"—the God of monotheism, the gods of polytheism, ancestor spirits, or the monistic abstractions of Dao and Void—are really "objects" in our normal sense of the word. None of them can quite be seen or touched, perhaps not even ultimately understood. Even where a tree or mountain—clearly objects—or a divine incarnation like Jesus or Krishna can be described in really physical terms, there is something still that defies our explanations. There is something more than human about Jesus, the Christians say, and something more than biological about a tree for the animist. It is no wonder, therefore, that our descriptions seem incomplete. Arguably, the incompleteness of the description is one useful way of understanding part of what we mean when we speak of Ultimate Being.

SUMMARIES

Summarizing what we have learned about Ultimate Beings is precarious, as just noted, but we can find trends and concepts and a vocabulary that are helpful for understanding the essence of religion and its relation to the various elements presented in the later chapters. We know at least that Ultimate Beings are ultimate, and though that sounds like a trivial thing to say, it means that there is often some sense in which we are trying to talk about that power or person that is beyond us all and is somehow the final glory and value of reality. Even when that power is within us, as with Hindu Brahman or Zen's Buddha Nature, we should see that this power, this essence, is something more than we think we are. It is hidden and glorious, somehow pure and eternal, often in contrast to the ego or individual identity that most of us think of as "me." Thus these realities, like God or nature spirits, are examples of a tremendous and fascinating mystery.

Coherent with this idea of mystery is the fact that, for all our effort, the Ultimate Being is to some extent beyond our ability to understand and describe. As noted previously, it is a bit ironic to point out that calling something ineffable or indescribable is in fact a description. Thus the philosophers and theologians, the prophets and sages of the world's religions have continued to speak of the unspeakable Ultimate even as they admit their words fall short. Arguably, words must fall short, for any great reality that I in my limited human way could describe completely would not be Ultimate Reality. Yet just as arguably (as we note in Chapter 4), perhaps the sages and prophets simply cannot stop offering merely human words as some kind of trans-human description.

We might notice in some of these descriptions that we often find ourselves using negative descriptions of God or Brahman. The latter, especially when described with the term *"nirguna,"* means It is without qualities, and even when we speak of God as infinite or uncaused, we are actually using negative terms. That is, we can see in the terms themselves that we are actually describing what God is not, rather than what God is: God is not-finite, not-caused, not-dependent on any finite thing. This strategy of describing Ultimate Being in negative terms has been called "**negative theology**," and one finds many examples of such descriptions in this chapter and in the world's religions in general.

Regarding more anthropomorphic descriptions, Thomas Aquinas, the thirteenth-century Christian theologian, has suggested we are describing God, not negatively, but **analogically**. That is, we say that God loves us or that God is angry, and we say that God is a mind or has intentions and ideas and emotions, but in a way this is false. It is false because, for us with our human vocabulary, all these descriptions are themselves words for finite and human things. In God, therefore, they must be something else: God is more than a mind, He loves in a way greater than we know, and so on. Yet it is not wrong, says Aquinas, to describe God in these ways, because God's mind is in some way *like* ours, his love is *like* ours. In general, then, we are describing God's traits as analogies, qualities that are more than we can know, but that are like something we do know.[4]

Other terms we might consider using would be those that describe the power and wisdom of the Ultimate Being. When theologians say God is all-powerful or all-knowing—or omnipotent and omniscient—they are saying that God's power and knowledge are, like his very being, unlimited and absolute. These terms seem more in place with theism than with monism, however, as it is difficult to say how Brahman or the Dao could "know" anything, insofar as neither is a personal being with thought and ideas analogically like ours. When we speak of the power of Brahman or Dao, we have a similar problem. While in some sense, both Brahman and the Dao are the ultimate basis for all that exists, it may be a mistake to think of them as creators in a theistic way. As we've seen, they do not make or execute plans nor have or carry out intentions. Similarly, we do not find there to be stories of miracles associated with Brahman or Dao. Yet all this is consistent with these concepts of Ultimate Being as impersonal. Yet we should not think of these monistic notions of Ultimate Being as powerless. As the *Daodejing*, the foundational text of Daoism declares, "The Dao does nothing, and yet all things are done through it."[5]

We have also, in this chapter, used terms like "**transcendent**" and "**immanent**" to describe the Ultimate Being. The former suggests we should think of a greater reality outside the universe, beyond and above all we know in nature. "Immanent," in contrast, suggests that the Ultimate Being is somehow in the here and now, like the animistic spirits of indigenous religion. The Dao, too, might be better described as immanent, inasmuch as its natural balances of *yin* and *yang* are definitely here in the world of nature, not in any distant, transcendent realm. Perhaps this immanence is notable in Brahman, too, although the sense of Brahman as being here in this world is quite different. As we've seen, Brahman is "here" in the world, yet this implies that the world is itself an illusion; Brahman is the only reality, and the "here" and the "now" are not truly real.

Some versions of this latter immanence might be called **pantheism**. This term, literally meaning that everything (*pan*) is God (*theos*), would suggest a monistic view of Ultimate Being while at the same time calling that power that infuses all of nature "God." Perhaps this concept suggests the effort to bring the mysterious immanent reality of monistic philosophy into closer relation with our normal human lives. More commonly, pantheism has been a philosophical effort to think of God less as a transcendent person and more as all of Nature, somehow considered a singular unity. As the capital "N" suggests, there is in pantheism a kind of mysterious ultimacy projected onto the natural world around us, but in practice this religious view strays quite far from traditional theism. We would see, for example, in the pantheism of philosophers like Baruch Spinoza or of poets like Goethe, a sense of the awesomeness of nature, but no tendency to worship or pray.[6]

Perhaps in a similarly complex mixture of transcendence and immanence, it is clear that in the indigenous religions there may be a High God, creator of the natural world, but there are also numerous spirits within the objects of nature. The Creator, it seems, having done His work in giving nature its spiritual being, is too transcendent to be active in human life, and thus the tribal cultures interact much more with the immanent nature spirits. The one creator God of Judaic monotheism, meanwhile, is similarly understood to be utterly transcendent, and yet in this case the Creator clearly interacts with humans as He wills, going so far as to take the Jewish tribe as "His own people." God in that sense may be intrinsically transcendent, yet immanent in his relation to the created world.

It is evident in this discussion that all of our vocabulary for speaking about the Ultimate Being may not be simple to use, but it still may be necessary. We are, after all, dealing with what religions say is true about their own understanding of reality, specifically of the ultimate, transmundane reality that is at the center of the religious phenomenon. We must, therefore, risk speaking throughout this text of Ultimate

Being, referring in this way to some impersonal power or person-like entity that is intrinsically mysterious and beyond our comprehension. It is power, though perhaps not like an active agent, and is somehow beyond the normal, measurable powers of nature, even if dwelling within nature. It may be transcendent or immanent, personal or impersonal, theistic or monistic, singular or plural, or some combination of these qualities. In the end, if we were engaged in Philosophy of Religion, we might enter into a debate about which concepts of Ultimate Being seem to be the most consistent and the most explanatory of the world we experience. Such a discussion is beyond the scope of this text, but such rational considerations are almost inevitable as we go on to study the other elements of religion that connect to each religion's concept of Ultimate Being.

Consequently, we shall find in the ensuing chapters regular references to how the ideas we study in the various elements and functions of religion work consistently with the religions' concepts of Ultimate Being. That is, we should find that the idea of God is interwoven with specific ideas of morality and selfhood and salvation in ways that are different from how the idea of the Dao is interwoven with those same general elements. We will discover that there is an internal logic to religious beliefs, actions, and experiences that can help us make sense of religion, whether we ourselves are believers or not. We shall thus discover that religions are not haphazard collections of ideas and values somehow jumbled together. They are rather more or less cohesive ways of life that encompass complex understandings of our world, intricate structures of behavior, and connected emotions and experiences, all of it centered around some notion of a mysterious, transmundane Something that we call Ultimate Being. This way of life is the great religious nexus of truth, goodness, and beauty.

KEY TERMS IN CHAPTER 2

analogical description The effort to describe Ultimate Being in human terms, acknowledging that divine qualities are only *like*, not equivalent to, human descriptions.

animism Belief in spirits that inhabit nature and interact with people.

anthropomorphic The quality of being like a human, in human shape, thus a potential criticism of theism for having God/gods that seem only like magnified human beings.

avatar The "descending" of a god, especially Vishnu in Hinduism, into physical form.

bodhisattva In Buddhism, an enlightened person, still living in this or other worlds, who serves as a teacher and savior figure.

Buddha Nature In some forms of Mahayana Buddhism, the innately pure, enlightened mind or "true self" of all persons, even all things.

Dao In China, the "Way," the final pattern and order of nature as exemplified (for Confucians) in human relationships like father to son, subject to ruler, or exemplified (for Daoists) by nature itself in the balance of night and day, male and female.

immanent A description of Ultimate Being emphasizing its quality as being within the world, perhaps diffused into all things or directly active in nature.

mana Polynesian monistic concept of Ultimate Being, taken to be a pervasive natural force that exists in nature and powerful persons.

monism Belief in an ultimate reality that is single and unique, a final single substance of being or existence, but not personified or relational.

monotheism Belief in one God

negative theology The effort to describe Ultimate Being not in terms of what it is, but in terms of what it is not, thus in contrast to the finite and worldly.

pantheism A monistic view of Ultimate Being that places "God" within the substance of nature, rather than as a distinct, relational being.

polytheism Belief in multiple gods.

theism Generally the belief in God or gods, transmundane power that is personal or personified.

transcendent A description of Ultimate Being emphasizing its quality as being outside and beyond the world.

ultimacy A quality of transmundane being suggesting finality, a greatness or power or existence that is the last and final thing that creates or makes sense of everything else.

void/emptiness A Buddhist notion of the ultimate reality, arguably a monistic concept considered as the true nature of all things, expressing the interdependence of all things.

CHAPTER 3

FOUNDERS AND MANIFESTATIONS

WE HAVE BEEN CONSIDERING religion as a system or way of life involving truth claims, behavioral ideals, and personal experiences all focused on some supernatural or transmundane reality. We then considered this transmundane reality as Ultimate Being, some existent person or force taken to be the final, mysterious reality behind and greater than all we know and see in the world. Yet we have also noted in this discussion that this Ultimate Being is, almost necessarily, something mysterious and beyond our ability to understand. Even so, the world is full of theologies and philosophies and books that give us some idea of this mystery. And this fact—this paradoxical fact that we can't stop talking about something that is more than we can talk about— must inspire us to press questions further. Perhaps most immediately, we might simply ask how the great mysteries that lie at the center of religion are revealed to our world in the first place. That is, if we cannot see or touch or hear the gods and spirits and ancestors that are venerated in religion, or if even nature itself is but a balance in the Dao or an illusion covering Brahman, how do we, the normal and mundane humans of this world, come to know this transmundane reality?

From the perspective of the religious phenomena themselves, this amounts to questioning the origins of religion in divine revelation and the manifestations of the gods among people. In other words, we shall begin to talk about how God or gods have spoken to people, or how they have appeared to groups of people in history. But, described this way, we should immediately see that these references to "God" and "gods" cannot apply to all religions and all concepts of Ultimate Being. For as we think about it, we see that there can be no divine revelation where there is no divine being that wishes to be revealed. That is, we can expect to find gods that speak or manifest themselves only where we, in fact, find "gods," and we can be left wondering how history gets its ideas of Ultimate Being in the non-theistic religions. For surely we must say that there is some kind of "revealing" of the religious truths also in the non-theistic religions.

The implication of all this is that we must find some variety in the ways that religions come to be revealed to humanity. Gods who speak and gods who manifest in the world can be part of it, but they cannot be the whole story. At the same time, we should expect that the variety of manifestations of religion in the world will be more or less consistent with the religions' ideas of Ultimate Being. This internal consistency within religions is something to look for throughout this text and through all the different elements of religion studied phenomenologically.

From another perspective, one less phenomenological, we study the origins of religions more historically and less as revelation or as manifestations of gods. That is, from a more external point of view, we can look at how religions begin in order to understand the contexts from which the central ideas developed. In a way, this violates our principle of trying to see religion from the inside, but in another way, it continues to benefit our understanding of religion precisely because it can help us understand the religious truth claims of the various faiths. We understand better what religious teachings mean by understanding the culture and the language from which they sprang. We can say, for example, that Christianity began with Jesus and the Apostles, but arguably we don't understand them unless we also realize that all these men were Jews of the first century CE, whose lives to various extents were influenced by Greek ideas and Roman government.

Consequently, in this chapter we look at the origins of religion in the history of the various religions' founders. Having said that, it rather quickly becomes apparent that not all religions have "founders" in the same sense, and perhaps no historical founders at all. Thus, once again, we should look for a kind of internal consistency within religions, even as we examine different kinds of religious origins.

PROPHETS

The word "prophet" may bring to mind an idea of prophecy that emphasizes telling something about the future and probably about the appearance of great heroes or the end of the world. More etymologically, however, it really just means "speaking forth," though in particularly religious contexts it means speaking forth the words of God. A **prophet**, therefore, is a man or a woman who hears, in some sense, what God would have people know and then speaks forth the message of God to humanity. He or she tells us what God would have us know, and thus religions are born.

Immediately we see in such a definition that the concept of the prophet fits best with theistic religion, perhaps especially monotheism. And, indeed, we find perhaps the paradigm of the concept of prophets in the Judaic religions, particularly in Islam, where the idea of prophets is a basic tenet of belief. That is, a good Muslim is expected to believe that God, Allah, has spoken to specific people throughout human history, though most particularly to one man, Muhammad. Thus in one sense, Muslims believe that the founding of the religion of Islam goes back to numerous prophets throughout history, ultimately to the first man, Adam, who heard God speak and who then revealed the words of God to those around him. More historically, Islam begins with the prophet Muhammad, an Arab of the seventh century, for it was through him and him alone that the final message to humanity was delivered and the content of the religion we know as Islam was revealed.

According to the stories, Muhammad was in the caves of Mount Hira above the city of Mecca in the year 610 when an angel spoke to him and told him to "recite" the words of God that would be given to him. Subsequently, Muhammad recited those words as they came to him over the next twenty-two years. We discuss in the next chapter the obvious relation between this prophetic role of Muhammad and the development of the Islamic scriptures, the Quran; for now we need only note the drama of Muhammad's call, how he was selected from all the men of his time to receive the words of God and be the conduit through which God's message to humanity would be revealed.

Seventh-century Arabia was not, however, an isolated backwater culture. Rather, it is evident historically and in the words of Muhammad himself that people in his time and place already knew of the concept of prophets from Judaism and Christianity. Indeed, for Judaism the paradigm of prophethood is found in Moses, who may have lived as long ago as the thirteenth century BCE. It was back then that Moses, like Muhammad two millennia later, was on a mountain when God spoke to him and he received his message from God. As one follows the Jewish scriptures through the next eight centuries or so, one finds the names of numerous prophets who continued to hear what God wanted people to know and delivered God's words to the world. Yet it was Moses who received God's law and set in stone—literally, according to the stories— the rules and directives that God commanded for his people. Thus Moses, like Muhammad, is the medium by which the world comes to know the invisible and intangible God, only because he was chosen by God for this purpose.

The call of these men as receivers of divine revelation must have been a powerful experience, one we discuss more in Chapter 10, and it is what made them prophets and the founders of their respective religions. As a prophetic founder, we might add Jesus chronologically in between Moses and Muhammad, especially inasmuch as Jesus said things like, "The words I say to you I do not speak on my own authority, rather it is the Father living in me who is doing His work" (John 14:10). Yet overall, Christians who speak of Jesus as the Son of God do not consider him only a prophet, and so we shall have to consider Jesus in a later section of this chapter. Similarly, the Guru **Nanak**, the founder of Sikhism, is a complex character, one whom we can call a prophet, even though within the faith he is called a guru, not a prophet. The title of guru comes from Nanak's Hindu context, where the word generally refers to a spiritual teacher, one whose wisdom and authority can hardly be overestimated. Indeed, within the Hindu tradition, one's personal guru should be obeyed, followed, and honored as one would honor a god. Even so, Nanak, appearing in Islam-ruled India in the fifteenth century, is like a prophet inasmuch as he, like Moses and Muhammad before him, is said to have heard God's words and in turn delivered them to humanity. His message, moreover, fits with the founding of a monotheistic faith. Thus the Guru Nanak seems to fit the prophetic model: a person who hears the words of God and reveals those words to humanity, and in so doing starts a religion.

Figure 3.1   Traditional depiction of Guru Nanak, the founder of Sikhism.

We might multiply these examples, although it would become a point of discussion whether or not all of them start new religions. Whether the prophet Joseph Smith started a new religion in his revelation of Mormonism is a problem that deserves discussion, even if only briefly, later in this chapter. We have already noted that there are other prophets in the Jewish tradition, recognized also by Christianity, that do not change the message of Moses and start some new faith. Even today, in some Christian churches, some believers claims that the "gift of prophecy" remains an active work of God in their congregations, yet they would insist that they are not starting any new religion, but only continuing what Moses or Jesus began long ago. Nevertheless, we might recognize in such claims that still some people claim to "hear" what God is saying and then tell the rest of us His truths. And we should then recognize that there is a logical connection between the idea of prophethood and the theistic idea of Ultimate Being. That is, it makes little sense to speak of prophets in Daoism or Buddhism where no God speaks, but it makes complete sense to speak of prophets where the Ultimate Being is a god that speaks and has a message for humanity to follow.

As a final critical point about prophets, we might confess that it seems audacious that someone would claim to have divine truths to reveal to the rest of us. How dare some merely finite human being declare to the rest of us—we being no more finite and human than the prophet—the divine message? It seems outrageous. But this outrage is ironic. For if God chooses to speak, surely it is God's prerogative to choose whom He will as his messenger. For the rest of us who must simply receive God's message through His chosen prophets, it would seem ironically audacious of us to refuse to listen simply because God didn't choose to speak to us. It would seem foolish of me to refuse to believe that the President of the United States is speaking to his cabinet just because the President is not speaking to me.

SAGES

It may seem clear that the idea of prophets is quite consistent with the idea of mono-theism, while in contrast, as noted, there would not be a prophet in a religion like Daoism or Buddhism. In these religions, we should speak not of prophets but of sages. In this context, the term **sage** refers to a person of great wisdom. In particular, a sage is any human being who has some kind of uncommon insight that reveals to the rest of us something of the nature of Ultimate Being. And here the best example is not Muhammad but the Buddha.

The man we know as the Buddha—sometimes, "the historical Buddha," to distin-guish him from other, more legendary Buddhas—was born Siddhartha Gautama in northern India perhaps around 563 BCE. Raised, according to the stories, as a prince in a luxurious palace, he eventually saw the sorrow and suffering of life and committed himself to finding the solution to suffering. His solution is examined more in Chapter 6. For our purposes here we might simply note that he finally saw the answer by achiev-ing a kind of special insight that clarified for him the meaning of life and the true nature of existence. This experience was not a prophetic call; it was his enlightenment. And that is the meaning of "Buddha": the Enlightened One.

The Buddha was not the first sage of India, nor, in fact, the first Buddha. Yet he is the founder of Buddhism because, as an historical figure, he is for us the source of what have come to be the teachings and rituals of that religion. We also find explicitly in his new understanding of Ultimate Being a clear rejection of earlier teachings. Most important, we noted in the previous chapter his denial of the abstract monism of Brahman in favor of what became perhaps the more abstract notion of Emptiness. He also rejected the Hindu caste system and apparently the meditation techniques of Hindu renunciants and the asceticism of Jainism. In these rejections, we do not need to argue that the Buddha was in fact right, but we do see that he understood his own insights to be revealing the truth of a transmundane reality. We also see, of course, that the Buddha did not appear in history without context or connection to other histories and religious teachings. Thus we place the teachings of the Buddha into an historical context in order to understand his ideas better, even as we see him as the great and authoritative founder of a new faith.

We could pursue a similar discussion of the founding of Confucianism and Daoism in China. The stories of Confucius, a low-level aristocrat who studied assiduously the wisdom of previous ages in order to solve the problems of society in his own time, do not seem to require the legendary materials one finds in the Indian sages or the miracles of the prophets of Judaism. Confucius himself insisted he was inventing no new ideas,[1] and yet it is clear that his own collections of the great wisdom of past Chinese dynasties, along with his own wise sayings, become the foundation for all that follows in the religion named for him.

Laozi, the purported founder of Daoism, is a more shadowy character. Modern scholars are dubious even of his existence, let alone of his being the author of Daoism's seminal text, the *Daodejing*. But, legendary or not, it is clear phenomenologically that Laozi is taken to have been a sage, a man of uncommon wisdom and insight into the nature of the Dao such that he, by himself (accord-

Figure 3.2   Traditional image of Confucius preserved as a rubbing from a stone carving in the Beilin Museum, Xi'an, China.

ing to the story), could sit at the roadside and write his wisdom into the poetic stanzas of the short text that, to this day, is the foundation of Daoist thought.

Whatever legendary accretions might accompany stories of the sages—and we should consider as well what legends might develop regarding the lives of prophets—we see in their stories that they are not receiving messages from a divine being, but discovering in their own wisdom the mysteries of Ultimate Being. This may happen, as with Confucius, by collecting the wisdom of earlier sages and mythic "Sage Kings," or, as with the Buddha, by having a dramatic religious experience of his own. In either case, neither the nature of the Dao nor the liberating truths of Emptiness are revelations in the sense noted with the prophets. But this should be obvious, since neither the Dao nor the Void should be called "God"; neither concept of Ultimate Being is a person of will and words that would choose its spokesman. Rather, in these monistic concepts, we see an impersonal force or substance that must be discovered by the sage, and thus the sage's own wisdom is the proper source of insight, not some divine revelation.

The honoring of the sages' wisdom does raise an interesting problem for this discussion, however, for we find that the sages of China and India can eventually be thought of as much more than human. That is, we have stressed so far, both with prophets and sages, that these men—and they are almost always men, not women—are not in themselves divine. They receive the message of God or understand the mystery of Ultimate Being through their own wisdom, but they are not incarnate deities themselves. Yet even so, we find in India that sages like the Buddha are devoutly venerated, and it does not take long before Buddhism develops a pantheon of Buddhas and Bodhisattvas, a list of great, enlightened persons that live in holy realms of perfection and are capable of hearing our prayers. In China, we find that both Confucius and Laozi are ultimately divinized, raised to the status of holy ancestors, such that temples and rituals develop around them. Perhaps for some, a merely human source of authority about Ultimate Being is not satisfying. Perhaps the impersonal nature of the Ultimate Being in these religions leaves followers with a desire to interact with a "god" more relational. Whatever the cause of these developments, it is interesting to wonder if these founders would themselves appreciate being raised to the status of gods. We discuss divine persons as founders later in this chapter.

Another issue we consider later in this chapter is the history of secondary founders, men and women who do not found a new religion but are instrumental in following the teachings of an original religion and developing new or renewed teachings within that religion. For this section, a case in point is in reference to the "sages" of Judaism. In the first few centuries of the Common Era, Judaism was in the process of transformation, changing from the ancient structures dependent upon the central authority of the temple in Jerusalem to a new emphasis on the details of Jewish life. The men who established these details, who over the course of several centuries discussed and debated the nuances of God's law, were called *Tannaim* and *Amoraim*, literally the "teachers" and "interpreters" of the law. Ultimately, these men contributed to the great collection of Rabbinical literature called the Talmud, which functions as scripture secondary only to the revelations given to Moses. Yet these men are not prophets in the same sense as Moses. Their insights are not a matter of receiving and reciting the words of God, but in establishing through human wisdom what the words of God mean. That is why they are the "sages" of Judaism.

Thus, while we have seen that monotheism is most consistent with the concept of the prophet, the world's religions are by no means so simple that we can establish easy one-to-one correspondences between basic concepts and their Ultimate Being. Nonetheless, we also see here a consistency in that sages remain something distinct from prophets, and we can continue to use such terms to understand the religions we study. We must only remember to use our terms carefully.

INCARNATIONS OF "GOD"

In some contexts, it is most evident that the Ultimate Being "speaks" to His chosen prophets, while in other contexts the common idea is that human sages gain special insight into the nature of the Ultimate Being. As a third possibility, we should consider whether or how the transmundane, supernatural power above all things might in fact appear directly in the mundane world. That is, the Ultimate Being can incarnate.

Incarnation literally means that the Ultimate Being enters into flesh (*carnem*, in Latin), and the world's best known example is probably Jesus within Christianity. Yet the idea of divine incarnation is much more common in various polytheistic religions, most notably Hinduism. In the latter, it is claimed that many of the gods have literally manifested in flesh, especially Vishnu, whose *avatars* are his "descents" into physical form. The legends of Vishnu's *avatars* include the gods Rama and Krishna, along with various animal and semi-animal manifestations that have appeared in flesh in order to achieve some great saving victory for mankind. Other Hindu gods, like the goddesses Kali and Durga, have likewise manifested in flesh, and their legends, too, focus on stories of their powerful exploits in the defeat of demons for the benefit of the world. Of course it is difficult to place any of these gods in human history, but within Hinduism it remains possible to this day that human beings, living and walking among us, whom we can visibly see in photos and videos, are gods. Sai Baba (1838–1918) and his more controversial reincarnation Satya Sai Baba (1926–2011), along with the goddess Anandamayi (1896–1982) and many others, are literally taken to be divine. Swami Narayan (1781–1830), who, as an eleven-year-old boy was already being recognized as a holy person, was considered a manifestation of divinity by the time he was twenty-five and was eventually taken to be an incarnation of Krishna, thus of Vishnu. Currently, he is worshiped as the deity of a new sect of Hinduism that has glorious temples and millions of followers throughout the world.[2]

Other manifestations of deity are less about "deity" (thus the quotation marks around "God" in the heading to this section). In a way, the spirit beings of basic animism are direct manifestations of deity in the world, inasmuch as any particular tree or mountain or river can be divine. It seems in fact that, although the spirit of water is not evident in the world, any particular running stream or pool of fresh water may be the presence of that spirit. Similarly, any particular animal killed for food may be more than just an individual animal; it may rather be a manifestation of the spirit of all the deer or buffalo. Thus, when hunting, the animists of Native American religion must respect the animal they kill, in order to avoid offending the spiritual presence of all such animals.

Ancestor spirits, too, may manifest among human beings, sometimes as other natural phenomena and sometimes as animals. In Australia, the aboriginal religion states that the great ancestors of the "Dreamtime" creation myth entered into the objects of nature and even today continue to be a real, physical presence in the world. In Native American myth, ancestor spirits, such as White Buffalo Woman, manifest as animals and as humans in order to teach the tribe the important lessons of ritual and social order.

In these cases of divine manifestation, we see the central role of myth as a form of story-telling, in order for us to know how and when the ancestors have come to be among us. Also, as we will see in Chapter 9, there remains within native traditions the need for a religious expert, the shaman, to interpret the intentions and emotions of the animist spirits. Shamans thus play the role, roughly, of prophets, receiving in their dreams the voice of ancestors and spirits, in order that the tribal group will know what these beings desire. Yet the spirits of animals and plants and ancestors remain a distinctly immanent form of Ultimate Being, present as physical manifestations in the world, whether as persons in myth or as the mountains and animals around us.

In all these examples, we can note how religions that accept the existence of many gods and spirits find it easy to incorporate incarnations of gods. That is, the incarnation of gods in polytheism is more common than the incarnation of God in monotheism. As already noted, among the monotheistic religions in the Judaic family, only Christianity dares to suggest that God, the one eternal Creator beyond the world and utterly independent of it, has become a human being, and according to their stories God did this only once and for a very singular purpose. For Christians, "the Word became flesh and dwelt among us," and in so doing God revealed Himself as merciful and gracious, offering to sinful humanity forgiveness of sin and a dramatic example of self-sacrificial love. Yet to Muslims, Jesus can only be a prophet, and to Jews he is taken to be a wayward Rabbi, one guilty of perverting the teachings of God and "leading Israel astray."[3] But to neither Judaism nor Islam is Jesus God, nor could he be. For to these related faiths, God simply does not manifest in any finite form. In some ways, understanding the difference in how these three closely-related faiths see the role of Jesus can be a straightforward way of getting to the root of what unites and divides them. All three religions insist that there is only one God, transcendent and absolute; Christians alone declare that this God entered physically into the world as a savior. We have already noted that this makes a difference in their respective theologies as Christians developed the idea of Trinity; we shall see that this difference will also have implications for ethics and ritual and salvation.

SECONDARY FOUNDERS

As we noted in the discussion of the Jewish sages, there are within the world's religions what can be called "**secondary founders**." The great sages of Judaism, who lived roughly from the beginning of the Common Era to the end of the fifth century, should not be considered founders of any new religion, since they are said to be as legitimately a part of the Jewish orthodox religion as Moses himself. Indeed, just as Moses was given by God the revelations that became the Torah, so the sages are said to have developed their own wisdom into collections of legal discussion called "Oral Torah." Thus the work of these sages is not any new faith. And yet clearly their work is foundational to Judaism, especially inasmuch as that religion was, during the time of the sages, faced with a crisis that forced upon the Jews a measure of change and redefinition that can seem radical from the outside. Even so, with wholly new emphases on new interpretations of the law of God, and even with new scriptures, the sages of Judaism are not founders in the way Moses was. They developed changes and emphases within the faith and thus are secondary.

Other important secondary founders would include the second-generation sages of China, such as Mengzi (Mencius) in Confucianism and Zhuangzi in Daoism. These men, living roughly two hundred years after Confucius and Laozi, became recognized as the greatest interpreters of their respective religions, and their writings became almost as influential as those of the great founders. This is possible within these religions partly because they have a more open view of scripture than do religions like Christianity and Islam, as we will see in the next chapter. In Christianity, it would be clear to most Christians that there are no new scriptures to add to the New Testament after the time of the direct followers of Jesus, and thus the writings of a secondary founder like Martin Luther would never be called "scriptures." Indeed, Luther, along with other major Reform-

Figure 3.3   Portrait of Martin Luther, German monk and theologian credited with starting the Protestant Reformation.

ers of his time, thought of himself as trying to get back to the origins of the faith. Thus even as Luther was trying to reform the Catholic tradition, which he thought had strayed terribly from the true teachings of Jesus, he was also very critical of those radical reformers of his time who seemed to want to remake Christianity according to their own prophetic insights.

It is possible, therefore, that some secondary founders might be considered to have developed their religion too far beyond the boundaries of accepted beliefs and practices, even if they would insist they are developing nothing new at all, while other secondary founders might end up with movements or denominations named after them, but still they would be considered as staying within the pale of the faith. We might ask, however, "Considered by whom?" For even a modern Catholic might consider Luther a heretic, and no doubt some rather radical secondary founders have considered themselves to be true followers of the original faith. Nichiren, a Buddhist reformer of thirteenth-century Japan, considered the Buddhism of his time so corrupted that he thought "true Buddhism" needed to be recovered by a new Buddha. His condemnations of the other Buddhist schools of Japan earned him significant disdain and exile from Japan at least twice, and yet he eventually prevailed in founding the Nichiren Shoshu sect that continues on—notably in various sub-denominations—to this day. The new Buddha, the sect teaches, was none other than Nichiren himself.

So at what point does a "secondary" founder become, in fact, the founder of a new religion? The answer to this question is rather complicated, depending a great deal on how open the religion itself is to new interpretations and how radical we may find those interpretations to be. Muhammad ibn Abd-al-Wahhab (1703–1792), the Islamic reformer who founded the conservative Wahabi sect and helped the Saud family establish the modern nation of Saudi Arabia, would by no means be considered the developer of a new faith, but was, like Luther, conscious of himself as trying to clean up the errors and laxity that had crept into his religion. He would never have thought of himself as establishing "Wahabism," any more than Luther saw himself as starting a "Lutheran Church." In contrast, Mirza Ghulam Ahmad (1835–1908) might have left the fold of orthodoxy when he delivered a sermon in Arabic and claimed it was an angel speaking through him, apparently like Muhammad himself. In Christianity, the equally challenging parallel would be Joseph Smith and the founding of Mormonism: As Smith received messages from God, left behind him a new scripture, and arguably changed key teachings of Christianity, shall we consider him the prophet of a new faith or the reformer of an already-established religion?

Clearly there is no intention of answering a question like this here, but we raise the question to recognize that religions have had various kinds of founders. Thus to a great extent it is difficult to establish when a new sect is really a new religion because the religions themselves are so complex. Yet religions themselves do have ways of settling—or trying to settle—such disputes, as they consider notions of **orthodoxy**. The term "orthodoxy" literally means "straight doctrine," and so becomes a term to suggest that there is some body of ideas or beliefs that function as a measuring rod for what does and does not fit into the religion. If a secondary founder steps beyond the realm of orthodoxy, he or she is a **heretic**, one who teaches false and possibly pernicious ideas under the title of the established religion. And, at their worst, religions that staunchly defend their orthodoxy may torture and kill its "heretics," whether they really are heretics or not.

In the end, the appeal to orthodoxy to help us understand what constitutes a founder of religion as opposed to a reformer is not without danger. Even more broadly considered, the notion of orthodoxy cannot always help us define our founders because the idea and application of orthodoxy is itself not very consistently valued across the world's religions. Indeed, as we have already seen in the way this text is set up, doctrine, a religion's claims about truth, is only part of the phenomenon of religion, and we shall note explicitly as we move through this book that some religions are much more focused on their practices or their religious experiences than they are on their truth claims. Thus we find across the world's religions considerable variation on how open or closed they might be to new interpretations and new emphases. This will begin to be evident in the next chapter, where we consider how much or how little religions develop and emphasize the use of scripture, along with how much or how little they can tolerate the appearance of new scriptures.

NON-HISTORICAL ORIGINS

We cannot end this chapter without taking some time to reconsider the historical issues surrounding the founders of the world's religions. That is, we have spoken of men like Jesus and Laozi as if they are historical persons, although we have also admitted that the historicity of such men can be questionable. It behooves us to reiterate, in fact, that when we spoke of ancestors of indigenous religions and the Sage Kings of China, we were content to consider these people as mythic, parts of grand stories of origins and meaning, but probably not considered historical even by believers. We reconsider in Chapter 5 how the distinction between myth and history can be a useful tool in understanding how to read scriptures.

Meanwhile, the point to stress here is that the historical basis of some of these founders may not only be more or less problematic; it might also be more or less important. The *rishis*, or seers, of ancient Hinduism were men and, possibly, women who are said to have heard the gods singing the Vedas, or perhaps to have entered ecstatic states of consciousness in which they "saw the truth." It is from these *rishis* that Hindus have their oldest, most foundational scriptures. And although there are a number of names associated with these seers, names that appear in later collections of the ritual texts of early Hinduism, there is very little chance any of them represent historical figures. Nor does it seem to matter. For the men (and women) themselves are not important; what is important is the poetry of the scriptures. Even the means by which they gained their insights—whether heard from gods like prophets, or gained from ecstatic insight like sages—may not be very important. For many Hindus, Hinduism itself is *sanatana dharma*, the eternal religion.

This eternal religion, while probably an idea developed rather recently even in Hinduism, is similar to the way Muslims understand Islam as it was delivered to Muhammad to be the same as the religion delivered to Jesus, Moses, Abraham, and even Adam. Thus for Muslims, Islam is also eternal religion, the primordial faith given by God to all humanity, starting with mythic Adam. But this, like the *sanatana dharma* of Hinduism, is impossible to verify in any historical sense and is almost certainly a projection backward of what early Muslims, like modern Hindus, wanted their religion to mean.

It seems, then, that the effort to establish historical depth in these religions aims at reaching deeply into the mythic mists of human origins. Currently, somewhat careless websites might well advertise Hinduism as the world's most ancient religion—perhaps ignoring Judaism and the arguably more ancient religions of various tribal groups—and it is interesting to wonder what one hopes to gain from such a claim. Perhaps it is the prestige of age. More likely, it seems, it is the authority of being the original religion, such that everything else can either be subsumed under this umbrella, as Hindus might claim, or can be seen as aberrations from the original message, as Muslims might say.

In any case, there does seem to be some connection between historical claims and the idea of authority. Yet it is precisely the difficulty of establishing history in these mythic cases that makes the authority also problematic. And we can see that this problem extends also to those cases of historical founders like Jesus. It is no accident that we have had a "search for the historical Jesus" in Western scholarship for about two hundred years, and that this search continues today in scholarly seminars and popular film. In contrast, scholars seem to have abandoned any search for an "historical Laozi," while only recently have Hindus tried to find an historical basis for the stories of Krishna or Rama.

Perhaps from our phenomenological perspective the point would be to ask what happens to a religion if, in fact, its claims of historical founding become unbelievable. That is, if there is no ancient core of Hinduism we could recognize as *sanatana dharma*, or if there is no indication that the message of Adam was indeed the Islam of Muhammad, what becomes of the authority of Hinduism and Islam, respectively? Notably, the answer varies depending on how much each religion's message depends on history. We shall find, for example, that a merely mythic Laozi is less problematic for Daoism than a merely mythic Jesus is for Christianity.

But this is to be expected. We note again in Chapter 5 that Christianity has a tendency to cast its message into historical terms, probably because that faith is a daughter of Judaism, which also has that tendency. That is, we find the God of Judaism referring to himself in historical terms: "I am the God that brought you out of Egypt," Yahweh declares, and He goes on to tell His people not to forget His great deeds and to commemorate those deeds with annual rituals. Rama never refers to himself in a similar way.

We see in such examples that there is a coherence between how a religion is founded and how much it takes its own historical claims to be necessary. We also see connections between historical emphasis and ritual, and we have already noted repeatedly how often the founding of religion gives rise to the development of scripture. In all these ways we begin to see the internal cohesion of religions, and as this text goes on, we should expect to see again and again how religions of the world gain a kind of internal logical coherence by relating their claims of history and scripture to behavioral activities of ritual and morality, while also relating all these elements to religious experience. And in the end, this entire nexus of ideas and actions and feelings relates back to Ultimate Being.

KEY TERMS IN CHAPTER 3

heretic   One who teaches false and pernicious ideas within an established religion, apparently violating that religion's orthodoxy.

incarnation   Literally to enter into flesh, thus the idea that the Ultimate Being may become a human being and reveal Himself or Itself to humanity.

Nanak (1469–1539)   The founder of the Sikh religion.

orthodoxy   Literally "straight doctrine," thus some body of ideas or beliefs that function as a standard for what does and does not fit into a particular religion.

prophet   A man or a woman who hears, in some sense, what God would have people know and then speaks forth the message of God to humanity.

rishis   Literally "seers"; in ancient Hinduism, the men and, possibly, women who heard from the gods, or discovered in their own ecstatic states of consciousness, the hymns that became the Vedas, the earliest scriptures of Hinduism.

sage   A human being that has some kind of uncommon insight that reveals to others something of the nature of Ultimate Being.

secondary founders   Men and women who do not found a new religion but who are instrumental in following the teachings of an original religion and developing new or renewed teachings within that religion.

CHAPTER 4

SCRIPTURE AS SOURCE AND AUTHORITY

WE NOTED A FEW times already that religions are not haphazard collections of ideas but more or less unified systems of thought and behavior with their own internal logic. Indeed, we have been suggesting from the outset of this text that religions all over the world find meaning in ideas and actions and experiences (truth, goodness, and beauty) that are intricately interwoven with a singular focus on something transmundane. We have therefore spent the last couple of chapters talking about that "Something" and about how, given that it transcends the world, it can become manifest into the world. Thus we have been seeing how religions become religions, not merely some personal "spirituality" but historically recognizable phenomena in human history. We have begun to see, in fact, the beginnings of the phenomenon of orthodoxy.

We noted already that this term, orthodoxy, literally means "straight doctrine," suggesting that religions often—perhaps inevitably—begin to develop systems of ideas and beliefs that define what are the truths of a particular religion. It should not be supposed, of course, that all religions have the same kind of focus on orthodoxy, or indeed that all religions would even want to use such a term to describe their system of beliefs. Indeed, as suggested by the title of this text, there may be religious phenomena that significantly downplay the "truth" aspect of religion in favor of "goodness" or "beauty." That is, we will see as we go along that orthodoxy is certainly not always at the center of religious phenomena but rather, in some cases, we find much more religious emphasis on proper behavior or an expected kind of experience. We shall risk later talking about "orthopraxis" (emphasizing the right kind of practice) and even "orthopathos" (emphasizing the right kind of experience). But for now let us look at how orthodoxy can become central in religious teaching, for it suggests that there are proper sources for our beliefs and ideas about the Transcendent, and that it is important that we get the doctrines straight.

Having already discussed the historical founding of religions, we have noted how the special status of a person as a prophet or a sage makes them the proper source for religious ideas, for the "straight doctrine" of orthodoxy. In this chapter, we continue from those historical foundations and begin to consider how many religions establish their beliefs, the "truths," in written form. After all, the founders eventually die. Even those founders who are thought to be direct manifestations of divinity (Jesus, Krishna, and others noted in the previous chapter) disappear from our world for one reason or another and leave behind them a kind of vacuum. That is, while the spiritual master is with us, we may be quite content to sit at his or her feet and learn. But when the master is gone, we might expect that followers would want to be sure they had the teachings right. They might want to be sure they could keep those teachings from being lost. And thus they might write them down. This would be the beginnings of scriptures.

SIKHISM AND THE *ADI GRANTH*: A CASE STUDY

It would be a mistake, of course, to imagine that all religious scripture comes about through the obviously necessary labor of recording the teachings of an historical founder. We know by now that the human phenomenon of religion is much too complicated to have only a single way of forming any of its many elements. But there is a useful kind of logic to the idea that scripture might often come about within a religion through the need to save and finalize the teachings of a living leader. The Sikh religion gives us an example.

We noted in the previous chapter that Sikhism started with the Guru Nanak in fifteenth-century India, appearing as a divinely revealed wisdom incorporating the Hindu and Islamic elements found in the Muslim-controlled, Hindu-majority culture from which it emerged. During his lifetime, Nanak wrote songs and poetry of worship, and when he died, his authority of leadership over the evolving Sikh community was believed to pass into another poet, the Guru Angad, and from him to Guru Amar Das. Over the next two centuries, the authority of the guru was thought to pass from teacher to a specially chosen successor until the time of the tenth guru, Gobind Singh. All this time, the poetry and songs of many of these gurus were being collected and eventually became the book known as the *Adi Granth*.

But the point here is not merely to note that writings can be collected. The important part of the story is the ending of the line of ten gurus. Sikhism, though an initially peaceful religion, began under the later gurus to take on a more and more military character in response to the military threats and violence of the Muslim authorities. Thus, as

Figure 4.1 Sikh man worships the text, the *Adi Granth*, where it is settled beneath the canopy and treated as a living teacher, the Guru Granth Sahib.

Gobind Singh saw his own life nearing its end, and as he had seen his own sons die in battle, he declared that the authority of the guru, the power to see and declare the words of God, no longer would be evident in a human being. Instead, the tenth guru declared, it was the text, the *Adi Granth*, that would henceforth be the living guru.

This brief telling of the story of the guru succession of Sikhism is meant to show that the text is not just a text. Within Sikhism, the book is Guru Granth Sahib, the book that is both Lord and Teacher. As noted in the previous chapter, one person may be no more or less human than another, yet somehow he or she is holy by virtue of his or her relation to the Ultimate Being. Similarly, the book called the *Adi Granth* is in one sense a book like any other book, with written script and words and pages. Yet in another and clearly more important sense, it is more than a book. It is Guru Granth Sahib, the text that is the link between the believer and the divine.

At the same time, the story of the Granth illustrates one other common thread of religious scripture: the relation of text to founder. It is, of course, not universally evident, but it is often the case that the scripture will be about or by a religion's primary founder. In this case, the writings of the Guru Nanak constitute nearly 1,000 of the almost 6,000 hymns of the holy text.[1] But even those hymns written by successor gurus have the authority of the founder because it is believed that the spirit of the original Guru has passed on into his successors. Thus the text has authority because of its connection to the holy founder who has his authority because of his connection to the Ultimate Being, and the Ultimate Being has authority just because he/she/it is Ultimate Being.

THE GENERAL CONCEPT OF SCRIPTURE

With the example of the development of the scriptures of Sikhism, we see two instructive qualities of **scripture**: the connection between scripture and founders and the general idea of authority. As we have noted, we cannot expect that all religions will have exactly the same kind of relation between scripture and founders—indeed, we will sometimes find no such connection at all—and we will similarly find that religions understand the authority of their scriptures in a variety of ways. Yet we might risk saying that religious scriptures in general are read and appealed to precisely because they can help followers, even generations after a religion's appearance, touch the roots of faith and practice, getting back to the words and works of persons most holy to the religion as a whole. Moreover, by having written words that are given somehow through a founder with a special relation to Ultimate Being, we find that such holy texts are right; that is, they have the authority to tell the followers about proper belief and ritual and about Ultimate Being itself. Thus if religions the world over help us consider an ultimate ideal in beauty, truth, and goodness, scripture is one of the key ways that religious believers come to embrace truth.

As is often helpful, let us consider a non-religious example of authoritative text. Consider, for example, this textbook you're reading now. In some ways, we might hope, the book is read with a certain expectation that you, the student, will learn something from it. We hope it contains valid information, even truth. In that sense, this book can be read with a certain trust in its authority. And yet no student would consider this text scripture. No student would guess that the writer of this book has any special relation to Ultimate Being, nor does the writer make any such claim. The writer is a mere human being with no special, numinous qualities, and, though we might all be dismayed, none of us would really be surprised if we found out that the writer had made some mistakes. In fact, even if every assertion made in this book were correct, precision of information is still not enough to make a claim of scripture. What is being claimed when a book is called scripture is that the writing, somehow, has a transcendent quality, a special significance that even the best mundane text cannot match. Of course we should expect that connection, seeing that it takes us back to our definition of "religion."

"But, wait," one might say, "aren't all scriptures just written by mere human beings?" Actually, from the phenomenological point of view, the answer to that question varies. But even if the answer is "Yes," one should not make the mistake of thinking that "mere human beings" cannot produce scripture. In a way, we saw this in the case of Sikhism. Another good example might be from the New Testament of Christianity. Much of the New Testament consists of **epistles**, letters written by important followers of Jesus. The letters of Saint Paul, for example, are just that, letters, complete with opening and closing greetings, Paul's personal reflections, and his specific responses to letters he received from others. And yet somehow, for the Christian, this is also scripture. How can that be? It is because Paul is an "Apostle," a person specifically chosen by Jesus to deliver to the world the teaching and instruction of the faith. "Apostle" means "sent." Sent by

Figure 4.2 Woodcut of Saint Matthew writing his gospel, with the angel representing the inspiration from God.

whom? By Jesus, who is Himself taken by Christians to be the Son of God, the second Person of the eternal, triune God. Moreover, Christians believe, Paul is "inspired." Inspired by whom? By the Holy Spirit, the third Person of the Trinity. Thus for the Christian the epistles of Paul can be both human letters and divine scripture.

SCRIPTURE AND PROPHETS

Perhaps one of the simplest ways to understand what we mean by a "holy text"—a writing especially related to Ultimate Being, making it more than any secular text— is to connect scripture to the concept of a prophet. As we've seen, prophets are one kind of founder that is himself or herself especially related to God by being the recipient (in some sense) of a divine call and an ensuing message from God. We saw in the previous chapter that the concept of the prophet is most closely related to the concept of Ultimate Being as God precisely because the prophet must be, in some way, in communication with God as an inter-relational, personal being. We noted that it is not quite correct to think of a "prophet of the Dao" simply because the Dao is not the kind of Ultimate Being that communicates its will to human individuals. Indeed, as we saw back in Chapter 2, it does not make much sense to say the Dao has a will at all. Thus we think of a prophet perhaps literally in communication with God and thus receiving from God a specific message. And, in turn, if this message is written down, we have scripture.

We have, perhaps, already seen how the prophetic role gives rise to scripture in the Gurus of Sikhism and the Apostles of Christianity. But, let us admit, both of these cases are not quite perfect examples of prophets; indeed, neither religion tends to call these writers "prophets." Let us therefore look at another example, where we find perhaps the clearest case of a prophet whose relation to God yields scripture: Islam.

We have already noted the call of Muhammad as the historical beginning of Islam. Not only is the story of Muhammad reciting the words of the angel in the caves of Hira a classic example of the prophetic call; it is also a paradigm example of how the words that Muhammad thereafter uttered were taken as something more than the mundane words of a man, even a very holy and righteous man. Rather, for Muslims, the words that Muhammad spoke from his encounters with God and angels are not his words at all. They are unmediated divine revelation, simply "recited" by Muhammad. Thus when these words are memorized and later collected, they are exactly that, "Recitation," which is what is meant by the term "**Quran**."

From the phenomenological perspective, then—for, of course, from the outside these claims are highly debated—the words that Muhammad received and recited to others are not his words at all. In contrast to Saint Paul, Muhammad is not writing what he is thinking about, however inspired that writing might be. Rather, Muslims say that it is more like dictation, with God (through an angel perhaps) simply saying what Muhammad is then supposed to repeat. Muhammad's vocabulary and his interests are not involved in the content of the text, Muslims say, insisting in fact that Muhammad himself was illiterate. Yet the Quran comes to humanity in an inimitable style, gloriously poetic, full of unfathomable wisdom, without contradiction, fluent in perfect Arabic. Thus the Quran is clearly divine revelation, sacred scripture, because it is the very words of God.

The story of Moses might be added here as another example of the way the words of a holy prophet become holy text. Indeed, Moses is recognized as perhaps the greatest prophet of Judaism not only by Jews but also by Muslims and Christians, and all three religions agree that the writings attributed to him, the "five books of Moses," are holy scripture. These five books are the same as the first five books of the Christian Old Testament, collectively called the **Torah**, which means something like "law" or "teaching." It reads somewhat differently from the Quran: much more narrative in many parts, though with long stretches of instruction; and it is certainly not like the epistle literature of the New Testament. Even so, for Jews it is the single most important revelation of God to humanity. God delivers to Moses on Mount Sinai all that mankind needs to know, and the rest, we might say, is interpretation.

Admittedly, there is much doubt among scholars about the authenticity of historical claims about Moses and the composition of the Torah; there are difficulties and nuances even about the revelation, organization, and preservation of the Quran after Muhammad. But for our purposes, again, it is important to see that what devout Jews and Muslims believe they have—alongside devout Christians with their New Testament, Sikhs with the *Adi Granth*, and others—is a divine word passed on to humanity. Human words, human language, of course; yet somehow different, unlike any human words because of the ultimate source. That source, whether through recitation or inspiration, is believed to be God, and thus these texts are "scripture."

SCRIPTURE AND SAGES

We have just seen that there is a kind of logical relation between the ideas of scripture, prophets, and the relation of those prophets to God. When we turn to a kind of non-theistic Ultimate Being, we find something a little different and yet we still find scripture. Indeed, if we recall the basic logic used in differentiating between prophets and sages in Chapter 3, we can guess the logical connection we now find between Ultimate Being concepts like the Dao and the kind of "revelation" that comes through a sage like Laozi. For we can say that there is a clear analogy between the relation of God and prophets and the scripture of theistic religions and the relation of other kinds of Ultimate Beings and sages and the scriptures of those religions. The logic suggests that the relation God/Moses/Torah is analogous to the relation Dao/ Laozi/*Daodejing*.

Let us be clear: It's analogous, not identical. For we saw in the previous chapter that it would not make sense to call Laozi a prophet, because he does not receive a call or a message from any Ultimate Being. Indeed, the Dao, as we've noted since Chapter 2, is not the kind of Being that could call or speak to Laozi. And yet Laozi has a message and it is something more than, say, a college textbook. It is right to call it Daoist scripture.

As one might guess, the situation with Confucius and books like his **Analects** or the *Doctrine of the Mean* (actually written by Confucius' grandson) is similar to that of Laozi. In both cases, the texts that emerge from the recognized sage carry a special kind of religious authority, such that if someone quotes these texts, he or she has made a statement about what is true for these religions. That is, the fact that the source of these words is a Chinese sage means that he knows something about these truths that most of us do not know, and thus to quote him is to say something authoritative.

Besides the scriptures of China, a useful third example is evident in the words of the Buddha. In this case, Buddhist tradition declares that the Buddha himself did not write the texts that became the scriptures of Buddhism, but, somewhat like Muhammad, his followers memorized and began to recite what the master said and, ultimately, to record his teaching in writing. Thus, for example, the most foundational texts of Buddhism are literally the Buddha's sermons, or what are usually called **sutras**. These sutras, in their earliest forms, often begin with an apparent reciter saying, "This is what I heard the Buddha say," and thus the authority of all that follows is established. Along with this sutra literature, early schools of Buddhism collected the Buddha's statements about monastic rules and his analyses of phenomena that help followers understand the soul-less nature of the self and, as Buddhism develops, the ultimately "empty" nature of all things. These three collections become the "Three Baskets" of early Buddhist scripture, and they carry religious authority because they are spoken by the Enlightened One. Here is the man who awakened to the truth of Emptiness; it only makes sense, therefore, to see his words as revelation of religious truth.

There are many complications to any discussion of Buddhist scripture, however, and, for that matter, some interesting complications in the way Muslims apply the Quran, Jews the Torah, and so on. We will talk in a moment about secondary scriptures and the possibility that there may be more scripture in a religion beyond what the founder spoke. But for now we should be able to see how authority in text can come from the authority of a founder, thus connecting the readers to the Ultimate Being. This is what makes scripture "holy." Again, it should not be assumed that all religions think of scripture or apply it the same way. Indeed, we should expect that the Quran of Islam and how it is used will be as different from, say, how the *Daodejing* is used as the sage Laozi is himself different from the prophet Muhammad. And they differ ultimately because Allah is not the same as the Dao, even if both are Ultimate Being.

CANON

The word "**canon**" refers to a kind of measuring stick, a standard by which other things are marked. In the area of religious texts, the word refers to a group of writings that, in one way or another, form a limited and defined group. We therefore can talk about the "canon of scripture" in order to discuss what exactly fits into a religion's list of authoritative texts and what does not.

Perhaps the easiest way to understand this concept is to look at an example. It is well known, perhaps, that the Christian New Testament consists of twenty-seven

separate "books," mostly letters (or epistles, as noted earlier), along with four accounts of Jesus' life (the four Gospels), one history of the early Christians ("Acts of
the Apostles"), and a final "apocalypse," the "Revelation of John." It may also be well
known in our time that there were other candidates, other letters, gospels, and even
apocalypses, that might have been selected to be part of the official New Testament.
But they weren't. Telling the story of precisely how these twenty-seven books came
to be the New Testament, and other pieces of literature, like the Gospel of Thomas
or the Epistle of Clement, did not is beyond the scope of this text. Suffice it to say
that, over time, it became clear to many Christians spread across the Roman Empire
in the second century that these twenty-seven books, and only these, should be
"read in the assembly." Later, within another two centuries or so, that list was finalized and declared complete by a group of church leaders from throughout the
Mediterranean area. And this, for most Christians, is what "closed the canon" of
the New Testament.

There are two points to get from this short tale. First, it helps to clarify what is
meant by "canon," namely the official list of scriptures, a kind of final designation
of what is in and what is out. That does not necessarily mean, in the case of the New
Testament, that something excluded is bad; it was well known that, for example, the
Letter of Clement was a strong, edifying piece of early Christian writing. But it was
generally believed among early Christians that to call a writing "scripture" meant it
had to be something written by one of the Apostles (or a close companion), and
Clement, even writing as early as the 90s of the first century, did not qualify. In
contrast, some texts were rejected because they just didn't seem to tell the right
story. This is the case with the Gospel of Thomas. For our purposes, it doesn't
matter whether we in the twenty-first century think these other writings are good
or "Christian" enough. The point is that early Christians knew they existed and
chose not to include them in the canon. And thus, to this day, if you pick up a
Christian Bible and turn to the New Testament, it will probably not contain either
the Gospel of Thomas or the Letter of Clement. You can find them elsewhere easily
enough, but we can't really just decide on our own to call them Christian scripture.
The canon is closed.

And that is the second point. When we speak of a **"closed canon,"** we mean that
new texts cannot be added to the original list as if claiming some equal authority. In
the case of the New Testament, the closing of the canon took centuries. In the case of
the Quran, the closing of the canon was relatively simple, since, once Muhammad
died, it was believed that there simply could be no new revelations from God. Thus the
canon closed with Muhammad's death. It was not quite that simple, of course, since
those who had followed Muhammad had to decide what they remembered and how it
was to be written, how the various parts should be organized, and even if, perhaps,
some verses might have gotten lost somewhere. But whatever revision and reorganiza-
tion might have been necessary over the next couple of decades, there was no dispute

about the closing of the canon. Muhammad, the last of the prophets, was dead, and therefore there was no more revelation to come.

With these two examples, it may seem intuitively obvious that a canon of scripture has to be closed, but interestingly, we might also see that the closing of the New Testament was much more challenging, in a way, than the closing of the Quran. And in fact, we might from there be led to ponder if, indeed, there is such a thing as an open canon. And the answer is yes.

Hinduism and Buddhism—at least some schools of the latter—make interesting examples of the possibility of an open canon. For Hinduism, the most authoritative texts (in theory) are the ancient **Vedas**. The foundation of these texts, appearing perhaps as early as 1200 BCE, is the Rig Veda, a collection of great hymns that were "heard" by the wise *rishis* long, long ago. As noted in Chapter 3, these *rishis* might be like prophets, hearing these hymns from the gods themselves, or they might be sages, so in tune with the great mysteries of nature that they spoke primarily from their own wisdom. Actually, we can't tell, because any historical information about these men is lost. More important for our concern in this chapter, the even more difficult issue with the Vedas is that they change and metamorphose from hymns praising ancient gods into ritual formulas and magic words for magic spells, like how to cure snake bite or encourage crops to grow. Strangely (at least for someone more used to the Bible or the Quran), the texts that eventually become the canon of the Vedas become several different collections, even some wholly new texts—the Upanishads—that seem to leave the ancient gods behind entirely and refocus the practice of Hinduism greatly.

And this is not the end. In Chapter 2, when we discussed Hinduism and polytheism, the ancient gods of the earliest texts were not even mentioned. Indeed, it is interesting and perhaps curious that the gods of the most ancient texts of Hinduism are largely forgotten to the worshipers within the modern faith. And by the same token, these ancient texts, still in some way the most authoritative texts of Hinduism, are mostly the interest of a priestly class that uses them for ritual magic. Meanwhile for the average Hindu worshiper today, new gods have replaced the ancient Vedic gods and other texts have become more important than the Vedas. For example, texts written much later than the Vedas—like the stories of the gods collected in the Purana literature, or like the great "epics" of human and divine heroes told in the *Ramayana* and the *Mahabharata*—are texts far better known and more directly accessible by the average Hindu than the Vedas. And they, too, are open to edition and revision, such that, for example, the ***Ramayana*** as read by a devout worshiper in south India might be intentionally different from one read by a Hindu of a different area or a different social class.[2] And no one seems to find this problematic. The canon, apparently, is open.

This is logical. We saw before that even the pantheon of Hinduism is, in a way, open. That is, we saw that, even today, it is possible that a great guru might arise, gain a large following, and be declared a manifestation of deity. Thus his or her words would have a valid claim to authority, a direct connection to the holy, and therefore be scripture. For example, we can find in the Hindu sect devoted to Swami Narayan, the nineteenth-century guru and divine manifestation mentioned in the previous chapter, a collection of his sermons and speeches called the *Vachanamrut*. And these, as the introduction to an English translation declares, are Lord Narayan's "divine words."[3]

With Buddhism, the story is a bit different. To some degree, we might assert that all schools of Buddhism accept as authoritative the Three Baskets of the Buddha's lessons. But in the later schools of Buddhism, the Mahayana schools, it was possible simply to assert that the Buddha had given other sermons besides those collected in the basket of sutras, and that these other sermons, even where they appeared to con-tradict the earlier teachings, were equally authoritative. Thus, some centuries after the life of the Buddha, there began to appear other texts: The Perfection of Wisdom Sutras, the Lotus Sutra, the Diamond Sutra, and others; and for the Mahayana schools who found the authority for their teachings in these texts, the fact that they could claim to have the words of the Buddha himself meant that their schools, too, were genuinely Buddhist, even if they seemed contrary to what had been delivered in the Three Baskets.

And Buddhism adds another possibility, one perhaps analogous to the openness of the canon in Hinduism. For if indeed it is possible that someone living long after the historical Buddha could likewise be enlightened and could be, so to speak, a Buddha himself, then it is possible to appeal to the words of the latter-day Buddha with equal authority. Indeed, this seems to happen in the seventh century CE when there arose in China a dispute about which great teacher should be the leader (or Patriarch) of the "real" Zen Buddhist school. In the middle of this dispute, there appeared a text called "The Platform Sutra of the Sixth Patriarch," and this text established for many in the history of Zen, a lineage of authentic teachers going back to this Patriarch and his words, as recorded in this text. It is interesting—and indeed ironic, as we note later in this chapter—that the possession of this text and its use in teaching became a hall-mark for genuine authority in Zen Buddhism.

SECONDARY SCRIPTURES

The many examples of the previous section illustrate the difference between an open canon and a closed canon of scripture. We have noted that, for example, in Islam, its relatively strict denial of other gods goes hand-in-hand with its relatively strong sense of its canon being closed. In contrast, the relatively open pantheon of Hinduism goes well with its relatively open sense of scriptural canon. Thus we might tend to expect that these two concepts, closed pantheon and a closed canon, are logically connected. By and large, we have seen that this is so, although it would be a mistake to think it a simple and unchanging relation. For, although we have looked for and found many important logical connections within religions of all kinds, we have also noted often enough that there is a great deal of variation in the religious world.

Indeed, as a kind of appendix to this discussion of open and closed canons, we should note that even the religion of Islam opened itself, interestingly enough, to a kind of second scripture. That is, we find in Islam that the Quran, considered by Muslims (as we've seen) to be the final, perfect, unchanged words of Allah, and therefore the absolutely final word of truth, is still not the only source of religious truth. In fact, it seems that as Islam developed, it became apparent that the detail of what the Quran teaches about how to submit one's life to God is not entirely clear in the Quran alone. We noted earlier that the text had to be arranged and organized after the death of the Prophet, and it is not often evident, therefore, what the context of a particular verse might have been, or exactly how it was meant to be applied to life. Therefore it became necessary within orthodox Islam to appeal not only to the Quran but also to the stories of Muhammad's life, as a source of authority. These stories, collectively called **Hadith** or Sunna, are described as "traditions," and they constitute a vast collection of words and actions by Muhammad that runs to multiple volumes. And, as Muhammad himself is taken to be a perfect example of worship and submission to Allah, these collections of traditions become essential in Islam for developing the detail of living according to the will of God.

In Judaism, there is a similar example, though interestingly quite different. In this faith, too, it became clear some 2,000 years ago that the ancient rules for establishing a priesthood and offering sacrifices in the Jerusalem temple would no longer be followed. Therefore, if Judaism was going to survive, it was necessary to clarify what it meant to follow the law of God in a new way, a way open to interpretation and development. Thus was born the **Mishnah**, the collection of laws from the Torah as understood and explained by the Rabbis of the first couple of centuries of the Common Era. Beyond the Mishnah, in fact, there developed more interpretations of these laws, exemplified, discussed, and debated by several more generations of scholars. All of this debate and clarification then became collected in another vast and detailed set of statements of religious law, the **Talmud**.

The Talmud, like the Hadith, is a secondary text, yet one with significant, even necessary, authority for the development of the religion. Unlike the Hadith, however, the Talmud is not a matter of seeing how one man, some great founder, lived and exemplified obedience to God. Quite the contrary. For the Talmud, authority lies in the general consensus of a group of scholars—the "sages" of Judaism noted in Chapter 3—and not in any one individual. Even so, the Talmud carries authority as the direction of God for Judaic life. In fact, the sages declared that this process of debate and the examination of religious law by scholars was a tradition going back to Moses himself, and therefore the opinions of scholars from the first to the sixth centuries CE had the same authority as Moses' original Torah. That is why the Rabbis call the Talmud the Oral Torah.

We might extend this section further with references to other secondary scriptures. We could note how the Confucian philosopher Mencius (372–289 BCE) became recognized as the greatest interpreter of Confucius, such that his own eponymous text, the *Mencius*, became recognized in China as the latest text alongside those of Confucius required to be studied by all Chinese scholars. Another eponymous text, the *Zhuangzi* (Zhuangzi, 369–286 BCE), is a similar example from Daoism. Exactly how much authority there is in these later-generation teachers varies. If we were to go on and add examples from the founders of different Christian sects, such as the writings of Martin Luther or the famous *Institutes* of John Calvin, we would have slowly slipped from the realm of scripture. That is, for a good Presbyterian Christian, the works of Calvin might be very important, quite foundational to what he or she believes and to the way he or she practices the faith; but no good Calvinist theologian would say Calvin's work is scripture. Someone might appeal to such a text very much, perhaps even more than the New Testament. But then someone might live less by the Bible than by, say, the works of Karl Marx or Tupac Shakur. But at that point we have the "functional equivalent" of scripture, just as we may have the functional equivalent of religion.[4]

CONCLUSIONS ON SCRIPTURE AND THE POSSIBILITY OF ANTI-SCRIPTURE

We have seen in this chapter that religious scriptures are a common element among many of the major world religions. They are generally a kind of writing that reveals to the reader something about Ultimate Being, yet they do so with a kind of authority not shared by just any scholarly or devotional text. A Christian might find the devotional writing by Thomas à Kempis or the philosophical ideas of C. S. Lewis more inspiring than the New Testament itself, and still only the latter is sacred scripture. And to repeat our common "logic of the sacred," we see that the scriptures have that authority because the writers are thought to be somehow special, whether sages or prophets or something in between, and they themselves are "holy" because of their special understanding of, and relation to, Ultimate Being.

We have also seen, of course, that exactly how authoritative a religious text may be is somewhat variable. The text of a prophet receiving a dictation of divine words might understandably be taken to have more authority than the wisdom of a sage, and of course we will find, even among those who follow the same sacred text, that some believers will follow it more strictly than others. All this is to admit, as usual, that our generalizations are just that: generalizations. And yet we can find threads of logic that tie the ideas of scripture, founder, and Ultimate Being together, such that we begin to discover how a religion comes to exist as a unified system, not just a haphazard collection of ideas.

Thus we come to the end of this discussion of religious scripture, seeing how, with a text in hand, a believer can know how to live and what to do and what to believe

Figure 4.3 Hui-neng, the Sixth Patriarch of Chinese Chan (Zen), tears up the Buddhist sutras, insisting that the written text is a distraction from the immediate experience of enlightenment.

because it is written. Indeed, we find that the words of scripture being written is precisely what allows people of a religion to hold onto important doctrines and practices from generation to generation. In many cases it allows believers to settle disputes by appealing to an authoritative source, and it allows people to gather into social units defined by their adherence to the authority of the text. Thus a religious text often helps define the content of the religion itself, its community, and its order and ritual. This is the strength of religious scripture.

It is also the weakness of scripture. For one might wish that a religion could change with the times, update itself so as to seem more relevant to the problems of the present. One might simply wish the language were not so archaic, so that we readers of the twenty-first century could actually understand what it says. An old, apocryphal tale from a tribal religious culture speaks of a tribal elder telling an ancient tale of ancestors and the founding of religious ritual, when a visiting anthropologist asks him where he reads this story. The elder replies that it is not written down, but handed down orally from generation to generation. "Then how can you know that it is the same tale told by your fathers' fathers?" the anthropologist inquires. The tribal elder replies: "It doesn't matter, for I am the one telling it now."

In other words, it might actually seem to some that scripture inhibits the transfer of religious wisdom, inasmuch as that wisdom is ancient, perhaps locked in cultural traditions not relevant a thousand years later. It is also possible that people might feel that writing in general, as a medium, simply cannot contain wisdom the way wisdom ought to be conveyed. Wisdom, one might suggest, is not something dead and frozen on a page, but something heartfelt, given from one person to another along with care and instruction. Or true wisdom, someone might say, shouldn't merely be read but rather enacted, more important, something *done* rather than something *said*. Perhaps scripture is really scripture only if it is sung.

All of this suggests that there might be reasons why written scripture is actually resisted in some cases. Notably, there are indeed indigenous groups whose religious myths and ritual rules have never been written down and which, perhaps, should not be. In one example, captured in the *Long Search* episode "The Way of the Ancestors," it was noted how the Toraja people of Indonesia had never had their religious stories written and did not want them written. Even so, the loss of native ways to the encroachments of modern life left many of the elders afraid that the ancient religious ways would be lost. And thus writing was being considered, reluctantly, for the first time.

In a different vein, the Zen tradition in Buddhism advertised itself as a transmission of the Buddha's teaching "outside the scriptures" and "not dependent on words and letters." At a time in China when various schools of Buddhism were in competition, each claiming that this or that Mahayana sutra was the Buddha's highest teaching, the Zen school made its own claim of superiority by insisting that the true center of Buddhism was the experience of enlightenment, the awakening of the mind, and that scripture merely gets in the way. Thus the Zen school would have us not read scripture, but sit at the feet of an enlightened master who will help us "point directly to the mind" and awaken to our innate Buddha Nature. Words are merely cognitive, we are told, and get in the way of enlightenment. That is why one hero of the Zen school in China, the Sixth Patriarch, Hui-neng, is said to have been proudly illiterate, and there exists a famous sketch by Liang Kai (1140–1210) that depicts Hui-neng tearing up pages of scriptures to teach his disciples the danger of relying on words.

Yet this is ironic. We already noted that the text called *The Platform Sutra* emerged within the Zen tradition and became the authoritative scripture that in a way defined orthodoxy. Notably, this scripture is said to be the words of the Sixth Patriarch, the same Hui-neng who tore up the scriptures in his disdain for the written word. This suggests perhaps that, even when we try not to rely on words, we often rely on words to tell us not to rely on words. In a sense, it seems we simply are beings of language and linguistic cognition, and we cannot help it that we find ourselves prone to construct beliefs and make truth claims, even about those things that transcend our language and thoughts. But this has been a hallmark of religion from the outset: that we focus on things that are ultimately beyond us, and yet which we cannot, it seems, ignore. Perhaps in the end we would be better off religiously if we could stop being concerned with words and texts, focusing instead on emotion or feelings or experiences, or if we instead focused our religious lives on what we do in ritual and in moral behavior. But these are points we shall consider later, when we have finished our unit on truth and turn to speak of goodness and beauty. But, be warned, we shall still be using words, and those words will appear here, in a written text.

KEY TERMS IN CHAPTER 4

Adi Granth   The primary holy text of Sikhism, being the poetry of the founder Guru Nanak and successive leaders. It is ultimately itself considered the holy guru.

Analects   The sayings of Confucius, collected to become one of the "Four Books" taken as scripture in Confucianism.

canon   A group of writings, especially scriptures, that form a limited and defined group, thus amounting to a list of a religion's authoritative texts.

closed canon   The sense within a religion that the list of authoritative texts, the scriptures, cannot be added to, in contrast to an "open canon," where some possibility of adding new scriptures exists.

Daodejing   The foundational scripture of Daoism attributed to the sage Laozi.

epistle   Literally, "letter." Particularly in Christianity, one of the letters of the New Testament scriptures written by those sent by Jesus to spread His teaching.

Hadith   A collection of written "traditions" that functions as a secondary scripture in Islam. It contains the words and actions of Muhammad, providing for Islam example and context for understanding proper submission to God.

Mishnah   The collection of laws from the Torah as understood and explained by the Jewish Rabbis of the first centuries of the Common Era.

Quran   The scriptures of Islam, literally the "recitation" of God's words to Muhammad.

scripture   "Holy text"; the writings within a religion that carry a special status of authority, based, often, on the direct relation between the recorded words and the founder, thus finally to Ultimate Being.

Ramayana   Scripture of popular Hinduism featuring the epic tale of the god Rama.

sutra   A sermon or teaching, especially by the Buddha, remembered and collected by generations of monks who compiled the earliest Buddhist scriptures.

Talmud   In Judaism, the multiple-volume collection of Mishnah and commentary, amounting to a secondary authority for studying divine law as revealed in the Torah. Also called the Oral Torah.

Torah   The holy scriptures of Judaism attributed to Moses, collected as the first five books of the Bible.

Veda   The oldest scriptural texts of Hinduism, evolving from approximately 1200 BCE through forms of hymns to ancient gods, ritual formulae, and magical mantras.

CHAPTER 5

THE LANGUAGES OF RELIGION

THE TITLE OF THIS chapter might make one think about specific human languages that have become, for one reason or another, important, even holy languages, within specific religions. But that would be a mistake. This chapter on the "languages" of religion isn't about Latin or Sanskrit or Arabic; it is really about myth and poetry and instruction.

This is not to say that the historical relationships between some religions and a specific language are unimportant or uninteresting. In connection with the previous chapter, it is often the case that languages somehow associated with scripture take on a kind of power or magic of their own and thus become holy. Sanskrit, the ancient language of the Hindu Vedas, is what can be called a "dead language," a language no one really speaks any more, but because it is the language of the ancient scriptures, the Brahmin priests of Hinduism to this day learn to read and chant the Sanskrit words of the Vedas. In fact, a young priest must learn very precise intonations and rhythms of the words of scripture—words that evolved into ritual formulas and even magical phrases for warding off evil—in order that the words have their effect.

In a similar way, Latin became the holy language of the Roman Catholic branch of Christianity, passing out of common ritual use only quite recently. There are many good Catholics still alive today who will remember when the Mass had to be said in the old Roman language; it was only in 1963 that the Second Vatican Council decided that the central Catholic Christian ritual could be spoken in the everyday language of the people. Notably, the original scriptures of Christianity were not in Latin but in Greek, and it was only the Western, Rome-centered church that translated their text and rituals into Latin in the fourth century and kept tight control of translation until the twentieth century.

Arabic, for Islam, is yet another interesting case of linguistic history, partly because it remains a living language. Indeed, it is precisely because the Quran was written in Arabic, and because the Quran (as we've seen) is believed to be a perfect and final dictation of God's words, that the language has been so stable. While Latin evolved into languages like Spanish and French, Sanskrit into Pali and Hindi and many others, the Arabic of the Quran has remained largely stable. In a way, the holy text made the Arabic language—giving Arabic its form from among many dialects—and keeps it still relatively unchanged. And the language remains "holy" inasmuch as any good Muslim will insist that the Quran can only be truly God's words in Arabic, that its ritual quotation during prayers must be in Arabic, and that the recitation of belief must be in Arabic. Many Muslims to this day will memorize much of the Quran in Arabic, even though they don't know Arabic and don't understand what it means.

For all this, the role of various human languages in the practice of religion is not the focus of this chapter, although some points about the magic power of words will be noted in Chapter 7. This chapter, rather, is about "language," in the sense of how we all speak in different ways, even if we all use English. That is, when you sing a song to the radio, you are, in a way, using a different kind of English than when you write a paper for your Religion course. When you tell a joke, you're using English differently from when you describe your recent injury to your doctor. They are all English, but in this chapter we will talk about them as different languages.

RELIGIOUS LANGUAGES AND THEIR IMPORTANCE

To understand the different languages of religion, it might help to explain why it is an important issue. In a way, the point of talking about these languages is an extension of the previous chapter, in which we talked about scripture. For it is not only important to know what a religious scripture says; it is also important to know what it means. There is often an issue in religious discussion, even when two people agree on quoting authoritatively the same text, that people can't agree on the text's interpretation. This chapter does not resolve all such disputes, but it might help us to think carefully about how to read scripture whether we accept its authority or not.

Here is a non-religious example. Joyce Kilmer in his poem wrote:

I think that I shall never see a poem as lovely as a tree,
A tree whose hungry mouth is pressed against the earth's sweet flowing breast.

Now there would be few of us who would read these lines and argue that they are simply wrong. That is, obviously trees don't have mouths and the earth isn't a breast, and yet we don't complain that Kilmer's words are misleading or erroneous. That is because we recognize that he is writing a poem. If one were to read a similar line in one's Botany textbook, there would be a grave problem. Imagine the biology text said, "The common pine tree known as blue spruce (*picea pungens*) presses its mouth into the soil from which it sucks milk for sustenance." That's bad science. But a poem isn't "bad science" because it isn't speaking the language of science. This is something we know intuitively.

Here is another example:

> Manwe considered, given a vision by Eru Iluvatar as he did so, then told Yavanna of what he had learned: "When the Children awake, then the thought of Yavanna will awake also, and it will summon spirits from afar, and they will go among the *kelvar* [animals] and the *olvar* [plants], and some will dwell therein, and be held in reverence, and their just anger shall be feared. . . . But in the forests shall walk the Shepherds of the Trees."[1]

Obviously this, too, is somehow about trees and yet it is neither a poem nor a biological description. It's something else, although our intuitions about exactly what kind of language it is might not be clear. In this textbook, I call it myth, and in a section later in this chapter, we shall see more clearly what that means. The point for now is only to note that you, the reader, probably felt almost at once that you were reading neither poetry nor science, though it might have felt more like poetry than science. And that's important. For one can intuitively get a feel for how to read something and how it ought to be understood. And this applies to religious scriptures as much as it applies to examples in a textbook on religion.

In the sections that follow, therefore, we will talk briefly about different kinds of religious language and about how to understand those languages so as not to misunderstand what the writing is trying to do. We will talk about myth and history and parables, but also about poetry and "wisdom," as well as simple, straightforward instruction. We shall find that we read these different genres, these "languages," differently, and that keeping such differences in mind can be the first step toward an intelligent reading of scripture.

STORIES: MYTH, HISTORY, AND PARABLES

There are stories about Abraham Lincoln growing up in the woods of Illinois; there are stories about the end of the world; and there's a story about "a boy who cried 'Wolf.'" All of these are stories, but they shouldn't be read in the same way. The first may be history, the second myth, and the third a parable.

Of these three kinds of stories, history may seem to be the most obvious. When a story is told that is intended as history, we are—more or less—expected to take the story as a reasonable description of something that actually happened. This is not to say that historical descriptions are ever objective and complete; one couldn't even describe what happened yesterday objectively and completely. But a piece of literature that is trying to be historical is an effort by the author to describe something that he or she believes happened in time and space. The author might be mistaken, might have only a peculiar perspective on the facts, and so on, but it is important to read the story as if the author intends us to get those facts. That is precisely why it makes sense to ask if the author is right; it makes no sense to ask if the author of the tree poem got the facts right.

A good example to ponder is the gospel narratives of Christianity, Luke's gospel in particular. Notably, Luke starts his story by pointing out that other people have tried to tell the story of Jesus, and that Luke himself considered it necessary that someone try to "draw up an orderly account." It is possible to gather from his prologue that he found some eyewitnesses to ask about Jesus, and most scholars believe that Luke had at least two, maybe three earlier written sources on his desk as he wrote his version of the life of Jesus. One doesn't have to believe that Luke got it all right; one does have to believe that Luke was trying to get it right.

This is in contrast to the **parables** of Jesus himself. When Jesus told stories about a man from Samaria who was kind to a stranger, or a story about a wealthy man with two sons, the younger of whom left home with his inheritance and squandered his money, or a story about the owner of a vineyard whose workers tried to steal his property—these stories are evidently illustrations of a point Jesus was trying to make and are not intended to be understood historically. That is, if we read the story of the "Good

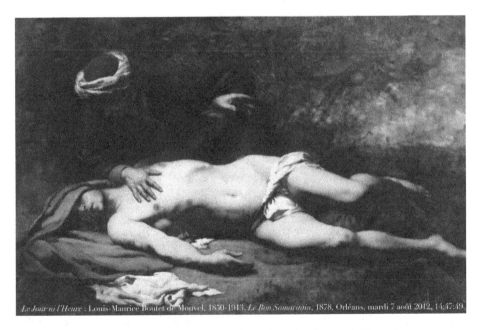

Figure 5.1   *The Good Samaritan*, painting by Louis-Maurice Boutet de Monvel.

Samaritan," it would be silly of us to ask what his name was or what town he came from. We don't ask if Jesus got his facts right, because there are no facts to get right. He's making a moral lesson about kindness, not telling the history of a man's life.

Myth is the more difficult category, as it falls somewhere in between parable and history. For many people, the word "myth" by itself seems to imply that the story being told is false, certainly not history. But the way the word is used in religious contexts, it refers to a story that is often of literally cosmic proportions, telling us something about humanity or the world or at least some important part of the world as we live with it every day. Think about the story of the American immigrant who comes to the United States penniless, but through hard work and frugal living gets an education, starts a business, and becomes a self-made millionaire. This is a myth of the "American dream," and, interestingly, it is not totally false. That is, it does actually happen sometimes. But the point is not to tell the story of one individual as if it's history; nor is the point to suggest that this happens to everyone that comes to the United States. Clearly in that sense it is false. But it does tell us something about how many Americans view America. It is a myth that defines who they are and the meaning they apply to their own existence. It's an American myth.

In religion, the myths that "define who we are" are as grand as stories of creation and as particular as stories among Native Americans of how the first corn was planted. In the Bible, the creation of the universe in six days is a common story that has been interpreted in a variety of ways. Surprisingly, perhaps, the literal sense of there being six 24-hour periods in which God created the listed objects on planet Earth has not been the most common understanding. As far back as Saint Augustine, writing in the fifth century, one finds interpretations of the creation story that suggest the "days" are metaphorical.[2] By the same token, Augustine almost certainly took the story of Adam and Eve and their first sin as not-metaphorical, since the historical fall of mankind into sin was an important part of his theology. The point here is not to explain which approach to which story—metaphorical or not—is the right one; the point rather is only to suggest that interpreting the story is more complicated than it seems on the surface.

When it comes to myth, therefore, we, as intelligent readers and interpreters of scripture, are navigating difficult seas. If one discusses the Apocalypse of John (more commonly known as "Revelation") in the New Testament, one might want to find all kinds of references to historical events predicted to be near the end of the world. Some Christian teachers have managed to construct very careful timelines of the end, predicting down to the day the "Second Coming of Christ." Apparently, so far they've all been wrong. But that's not to say that the Revelation of John is a useless piece of Christian literature. Like the creation story at the other end of the Bible, it tells the believers something important about the world and about themselves. They learn from these stories (at least) that God is above all things, that the universe itself and the history of humanity are not meaningless chaos but a good and purposeful reality in which the goodness of God is the final word. Consequently, one might meet a very "scientific" Christian who holds a firm belief in an ancient Big Bang as the true source of the universe while also holding that these statements about the relation of God to creation might in fact be philosophically true. And this would not seem a contradiction but rather an effort to read the languages of the Bible with care and interpret intelligently.

POETRY

Poetry seems to exist in all cultures across the world and may be some of the most ancient forms of religious ritual, as people sang and chanted words from and to their gods. There is something about poetry that takes the expressions of belief and enhances them, making them emotional and deep in a way that perhaps tired prose cannot. We noted at the beginning of Chapter 4 that the Sikh religion began with songs and poems, and that its scripture ultimately is the collection of those poems taken to be, in some sense, divine revelation. Similarly, the Quran is believed by Muslims to be the most beautiful poetry in the world, its Arabic perfect and fluid, much of it in a kind of rhythmic, rhyming prose. And the beauty of this poetry is said to be part of the proof of its divine origins. Poetry, we might say, brings beauty to truth; we speak more of this in Chapter 10.

But poetry also has problems. The nature of poetry as often being full of powerful and moving imagery, often in brief and dense language, leaves the reader with significant challenges for interpretation, especially when one takes such poems to be somehow holy text. In China, the *Daodejing*, the *Book of the Dao and Its Power*, is a very brief text, about 5,000 words long—shorter than many college research papers. And yet its eighty-one chapters contain the wisdom of Daoism attributed to the great sage Laozi. Picking almost randomly, one finds, for example, Chapter 12 saying,

> The five colors make man's eyes blind;
> The five notes make his ears deaf;
> The five tastes injure his palate;
> Riding and hunting make his mind go wild with excitement;
> Goods hard to come by serve to hinder his progress.
> Hence the sage is for the belly, not for the eye.
> Therefore he discards the one and takes the other.[3]

But what does it all mean? That's hard to say, and in any case, interpreting specific passages for us isn't quite the point of this chapter. But we can note that there are hundreds of commentaries on the text of the *Daodejing*, and many of them are much, much longer than the text itself.

In the Jewish scriptures, what Christians call the Old Testament, there is a significant collection of poems generally called the Psalms. Many of them have traditional poetic styles, such as using each letter of the Hebrew alphabet in alphabetical order as its initial letter, and many others are evidently the lyrics to specific tunes. Others are clearly intended to be sung by priests at specific places in the temple rituals. Unfortunately, the tunes and chants are lost to us—we talk about the religious roots of musical notation in a later chapter—but for our purposes here, the point to remember is what we already noted with the Kilmer poem: that reading poetry is different from reading for information. People realize, for instance, that when reading the famous 23rd Psalm, saying, "The Lord is my shepherd," we are dealing with symbolism and evoking feelings and emotions about being guided and protected by God. It's a mistake to think God is a physical person with a shepherd's hook that he uses to protect sheep.

A more engaging and provocative example is Psalm 137. This poem was evidently written at a time when the Jewish people had just suffered the conquest of their great city Jerusalem, along with the destruction of the temple built by King Solomon. Many of the people of the city were then taken away as slaves to Babylon, and in the anguish of that time someone wrote,

> Beside the rivers of Babylon, we sat and wept
> as we thought of Jerusalem.
> We put away our harps,
> hanging them on the branches of poplar trees. (Psalm 137:1–2, New Living
>   Translation)

One realizes, of course, that this is not a God-praising hymn, like Psalm 23. Yet it is the ending of the poem that is troubling. There the poet writes of vindication, saying:

> O Babylon, you will be destroyed.
> Happy is the one who pays you back
> for what you have done to us.
> Happy is the one who takes your babies
> and smashes them against the rocks! (Psalm 137:8–9, NLT)

This is horrific imagery! And yet, that is the point: it is imagery. Its horrific character is precisely what we ought to feel, as we ponder the anguish of those whose homes and religion were destroyed, their freedom taken away, and their captors mocking them, asking them to sing happy songs from home. The poet instead sings a lamentation and a song of vengeful anger. We might be able to understand that anger, but, at the same time, it would be a mistake to take Psalm 137 as moral instruction. Even if one takes these Psalms to be "divinely inspired," to be genuine scripture and revelation from God, as discussed in the previous chapter, it would be wrong to read it as if it were actually justifying the killing of one's enemy's children. No doubt religious people have all-too-often found scriptural reasons to kill their enemies, even children, but happily, that is not the conclusion of an intelligent reader of Psalm 137 who understands that poetry is a kind of literature to be read for what it is: poetry. At the same time, Christians and Jews do quote the Psalms to defend doctrinal claims, and so it is evident that these poems are meant to convey truths, in some sense, revealed by God. So the point is not that believers never use poetry to convey religious truths. Certainly the opposite is true. But as intelligent readers, we need to be careful about what happens to the meaning of the words when a poem "brings beauty to truth."

WISDOM AND INSTRUCTION

Perhaps what people naively expect from religious scripture is straightforward teaching. Perhaps, if God were going to speak to us, we would just expect that God would tell us what to believe and tell us what to do. But as we're seeing, language is more complicated than that, and religion—as human experience in general—is not only about claims of truth and directions for goodness.

Even so, it is evident that much scripture does indeed contain straightforward instruction. We already noted how the letters of Saint Paul that make up a large portion of the Christian New Testament are his direct statements of belief and behavior written to the fledgling churches of the first generation of believers. Much in those letters was responding to specific needs and concerns of those congregations, some of them in fact responses to letters they had written to him with specific questions he needed to answer. What is the right teaching regarding salvation? What is the right way to practice the Lord's Supper? Paul tells you.

A different kind of "instruction" that one often finds in religious texts is sometimes called "**wisdom literature**." Wisdom literature often consists of short sentences

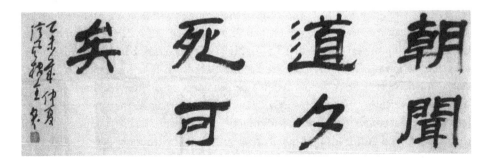

Figure 5.2   The Confucian aphorism reads, "In the morning hear the Dao, in the evening die content," from the Analects 4:8. (Calligraphy generously created by Liu Weiwei, Xi'an, China; photo by author.)

or aphorisms that contain advice on how to live or how to succeed in the world. They can come across as "old sayings," such as "pretty is as pretty does," or "a penny saved is a penny earned." Evidently such sayings are not necessarily very religious, as these examples, often falsely attributed to Benjamin Franklin, indicate. But other such life instructions apparently are trying to help the reader understand Ultimate Reality or offer us advice that comes not just from Franklin but from God.

One great and very influential example of such writing is the Analects of Confucius. Obviously (as we've noted in several contexts already), the "religion" of Confucius does not focus on God, and the revelations that flow from his pen are the words of a sage, not a prophet. But Confucius' aphorisms do contain religious material. "In the morning hear the Dao; in the evening die content," he says, and this wisdom seems to be telling us that we find prosperity and meaning in a life lived in harmony with the Dao. Other passages are clearly more like ethical instruction, for example, as he says, "A son who obeys his father three years after his father's death is a good son indeed," or "Guard virtue with propriety." But even here—as we shall see in Chapter 8—the ethics of Confucius are not without religious importance, for these instructions have their power and authority because they ultimately tell us how to live in harmony with the Dao, the Way of Heaven.

Other pieces of the central Confucian writings, such as the *Doctrine of the Mean*, seem more straightforwardly philosophical, more explanatory of ideas and truth-claims about the nature of the Dao and human character. But the pithy and wise sayings of Confucius' Analects remain the most influential literature of China, perhaps precisely because these sayings are so memorable. But they are also wise, telling us how to live, not like the lectures of a science teacher, but like the suggestions of a father.

In the Bible, one finds this kind of instruction especially in the Proverbs, but also in other books like Ecclesiastes. Here one reads phrases like: "We can make our own plans, but the Lord gives the right answer. People may be pure in their own eyes, but the Lord examines their motives" (Proverbs 16:1–2, NLT). Other bits of wisdom are less evidently religious: "Those who control their tongue will have a long life; opening your mouth can ruin everything. Lazy people want much but get little, but those that work hard will prosper" (Proverbs 13:3–4, NLT). These verses, besides having no evident connection to show why they are back-to-back, seem like nice, worldly suggestions, but there is little to recommend such sentences as divine wisdom. Moreover, they aren't evidently true, since, surely, many of us can imagine that there are indeed lazy people that somehow succeed, and sometimes hard work just isn't enough. But all this is to admit that this kind of literature is not simple instruction, even though it is, in fact, instructive.

Wisdom literature then, whether Biblical or Confucian, is indeed instruction, but it would be a mistake to think of it as simple statements of universal rules. A notable case in the Biblical Proverbs can be found in Chapter 26, where the writer says, "Don't answer the foolish arguments of fools, or you will become as foolish as they are; be sure to answer the foolish arguments of fools, or they will become wise in their own estimation" (26:4–5, NLT). In one sense, this might be read as a simple self-contradiction. But, again, this is not the simple instruction of universal statements. Evidently, the teacher is trying to tell us that there are reasons to avoid stupid argument, but also that people involved in foolish arguments may need to be corrected. Clearly, both these statements might be true. To take Proverbs 26:4–5 as a contradiction is simply to misread wisdom literature.

EXEGESIS AND HERMENEUTICS: THE SCIENCE OF INTERPRETATION

All of this information about different kinds of religious languages has been to suggest that part of an intelligent understanding of religious stories and religious teaching is reading and listening with some subtlety. Remember to read a poem like it's a poem and a myth like it's a myth, and you might avoid some confusions and misunderstandings. I say "might," because scriptures often are thought to have several levels of meaning, and there can be symbolism and metaphor, instruction and history all in the same piece of text. Interesting examples appear where Christians, who, as we've noted, keep and use in their own Bible the scriptures of Judaism, read the stories of Judaism and treat them as both the history of God's covenant with the Jewish people and as allegorical or symbolic promises of specifically Christian truths. Thus the Passover, the key event of the Exodus, when God saved the Jewish people from slavery in Egypt, is to Christians a story both of how the Hebrews put lamb's blood over their doors in order to be saved from "the angel of death," and a symbol of how the blood of Jesus, the "Lamb of God," would be the salvation of all humanity. Jews read the great prophetic poems of Isaiah 53 as descriptions of how Israel suffers in keeping her covenant with God, while Christians read the same poems as promises of the coming of Jesus. So keeping in mind the different languages of religion won't solve all our problems; it is, however, part of intelligent interpretation.

Generally, the art of intelligent interpretation, often involving explicit theories and methods for deriving meaning from a text, is called "**hermeneutics.**" The other difficult term in this section's title, "**exegesis,**" suggests a similar idea. It literally means "to draw out," referring to the process of deriving doctrine and truth claims from a religion's authoritative writings. In the process of developing such doctrine, there is almost inevitably some need to select from a sacred text or a body of sacred literature the pieces that one wants to use. This can lead to what may be called a reliance on "**proof texts,**" those selected pieces of sacred text that support one's doctrinal position. We find some creative—and perhaps frustrating—arguments of this kind, often between people of the same faith, as each side tries to support a favored position. Within Islam, for example, current debates about religious justifications of war choose texts from the

Quran that say, on the one hand, "There is no compulsion in religion," and, on the other hand, "Fight until there is no religion other than Islam." Both verses—and many more that complicate things further—are in the Quran, so one is forced either just to choose the verses one wants to assert (selecting proof texts) or to show reasons for interpreting these verses in specific ways (hermeneutics). In Islam, it is sometimes asserted, for example, that a verse revealed to Muhammad later in his life abrogates, or overrules, a verse received earlier, so that, in this case, the later verse about fighting overrules the earlier one declaring "no compulsion." It is also possible that one can interpret the two verses as compatible if the fighting is not meant to compel anyone toward Islam. Perhaps "fighting" doesn't have to mean forcing religion on anyone, and perhaps other verses in the Quran or in the life of Muhammad suggest that "fighting" mostly refers to defending one's faith against those who would try to suppress the Muslim's free practice of Islam.

We by no means can settle this matter here; it is merely an example of how interpretation—the work of hermeneutics and exegesis—works. It shows—and examples from many faith traditions could be added—that interpreting scripture is a challenge even when people already agree that their source is authoritative. When Mahayana Buddhism appears with new texts attributed to the Buddha, they solve the problem of how to apply these teachings by suggesting that some of the Buddha's sermons were meant for some listeners and other sermons were meant for others. Within the *Platform Sutra*, the Zen text mentioned in the last chapter, the dispute between "sudden enlightenment" and "gradual enlightenment" was solved simply by insisting that the former teaching is meant for superior students, the latter for inferior.[4] In more radical cases, the solution to resolving questions about the teaching of a religion can come down to someone claiming to find a new understanding of an old text, as when Mary Baker Eddy founded the Christian Science movement. The title of her famous book says it all: *Science and Health with Key to the Scriptures.*

So, in the midst of all this difficult work to interpret scriptures, how shall we ever know what is true about a religion? Answering that question is far beyond the scope of this textbook. But it is clearly within the scope of this book to emphasize that interpretation is not random or entirely subjective. Recognizing the difficulty and the many-sided disputes that go along with reading scripture and interpreting its meaning, we should not leap to the opposite error of declaring that any scripture can mean anything we want. While anyone may be entitled to any interpretation he or she likes, that does not mean that every interpretation is equally plausible or equally grounded in good thinking and good history. When Saint John opened his Gospel narrative about Jesus by saying, "In the beginning was the Word and . . . the Word became flesh and dwelt among us," it seems clear that John meant that somehow Jesus was himself the incarnation of some divine power, the Word. When Muslims read this passage, they may instead think only, as the Quran directs them, that Jesus received a word from God. As usual, it is not the purpose of this text to decide which is right, but it is clear from an historical understanding of the Greek language and Greek philosophy that John was not saying what the Muslims say. Right or wrong, John thought Jesus was a divine being. It is difficult to interpret him any other way.

The point, then, is not to give up on reading religious scripture, but to take on the heavy and difficult task of being intelligent readers. Even those of us who do not know the history of languages or the philosophical contexts of various religious writings can certainly find other people who do have this expertise, and when we find them, we can use what they know to help us all interpret scriptures well. We can look for internal consistency within religions, expect there to be rules of interpretation, and find ample commentary on difficult passages given to us by intelligent readers who have gone before us. Thus the difficulty of interpreting the content of religious texts is not solved by simple reading nor by giving up, but by a kind of combination of humility and effort that digs through tough ideas and searches for the best understanding available to us today. No, the text cannot just "mean anything you want it to mean," but neither is it always clear and unambiguous. One might be tempted, because of the labor involved, to give up on reading scripture and listening to the religious authority of stories and texts, but that would be to give up on something central to various religions all over the world. As we've seen, different religions apply different levels of authority to their stories and scriptures, but it is a mistake to abandon entirely such sources of religious truth.

KEY TERMS IN CHAPTER 5

exegesis   Literally "to draw out," referring to the process of deriving doctrine and truth claims from a religion's authoritative writings.

hermeneutics   The art of interpretation, often involving explicit theories and methods for deriving meaning from a text.

myth   A story culturally or religiously used to define the nature of life or a particular group of people; the story may be of literally cosmic proportions, telling us something about the origins or meaning of humanity or the world or some specific cultural phenomenon.

parable   A story invented to illustrate a moral or ideological point, thus stories not intended to be understood historically.

proof texts   Selected pieces of scripture used to defend a particular doctrinal point.

wisdom literature   Short statements and aphorisms collected like wise old sayings to give advice or teaching, such as "Proverbs" of the Bible or the sayings from Confucius' Analects.

CHAPTER 6

MISCELLANEOUS DOCTRINES: THE TRUTH OF SELF, SUFFERING, AND SALVATION

AS WE BEGIN TO wrap up the discussion of religious truth, it is important to re-emphasize that religious beliefs are not just haphazard collections of ideas. There is a logic and consistency to religious beliefs, whether one believes them or not, such that the acceptance of some beliefs makes others more acceptable. Believing that God exists, a God who is personal and interactive with humanity, makes the idea of prophets more reasonable, and perhaps also makes the stories of miracles more possibly historical. This logical coherence extends beyond the arena of truth claims and applies as well to how religions prescribe behavior and religious experience, the good and the beautiful.

Before getting to those other ideals, however, let us consider as briefly as possible a few other ideas that religions tend to emphasize in their constructions of truth. It should come as no surprise that the coherent collections of ideas that become major world religions often do more than merely point to the reality of Ultimate Being. They often connect this idea of the transmundane with ideas about ourselves and the nature of the world we live in. For example, they try to tell us not only who God is but who we are, why we live the complex and sometimes troubling lives we know, and what our ultimate purpose might be. That is, religions often construct for us an entire worldview.

Of course, such a generalization about religion has its exceptions. Some religions—Buddhism, for example—resist our efforts to systematize a philosophy of existence and warn us about becoming attached to philosophical positions. At the same time, even Buddhism in its various forms develops a very elaborate and sophisticated doctrine of the self, and its most basic message, the Four Noble Truths, is a careful and logical effort to explain the nature of our existence in the world. Ironically, perhaps, as the Buddhist is careful not to be "attached to views," so are "right views" part of the Noble Eight-fold Path that leads the Buddhist to liberation.

In this chapter, therefore, we consider "views," specific beliefs that flow out of religion about who we are and what we are here for. It has already been hinted that part of this discussion will focus on the nature of the self and will go on to talk about our ultimate purpose. In between, we discuss how religions deal with the infamous Problem of Evil. We should expect that these three ideas will be logically connected, as we begin to consider who we truly are, what seems to be our human condition, and what better possibility awaits us: self, suffering, and salvation.

THE SELF

Each of us is an individual. We have our own thoughts and experiences, and we each make our own decisions for which we alone are responsible. When I ponder new ideas, I "hear" me thinking, and I presume the same is true for you, though I can't be certain. After all, I don't "hear" you thinking unless you choose to talk or write down what you are thinking. On this level, each of us is a kind of lonely, individual consciousness: I am I, and you are you.

The "I" that I hear in my thoughts and the person that I recognize myself to be through reflection on my own character and beliefs we can call the **empirical self**. This self is "empirical" inasmuch as I am the object of my own thinking, and yet my "self" is not empirical in the same way that physical objects, known to us through the senses, are empirical. Thus the "I" and "you" we seem to know so clearly may really seem quite mysterious. In one sense, each of us is uniquely himself or herself because each person's DNA is unique, and yet we don't identify ourselves by our DNA any more than we do by our fingerprints. We know ourselves in some deeper, more internal and mysterious way than the way a detective in a murder investigation finds the suspect. This deeper and more mysterious self is therefore often the object of religion, as the mystery of the self comes to be explained in its relation to the other mysteries of belief. We might be saying, "I know I am unique genetic material and I know I've had a unique upbringing, but what am I really?" Religions try to answer this question, and, as we should expect, they do so by more or less consistently connecting our concept of self with a concept of Ultimate Being.

Soul and God

In the traditional creation myth of Judaism, a myth adopted essentially by both Christianity and Islam, we find that God created human beings by forming them from clay and then breathing into them "the breath of life." On one level this myth seems to describe us quite accurately: we are flesh and blood on the one hand but also spirit, one literal meaning of "breath." The same myth also says that God created us human beings "in his image." Within the Judaic religions, this has long been the basis for understanding ourselves as somehow specially created and distinct from all other animals. Of course, we share with all animals our biological nature, but we also have strange and wonderful capacities for thought and belief, experience and emotion, choice and intention. God therefore—as the myth continues—blesses humanity and gives them dominion over all other living things on earth. And however we have environmentally abused this dominion, that dominion seems to be a fact.[1]

Thus, within the religions of Abraham, humans are often thought to have a special kind of spirit, a soul that makes us truly thinkers of truth and choosers of our future. We are thus "*Imago Dei*," the image of God. We have a soul, they say, that bears identity and responsibility along with its ability to be rational. And while the physical flesh, this living body, may die, the soul does not. The Greek philosopher Plato, without the contextual benefit of Judaism, thought that our ability to think in terms of universal ideas and ideal truth, along with the command of our lives by choice and thought, indicated that there is an eternal element in the soul that outlives the mortal body. Even Yoda, in *The Empire Strikes Back*, tells Luke Skywalker, "Luminous beings are we, not this crude matter."

Figure 6.1   The famous painting of "The Creation of Adam" by Michelangelo (on the ceiling of the Sistine Chapel).

Unfortunately, George Lucas is not a particularly careful philosopher, and arguably his concept of self is not altogether consistent with his "religion" of the Force. In the Judaic religions, the focus on the individuality of the soul and its eternal nature as an individual seems to be consistent with its focus on God as an individual and relational spirit. "The chief end of man," declares one early Protestant catechism, "is to glorify God and to enjoy Him forever."[2] As Adam and Eve—going back to the creation myth—were created as individuals to walk with God in the Garden of Eden, so are we all individual and god-like souls, meant for eternal relationship with one another and with the Ultimate Being.

Self as Impersonal Essence

Inasmuch as the Force, for Lucas, is less like God and more like an impersonal energy that permeates all things, we might argue that his notion of the self should have been more like that of philosophical Hinduism. In Hinduism, the self is also a kind of soul, the **Atman**, which is indeed eternal and god-like. But, as we saw in Chapter 2, Brahman is a very different kind of Ultimate Being, not really "He," but more "It." Thus we should expect that the Atman is also not really like the soul as that idea is understood in monotheistic religions. We find instead that the Atman, like Brahman, is really impersonal, not so individual as we tend to think. Thus the Hindu philosophers, in fact, make the distinction between the self and the Self: The first is the empirical self, temporary and finite, and the second is the real you, the spirit that is eternal, unchanging, and quite different from the you you think you are.[3]

This view of the self is interestingly consistent with, and can therefore be further explained through, its connection with the idea of reincarnation. Through most of the religions of India, reincarnation is an understanding of what happens to most individuals when they die. The doctrine declares that all of us are simply reborn, but not as ourselves. For example, when I die, perhaps I will be reborn as an American child who will be named John. Perhaps he will be African American. Perhaps instead, I will be reborn as a woman. Perhaps as a duck. Notably, the reincarnation of "me" will in no sense be "me," if by this pronoun we are referring to the aged white American male now typing these words. What is reincarnated therefore is not "me," but the soul, the Atman, which is not really "me." The soul, according to Hinduism, therefore is not really the empirical self that I identify as myself, but is rather some impersonal "consciousness" that is, in the final analysis, utterly identical with your Atman and the Atman of my brother. Indeed, all are identical with the impersonal absolute being called Brahman, and, to a great extent, our individual selves are merely illusions keeping us from seeing this greater reality.

This notion of reincarnation can be found in other religions of India, like Jainism and Sikhism. For the Buddhists, however, the idea is different. The Buddha, reacting against the teachings of Hinduism, claimed rather that there is "no self." Instead of

Figure 6.2 Reincarnation depicted as the transmigration of a mysterious light from lifetime to lifetime, even between different kinds of living things.

Atman, he taught *anatman*, the denial of Atman, in order to dissuade his followers from seeking some eternal soul within. All we refer to when we talk about ourselves, the Buddha taught, is a temporary collection of pieces that, for the moment, constitute our physical and mental being. At this moment, I have this body and these beliefs and a specific set of ideas, but ten years from now, I will have an older and slower body, some different beliefs and a different set of ideas. No doubt some of the physical and mental characteristics will be the same as now; certainly most will be similar. But according to the Buddha's teaching, there is nothing in ourselves that stays the same, nothing that reincarnates from lifetime to lifetime.

Even so, the Buddha believed in reincarnation. Even without a soul, he thought, the force of karma can carry on from one life to the next, making the next "self" somehow the effect of a previous self. And if this sounds mysterious, that is also—ironically, perhaps—consistent with what we saw in the second chapter, namely that the notion of Ultimate Being was itself vague for early Buddhism. Evidently, as we noted then, there is something ultimate about Emptiness and about the pure state of the enlightened mind that identifies with Emptiness. In later forms of Buddhism, these ideas become more explicitly denoted in terms of a Buddha Mind or Buddha Nature that is somehow inherent and perfect in all living beings. And once stated in these terms, it may seem that, like Hinduism, Buddhism is referring vaguely to something more perfect and eternal in ourselves that is, at the same time, not really me. Indeed, later Buddhist texts will tell students about the need to find the "True Self."[4] Like in Hinduism, this "True Self" is something deeper and more impersonal than the empirical self and in some ways opposed to it.

This latter point deserves a final comment. It is notable that we started this chapter talking about the mystery of being a conscious and responsible individual, and yet in some religious philosophies, particularly those that would point us to an Absolute Being more monistic than theistic (more "It" than "He"), these philosophies ultimately direct us to abandon the focus on the individual empirical self. Indeed, they would tend to say that there is something inherently wrong about any focus on ourselves as finite individuals and that our usual, daily notion of "ego" is somehow inherently "egoistic." There is some evident logic to this. At the same time, we find ourselves brought to paradoxes that urge us to consider how "I" can transcend individuality, how "I" am reincarnated into a different "I," and, ultimately, how "I" am supposed to achieve some ideal state of liberation. We talk more about these paradoxes later in the chapter.

The point of this subsection has been to show how a kind of monistic Ultimate Being is, in many ways, most consistent with a view of the self that gives us an opposition between the empirical self and a deeper, more spiritual self. Thus the Indian religions will emphasize that the finite self, the ego-identity you know as yourself, is false, a distraction, an illusion, while the true Self is an impersonal and more mysterious consciousness of pure mind. Thus the question, "Who am I?" becomes very mysterious, as mysterious as the Ultimate Being itself. And this is an entirely consistent implication. For in the final analysis, you are the Ultimate Being, but you just don't realize it. Or rather, to embrace the mystery, we might say You (capital "Y") are the Ultimate Being, but you (small "y") don't realize it.

SUFFERING AND THE RELIGIOUS PROBLEM OF EVIL

It might have been evident in the preceding discussion of the self that we can often make connections between these ideas and beliefs in the afterlife. Of course, the concept of salvation is the topic of this book's final chapter, where we discuss these religious ideas in detail. But even before we briefly touch on the topic in this chapter, we must consider another topic, one more subtle, but still evident in the previous section: the Problem of Evil.

What we can notice in the preceding section is that, while the religions of India tell us that there is some perfect and "True Self" within in us, they also note that we are all, in some way, corrupted by the ego. Similarly, we might note that while Christianity shares with Islam and Judaism the notion that we are all created in the image of God, Christianity goes on to note that we are all also "fallen," somehow corrupted by sin. Thus we find that the religious concept of the self may well remind us of how good and glorious we are in our inner souls, and yet they may also tell us that something is wrong with us. When one considers the Problem of Evil, we are, by applying religious concepts, trying to understand what is wrong.

On another level, the problem of evil is even more obvious: suffering. It is obvious that there is suffering in this world, whether from the horrors of war and oppression or from the disasters of nature, and thus people are hurt, scared, and deprived of loved ones. In fact, what makes this problem so intractable is that it is often the innocent that suffer, not those who start the wars nor those who somehow create disease, but anyone, at any time. Some scholars of religion have suggested that this fact, that evil surrounds us and strikes at us almost haphazardly, may be the psychological beginnings of all religious thinking, so that, in a way, all religion is trying to answer the basic question: Why does such evil occur? In his book *The Sacred Canopy*, Peter Berger argues that all humans are faced with "marginal situations," or "anomies," events in life showing us that the world cannot be controlled and that its chaos intrudes into our lives no matter what we do.[5] And therefore, as we look for meaning behind what happens, we search beyond the mere description of wars and earthquakes, look outside the realm of power politics and plate tectonics, to try to understand what it all means. It has been said that we can endure tremendous suffering if we just think it has meaning.

Within the religions of the world, myth is often one way to make sense of suffering. We've already noted that the Christian tradition explains our suffering in terms of the "fallen" nature of the world and of ourselves, and this "**fallenness**" is described in the classic myth of Adam and Eve. The familiar story tells us that God created human beings with value and innocence—persons made, as we noted, in the image of God. But, as the story goes on to say, God also gave them a choice to obey or disobey, and, in the end, they disobeyed God by eating fruit from the "Tree of the Knowledge of Good and Evil." With this choice, their innocence was lost, they were expelled from the perfect, peaceful garden, and they were cursed with living in a world of labor and pain. As a myth, it may be hard to interpret this story accurately, but one thing seems clear: the trouble with the world and with ourselves is ultimately our own fault and a disruption of God's ideal world.

In some forms of Christianity, this story becomes the basis for the doctrine of "original sin." While Adam and Eve committed *the* original sin, Christian doctrine tells us that all of us now are tainted with this tendency to foolishness, rebellion, and sin. All of us, it seems, find it much easier to do evil than to do good, the doctrine tells us, and this may seem to many of us an all-too-accurate description of the human condition.

Yet this apparently pessimistic view is not only Christian. Following a similar line of thought—starting with innate goodness, but ending with the commonality of evil— the Confucian philosopher, Mengzi, tells the story of Ox Mountain. Ox Mountain, he says, was once covered with forest and lush grasses, but now it is bald and barren. Why? Because people have chopped down the trees and let their animals graze the grasses to stubble. And though the night air and the sweet dew of heaven would revive the soil and help the plants grow again, humanity's repeated abuse of the mountain's resources has left it a wasteland. This parable, Mengzi explains, represents human character: we are good by nature, but so abused by evil choices and bad habits that it seems we are some-how spoiled and broken creatures, a wasteland of vice and depravity.[6]

Many myths in native traditions also seem to carry this theme of explaining why the world and we, ourselves, are not as they should be. **Trickster** stories of Native American religions sometimes suggest that human life used to be easier, until the trickster, often the coyote, came along. Not malicious, but often deceitful or foolish, Coyote once was told that humans could lie down and let their spirits depart for a time, returning later to bring the body back to life. One time a man lay down in his hut and let his spirit depart, and Coyote made the mistake of closing the door of the hut, so that when the spirit returned, it could not find its way back to the body. And that, the story tells us, is why people die.[7]

As a final example, but one that does not try to find any explanation in myth, we already saw in the religions of India the idea that human beings seem to have the nat-ural tendency to focus on the individual self and are ignorant, somehow, of the deeper reality of Self. This **ignorance**, or a "nescience" called *avidya* in the Hindu philosophy of thinkers like Sankara,[8] apparently cannot be explained. "Beginningless ignorance," it is called, and no myth is invoked to try to explain how the pure nature of the Atman could become clouded with the foolish illusion of ego. Similarly, in the early Mahayana Buddhist text, *The Awakening of Faith*, it is declared that our original nature is the perfect consciousness of the Buddha Mind, and yet, somehow, illusion appears. No explanation is given; the text merely says, "Suddenly, there is ignorance."[9]

These examples show us how religions, through myth and philosophy, try to ex-plain for us why the world and we ourselves are apparently "fallen" or imperfect. But the problem of evil also challenges us more directly when we consider specific evils, not asking only why there is evil in the world, but why this particular evil happened to me. If a group of friends is in a car accident and only one survives, he might ask, "Why?" And it is no comfort to explain that he happened to be in that part of the car that was least damaged. He is not asking a question of physics; he's asking a question of meaning and purpose.

Once again, religion comes along to help us understand these events. Sometimes they tell us these things are "tests of faith," and we are expected to trust in divine love, even when challenged with a situation that suggests the universe is rather unloving. Some philosophers, like Thomas Aquinas, have argued that God does not prevent the haphazard evils of the world, but God is able to bring good out of the evils. Thus we are called upon to learn lessons of compassion or to devote ourselves more to campaigns against drunk driving. Yes, there are evils in our lives, the explanation seems to say, but in the larger picture God sees, there come from these evils "greater goods."

While "greater good" arguments suggest that the evils of life can be redeemed by growth and moral choices made after the experience, doctrines of **karma** seem to suggest that the reason for individual suffering comes before the event. That is, karma theories claim that every harmful and beneficial event in our lives and in the lives of all people is ultimately caused by choices made in previous lives. In a famous Buddhist story, a great monk named Mogallana, known for his devotion to self-discipline and the Buddha's teaching, was murdered in the forest by rivals, and the other monks in the Buddha's community asked the classic question of how something so bad could happen to a man so good. The Buddha, using his presumably omniscient, enlightened mind, declared that Mogallana had, in a previous lifetime, killed his own parents, and the result was that his successive reincarnations would be themselves murdered for the next fifty lives. We can question the justice of such a punishment, especially given the fact that the individual person who committed the parricide was not the one successively beaten to death in the forest, but the point of karma remains clear: What happens to us and what seems random injustice are really the inevitable results of other specific human actions.

A third example of a religious explanation for suffering comes from the fascinating parables of the Daoist philosopher Zhuangzi. In his writings, he tells stories of sages like Master Li and Master Lai who understand the flow of *yin* and *yang* and see all events and changes as harmonies of the Dao. And then Master Lai gets ill. Coughing and wheezing, Master Lai nevertheless is quiet and calm, while his wife and children are weeping and wailing. As Master Li comes to visit, he says to the wife and children, "Shoo, get back; don't disturb the process of change," while the sick Master Lai himself says, "If I think well of my life, for the same reason I must think well of my death."[10] Thus for the Daoist, suffering is understood and accepted as merely one more change in the great movement of the Dao.

A general term for all of these more-or-less philosophical efforts to explain human suffering, whether in the grand cosmic sense or as individual, isolated events, is "**theodicy.**" This term actually is rather imprecise for our general purposes, as its root meaning suggests an effort to show God's justice; and we have seen that not every religion speaks of "God." Admitting this, we can still use the term to name any effort to explain how the apparent injustices of human suffering occur, and why the world is not as perfect as it should be. This "should be" itself, of course, is a presumption. It is the presumption that the perfection of Ultimate Being should somehow be evident in our clearly imperfect world. Consequently, the problem of evil is a problem for religion precisely because religion seems to presume that there is a greater wholeness to things, a meaning and order to our lives and to the universe that is contradicted by the capricious tortures of mundane life.

To state this point the opposite way, if the world and our lives are ultimately meaningless accidents in an accidental universe, then we have no reason, perhaps, to expect that any innocent person should have a good life, or that any particular species, be it humans or vipers or velociraptors, would be nice. But if there is a God, or if we are all truly Buddhas, or if all things are truly in harmony with the Dao, then it seems we must explain how there can be disharmony. Perhaps it is easier for us just to give up the problem by giving up the idea of an Ultimate Being that somehow suggests things ought to be better. At the same time, human oppression and war, disease and the death of children are difficult phenomena simply to shrug off as the meaningless events of a meaningless universe. Indeed, we must realize that these mythic and philosophical ideas about the problem of evil are directly connected to our ideas of morality and human purpose. And so, once again, we find that religions are not merely collections of ideas but interconnected directions for life, in this case telling us not only what to believe about evil but also what to do about it.

One great example of this basic logic is evident in the most fundamental of the teachings of Buddhism: the **Four Noble Truths**. In this teaching—arguably the cornerstone of early Buddhist philosophy—the Buddha begins with the foundational assertion that life is characterized by suffering. He does not seek to explain how this has come about, but he is intently focused on what causes our suffering. Ultimately, he says, all things are impermanent, dependent, lacking in substance—early hints of the concept of Emptiness—and yet we cling to them as if we could own them, keep them from decay. But inevitably, we must be disappointed. And the problem, therefore, is that we desire what cannot please us as we fail to see the impermanence of all we have and all we are. So—and here is the basic, almost obvious logic—if suffering is caused by our desires and our clinging to what is impermanent, the solution to suffering is to seek a state of desirelessness, a state of inner quiet awakened to the Emptiness of things. Clearly we do not escape suffering by working harder to gain possessions or to live a longer life; we escape suffering through insight into the impermanence of things and through the desireless state of Nirvana.

This logic can be mirrored in different ways in other religious explanations of suffering. If the evils of the world are the result of sin, then it seems we should strive for moral improvement and seek redemption from sin. If the world's ills are the result of social forces that corrupt our good natures and create disharmony with Dao, then we resolve these problems through wisdom and virtue. In examples like these we might see the beginnings of a logical connection between understandings of the suffering world and our own necessary moral effort. We consider this connection again in Chapter 8.

SALVATION

In a way, this topic is that of the entire last chapter of this text, so I will be brief here. The point is only to admit, now at the end of Part I of the text, that religions make many truth claims, not only about the nature of Ultimate Being and the historical founders of the faith, but also about the nature of our souls, the purpose of our suffering, and even the very meaning of our lives. Connected—logically, as we might expect—with beliefs about the nature of our true selves and about the causes and purposes of our suffering are other implications about human life in its relation to Ultimate Being. We've already hinted at how certain views of suffering will have implications about human morality, and some views of the soul will suggest implications regarding what happens to us after death. It is not accidental, for example, that the Indian concept of karma is directly tied to the general belief in reincarnation. We saw in the story of Mogallana how the Buddha's explanation for what happened to the monk presumed previous existences and specific ideals of moral action. One would never find this explanation, for example, in the famous Jewish story of Job, the good and devout man who is made to suffer at the request of Satan. In this Jewish, Christian, and Islamic story, Job's friends do not try to explain that he suffers because of some evil done in a previous life, although they generally do think he must have done something evil in this life.[11]

Similarly, we can find in those philosophies from farther west, especially those religious views of many Christians, Jews, and Muslims today, a belief that the soul, given its god-like nature, cannot die when the body dies. The afterlife, therefore, is understood to be the continuation of the individual self in some other form. Perhaps the soul, which is the immaterial self and carries one's identity, exists without a body; perhaps the body itself is "resurrected," and the soul is, in some way, implanted in the body once again. Perhaps it is something in between. Whatever the precise understanding of the soul in the afterlife, it is important to realize that this idea of the afterlife is importantly different from the idea of reincarnation, yet both are consistent with a certain set of ideas about the nature of self-identity and the value of the physical world. We see this perhaps especially in the very physical and even sensual images of heaven and hell given in the Quran: heaven is a place of soft couches and cool breezes, wine and sex, while hell is a place where one's skin burns off.[12]

When it comes to a more monistic sense of Ultimate Being, one finds—again, as we would expect, given the drive to consistency and the internal logic of religions—a sense in which the self is finally merged with Ultimate Being and ego identity is left behind. If Atman is truly of the same essence as Brahman, then with enlightenment and liberation from the world, the soul does not awaken to some physical paradise or painful hell, nor does the soul move on to animate a new body, forgetting its former individuality. Rather, the soul simply and finally merges back into the oneness of Ultimate Being, like a cup of water being poured into a lake. It may seem contradictory that this view of final salvation and the idea of reincarnation both exist in Hinduism, but in fact, the general understanding is that reincarnation takes place over and over until one has achieved a kind of final liberation. Thus the merging of the soul with Ultimate Being ends the cycle of reincarnation. And in both reincarnation and liberation, individual identity is denied.

There are other views of the afterlife that we might consider here, but much of the detail of these ideas is reserved for Chapter 12. Here, we can briefly note that in many indigenous religions the most basic idea of the afterlife is something like a continuation of this life, a world in which one rejoins one's ancestors in a kind of spiritual existence that does not contradict the possibility of still interacting with the living through dreams and visions. In the Chinese religions, the concept of the Dao that informs both Confucianism and Daoism is, as discussed in Chapter 2, a rather this-worldly notion of Ultimate Being. Correspondingly, the notion of the afterlife is, for these philosophies, significantly downplayed. Confucius, when asked about life after death, said, "You do not yet know how to deal with the living; how can you know how to deal with death?" At the same time, it is clear that Confucius had a very strong sense of there being "ancestors," as he emphasized the crucial virtue of venerating ancestors with rituals that treat them with the same dignity they had when alive.[13]

Each of these teachings, these views of what different religions think is true about the afterlife, shows an internal consistency with various other beliefs within the religion. As we keep emphasizing in this book, that internal consistency should not surprise us. Thus when we examine these ideas of death and the afterlife, we find how they are interwoven with ideas of the self. Upon further examination, we would also find them interwoven with ideas of suffering and how suffering is overcome. We would find that afterlife ideas are deeply connected to ideas of human morality, sometimes (but not always) declaring that the way to achieve an ideal afterlife is to live a morally upright and exemplary life. Afterlife ideas are also very often (but not always) connected to some ideal image of what it means to live purposefully. That is, we shall see by the end of the text that "salvation" can mean much more than going to heaven, and that the final description of what it means to find the meaning of life will be dependent on what we think truly makes us fulfilled and meaningful beings. Unsurprisingly, these ideas of final purpose and meaning—what I call in the last chapter our "beatitude"—will be in some way a description of how we are finally and fully connected to Ultimate Being.

KEY TERMS IN CHAPTER 6

anatman   In Buddhist teaching, the claim that there is "no self," denying the Hindu concept of Atman and insisting instead that the self is nothing more than a temporary collection of parts.

Atman   In Hinduism, the Self, eternal and unchanging essence of the individual, yet different from the finite and limited empirical self. Ultimately, Atman is the same essence as Brahman, the eternal and impersonal Ultimate Being.

empirical self   The "I" that one hears in one's thoughts, the person that one recognizes oneself to be through reflection on one's character and beliefs.

fallenness   From the Christian interpretation of the myth of Adam and Eve, the claim that the perfectly created state of humanity in the Garden of Eden was lost due to human disobedience, and that this sinfulness still corrupts the human will.

Four Noble Truths   Fundamental Buddhist teaching about the inevitability of suffering and its ultimate causes in our own desires for the temporary, unsatisfying things of the world.

ignorance   Specifically in Indian Hindu and Buddhist philosophies, the understanding that an innate purity of self or mind is nonetheless clouded by humanity's tendency to identify with the ego and thus our inability to see and live out the ideal of the deeper self.

Imago Dei   Literally the "image of God," the idea from Judaic creation myth that the human soul, with reason and responsibility, somehow reflects the individual and conscious nature of God Himself.

karma   Literally, "action," the concept that actions done previously in life and, especially, in prior lifetimes, have consequences in later lifetimes, thus explaining suffering and good fortune as the effects of prior acts.

theodicy   Specifically trying to explain suffering in terms of divine justice; more generally, any effort to explain how the apparent injustices of human suffering occur, and why the world is not as perfect as it should be.

trickster   In some native traditions, a mythic person or animal that, through foolishness or ignorance, brings about problems for humanity.

EPILOGUE TO PART I:
The Promise and the Problems of Religious Truth

At the risk of tedious repetition, I keep noting in this text that religious truth claims have a kind of logical interconnectedness. It is a mistake to think that religions are simply irrational, as if anyone can believe anything just by deciding to do so. That is not to say that people are, on an individual level, consistent in what they believe. We find among those around us, perhaps even in ourselves, a tendency at times to clump religious ideas together in an eclectic mass and call it "my personal religion." But on a larger, more historical scale, we also find that in what we call the named and designated religions of the world, there is much more form and reason involved. Generally, one needn't give up reason in order to be religious.

But it is also true that not all religions emphasize belief and truth claims. We noted in the prologue to this section that orthodoxy—the idea that there are right teachings or true doctrines that go with specific religions—is sometimes significantly less important than what one ought to do in that religion, or what one ought to experience. That is why, in this text, we must go on to Parts II and III, where we talk less about "truth" and more about "goodness" and "beauty."

Even so, the idea of rational consistency will not be abandoned. It has already been hinted at in a number of places that, when we move into Parts II and III, we will find that rituals and morality, religious experience and a sense of "beatitude," will also bear recognizable logical connections to certain truth claims in specific religions. For example, the kind of religious experiences that are emphasized in one religion will often be quite different from the kind of religious experiences emphasized in another, and those differences will again be consistent with certain ideas, certain religious "truths," within those faiths.

Thus we never quite escape the problem of discussing religious truth. It is called a problem here because, as we will see, a focus on religious truth claims can bother some people precisely because of its dependence on language and argument. We have already noted, and will discuss in more detail in Chapter 10, that Zen Buddhism, for example, claims to reject "dependence on words and letters." The reason for this is complicated, having to do with the "dualistic nature of language" and other technical notions we can consider later. But generally, the Zen Buddhist would say his or her religion is really more about gaining the religious experience of Enlightenment than about believing some truth claim. Even in a religion more accustomed to doctrinal focus, like Christianity, we find believers who emphasize that we should not get drawn

continued . . .

continued...

into discussion and philosophical disputes. "What has Jerusalem to do with Athens?" the early Christian writer Tertullian asked rhetorically. His point: Our beliefs focus on the person of Jesus, not on ideas and arguments.

Related to the last point, another problem with a focus on ideas and truth claims is that it may seem to force us into interreligious argument. If we could all just focus on our own experiences, or if we could join in the good moral works of society, with Christians and Buddhists and Muslims all working side by side, for example, to help the poor, surely we could—and should—just avoid the disputes that inevitably arise from a focus on doctrines and beliefs. There is some good sense to these suggestions, and one can find movements toward religious cooperation that focus exactly on these things: joint meditation and prayer groups, social projects of the Interfaith Youth Core, and so on. Maybe we could all get along better if we would focus less on truth and more on goodness and beauty.

This might be true. But there we have still the problem: It might be true. In some ways we just cannot escape religious truth claims, and it seems folly to think we can. Therefore it is wiser, perhaps, to continue to look for logical consistency within religions and indeed between them. It may seem unfortunate, but it is the same logical thought that would help us to appreciate the internal consistency of religions that forces us to acknowledge that religions do contradict one another. No, unfortunately, it seems that all religions cannot be true, and we can dislike or mistrust doctrinal disputes as much as we like, but we cannot escape them. It is better, perhaps, to take the logic of religion seriously, to look carefully at where religions agree and disagree, and to worry a bit that we can't all be right. We can't all be right even about whether or not it's important that we disagree about whether we can all be right.

We can, of course, select the option of de-emphasizing truth claims and emphasizing instead the active or the experiential aspects of religion. We can acknowledge, for example, that truth claims in religion, along with disputes between religions, are to some extent unavoidable, but we can still choose to say that the moral teachings of religions can bring us all back together. Again, that might be true (there is that tricky word again!), and so, in this text, we must take seriously the importance not only of what religions believe but also what religions tell us to do and to experience. And that is the purpose of Parts II and III. ❈

PART II

GOODNESS, OR WHAT RELIGION WOULD HAVE US DO

ACCORDING TO OUR WORKING definition, religion relates us to some kind of supernatural reality in a broad range of ways. We have been examining how it can emphasize belief, or ideas that we should, in some sense, hold as true. This might seem obvious when we think of those who follow a religion as "believers," a term that immediately suggests that the focus of religion is on the truth claims that are, apparently, meant to be believed. But we have seen from the outset that the broad range of human elements in our definition does not focus only on the cognitive aspects of life. The ideas and beliefs might indeed be unavoidable, even central in ways that some religions would not particularly like. But it would be a mistake to think that ideas and beliefs are the sum total of religion. For religion is not only about what we think; it is also clearly about what we do.

A good example here can be found in Christianity, especially inasmuch as this faith seems particularly focused on belief. Indeed, it may be largely because of the Christian history behind much of the English-speaking world that we tend to use the term "faith" as synonymous with "religion." Even so, while Christians often talk about the centrality of belief, we find in the Christian scriptures the famous exhortations from the Letter of James stating that "faith is dead without good works." Jesus himself is quoted in the Gospel narratives as asking rhetorically, "Why do you keep calling me 'Lord, Lord' when you don't do what I say?"[1]

Even more emphatically dealing with action rather than belief, we can study Confucius. We have noted already that some scholars might not consider Confucianism a religion at all, but something more like a political and ethical system. We needn't pursue this argument here, nor try to defend again the inclusion of Confucianism in this book on religion. We can certainly note, however, that those who emphasize the ethical and political side of Confucius' teaching are not mistaken at all. Confucius' focus, we will see, was indeed on how to cultivate a certain kind of ethical character in tune with the Way of Heaven, such that all of society would run smoothly and harmoniously. He did not seem very focused on the metaphysical questions of religion. As noted previously, when asked about life after death, he replied, "You do not yet know how to deal with living. How can you understand dealing with death?"[2]

So it is certainly true that in many cases the behavioral aspect of religion—and it may seem especially those ethical components that would instruct us in how to live rightly—are central to religion. I have already argued that, in some ways, the moral claims are dependent upon truth claims, but it is also true that the behavioral emphases in religion cannot be ignored, and sometimes they are more central to the focus of a particular religion than any doctrinal assertions. Again, the ethical component of religion seems prominent here. But we must also note the ritual aspects of religion, those behaviors commanded by religion that tell us particularly how to behave in relation to the Holy and that may not, in themselves, seem like moral issues. Indeed, how shall we understand singing hymns or bowing in prayer or the washing of a statue as an ethical issue? Yet these behaviors, too, are commanded in religion, and they are an essential element of what it means to behave religiously.

Consequently, in this unit on "goodness," we consider how religions direct human behavior, both in terms of what we ought to do ethically and in terms of the actions we are directed to perform as part of religious ritual. The line between these two aspects of "goodness" is sometimes rather thin, and it is at times difficult to tell where ritual ends and moral directives begin. In addition to these two elements of religious behavior, we shall add a third: the relationship between religion and the social or political order. That is, we have to consider how religion affects government and social structures, particularly in areas dealing with justice and equality. For religions often have a great deal to say about how to treat the members of society, how to run government, the proper relations between men and women, rich and poor, members of different social classes, and so on. For good or ill, history in countries all over the world shows evidence of how religion has determined not only what people ought to do morally and what rituals they should perform, but also how people should be governed, what we owe to the poor, and what is the proper role of women in society. All these ideas will be considered in the context of discussing what religion defines as "goodness." We shall study this goodness for its own sake, but inevitably we must finish this section discussing how goodness and truth become mutually dependent, or we will fail to understand the complex interwovenness that is human religion.

CHAPTER 7

RITUAL

WE HAVE ALREADY NOTED that it is somewhat difficult to distinguish ritual from morality. Both are included in this discussion of "what religion would have us do" because it is rather obvious that religions prescribe specific behaviors that we might call morally right, and religions similarly prescribe specific behaviors that somehow don't quite fit the moral category and yet are nonetheless commanded. It seems, for example, that when a Muslim is commanded to give 2.5 percent of his wealth as charity, there is something in such a command that we would recognize as moral. When the Muslim is likewise commanded to pray five times a day, there is no similar, obvious moral dimension. Yet it is the same God that commands both actions.

Having confessed the difficulty of distinguishing ritual and morality, yet also confessing that they are somehow quite different elements of religion, I have simply chosen to consider ritual first and morality in the next chapter. Here, therefore, we shall try to define what we mean by ritual and then go on to discuss various kinds of rituals and how they fit into their respective religions. We can expect, of course, that religious ritual will have some connection to a religion's Ultimate Being.

Let us then define **ritual** in general as any kind of formal, regularized behavior that goes with specific occasions or conditions. Ritual behavior, therefore, is a kind of habitual behavior, stylized and formal, not in the sense of requiring a suit and tie, but formal in the sense of having a regular form. Indeed, being expected to wear a suit and tie to a fancy restaurant or to a wedding is indeed ritual and "formal," but being expected to wear a baseball cap and a shirt with the home-team logo to a local game is also a ritual and is also, in our sense, "formal." In both cases, the specific conditions imply a specified behavior. And when we obey those expectations and become comfortable with that behavior, ritual becomes habit.

It may be evident in this definition so far that "ritual" is a term with a much broader application than religion. Inasmuch as we are creatures of habit, we are creatures of ritual, and to varying degrees rituals of one kind or another pervade all aspects of our lives. All forms of politeness—saying "please" and "thank you," saying "bless you" or "Gesundheit" when someone sneezes—are ritual actions. Shaking hands when we meet someone is a ritual, too, and with such rituals we can note two things. First, it fits our definition because the action is repeated, stylized, and formal and goes with the specific situation of meeting. We might also note, however, that there can be many forms of such a ritual. Some people shake hands, some kiss on the cheek, friends on campus might "fist bump," and football players might slap each other on the butt. One sees the power of ritual when one imagines getting it wrong: kissing Grandma on the cheek would be quite proper, perhaps, but if the football players tried this ritual greeting, we might be rather shocked. And Grandma would be shocked if we slapped her bottom.

Religious ritual, as we should expect by now, will take its specific definition from the fact that the regular, formal, and habitual behaviors that go with a specific situation will have some connection to Ultimate Being. One does not shake hands with God, but one might, upon coming into a Catholic church, for example, embrace the habit of dipping one's fingers in holy water and making the sign of the cross. Upon entering a Shinto temple, preparing to worship or pray to one of the *kami*, the gods of native Japan, one would likely clap one's hands and bow, but only after undergoing a ritual rinsing of one's mouth and hands. Like handshakes and fist bumps, these rituals are quite different, and yet they are also quite similar, fulfilling a certain regularized function in one's relationship with God and with *kami*.

So it is quite clear that there is a great deal of non-religious ritual in our lives, but our focus on religious ritual brings us to emphasize those standardized actions and words that accompany specific situations in religious contexts, those habitual behaviors that in some way or another affect or express our relation to the transmundane reality. Our habits of behavior help us to get along with our friends, root for our favorite sports team, and keep our teeth free of cavities; our religious habits of behavior help us to relate to God and to find enlightenment.

THE RELIGIOUS USES OF RITUAL

That religions all over the world make use of ritual is simply a fact, but before we go on to develop a vocabulary for describing religious rituals, we might briefly consider the function of such ritual. What do rituals do for us? In raising this question, we risk a certain amount of reductionist thinking, reducing ritual to its psychological and social needs. But with that risk in mind, we can consider the social and psychological effects of ritual without perhaps merely reducing religion to those functions. After all, as we've seen since defining "ritual" in the first paragraph, there are perhaps many other, non-religious activities that can also provide various effects of social cohesion and psychological assurance, but that doesn't mean that religion can be reduced to those functions.

Having taken that caution, we can note that one valued function of ritual activity, whether religious or not, is a regularization and normalization of those activities. Even when we simply make a habit of brushing our teeth regularly, such that the tooth-brushing does indeed become ritualized, the regularity of the habit itself is helpful. We gain a certain confidence about our dental health through ritualized behavior. Similarly, we gain confidence about our relation to Ultimate Being by having a ritual structure that we know—somehow—has worked in the past. A particular system of prayer or of ritual magic, a liturgical style of worship, or a form of chanting can all be depended upon to be "right," because they are the rituals that have been built into the religion itself. Moreover, the rituals themselves, as we shall see in this chapter, have a kind of consistency and logical relation to the religion's doctrines and experiences that help one participate in one's religion in general. One can be quite confused about, say, one's relationship to a spouse or lover, but, when in doubt, bring flowers. Similarly, a Christian might not be sure how to pray, but when in doubt, he or she can pray the Lord's Prayer. In both cases, there is some hope and confidence in the ritual nature of the behavior itself.

Let us also quickly notice in these examples of regular ritual behavior that context and culture supply the needed meaning for any ritual to make sense. You will notice, for example, that both the flowers and the Lord's Prayer will apply only to some specific contexts of some specific cultures. One presumes to give flowers probably in the context of a traditional Western heterosexual relationship, and probably only in the direction of the male giving flowers to the female. Similarly, the ritual recitation of the Lord's Prayer is clearly and exclusively Christian. The flowers won't "work" for a traditional Chinese male, and the Lord's Prayer won't make any sense to a Buddhist. But within their proper contexts, people can count on ritual practices to do what needs to be done. Thus ritual gives us a sense of assurance and a proper sense of confidence that, whatever other concerns we might have, we can fulfill our religious and relational obligations best by falling back on ritual.

In a similar way, ritual helps a religious group to define its own boundaries. That is, just as ritual can give an individual a certain amount of confidence that he or she is doing what needs to be done religiously, so does ritual give a community a sense of confidence that its members are genuine members. We might think that one's religious life is somehow purely individual and internal, but in fact much religious ritual reveals how religious life is woven into the life of a community. For we see quickly in the observation of religious ritual that much of it is done in groups, often in unison. Indeed, the standardization of ritual is what makes it possible to perform such actions in unison. When Muslims do their traditional prayers, for example, they line up, shoulder to shoulder, all facing Mecca, and as the *imam* chants scripture and declares the greatness of Allah, all of them in unison bow and kneel and place their foreheads on the floor in front of them in a single, united action of submission to God. Of course, one can do the same prayer alone, but when one performs this ritual in the group, there is a literal unity of the body of believers that can be seen. We can note in the *Autobiography* of Malcolm X, that when he went to Mecca to perform the ritual pilgrimage, he for the first time prayed alongside a white man. And that experience, he said, helped him see that the community of his religion was bigger than the racially divided context in which he had learned his faith. The ritual defined his community.[3]

Similarly, when a Christian takes the Lord's Supper or when a Buddhist chants the traditional "Three Jewels," thereby "taking refuge" in the teachings of Buddhism, the participants are literally defining themselves as a community. Although once again a person can perform these rituals alone, they are mostly performed in unison, in community, and the ritual thus makes visible the spiritual unity that belief alone cannot.

In all these ways, ritual helps us to know who we are. We can use ritual to gain some assurance that we are right with God, that we have satisfied the ancestors, or that we have achieved or are on the way to achieving enlightenment. We can gain a full sense of being in proper relation to Ultimate Being because of the ritual performed. Also, we can gain a full sense of belonging to a community because of ritual performance. Like a secret handshake known and shared by only a few, ritual performance helps us know who our friends are and helps us know with whom we share religious conviction and religious hope. Religious ritual therefore offers psychological comfort and social cohesion. It should not surprise us that ritual is so strongly and prominently evident in religious life; indeed, ritual performs the same functions outside of religion and is just as strong and prominent in secular life.

TYPES OF RITUAL: COMMEMORATIONS AND HOLIDAYS

Having tried to understand the value and commonality—if not simply the inevitability—of ritual in general and of religious ritual in particular, we may now turn to develop a vocabulary for describing different types of ritual and considering how ritual is logically related to other elements in the religious phenomenon. In noting that there are types of rituals in religion, we are only recognizing that different rituals have different kinds of sources and purposes. For example, some rituals seem to be performed in order to change the world, or at least to change ourselves, while other rituals seem to be more about celebrating or recognizing simple facts, such as the greatness of God or the birthday of a founder.

The latter example often gives religions something we can call "**commemorative ritual**." As the word suggests, there is something of "memory" in a commemorative ritual, thus often a legendary or historical event celebrated or sometimes re-enacted. An obvious example of such ritual, already mentioned, is the celebration of the birthday of a religion's founder, such as Christmas. The Vesak festival in the Buddhist religion is likewise a celebration of the founder's birthday, although Buddhist tradition also takes it to be the day of the Buddha's death and of his awakening to enlightenment. Thus the

Vesak holiday rituals celebrate a good deal more than a supposedly historical birthday, but the basic idea of commemoration is the same. Similarly, one finds in the Christian celebration of "Holy Week" a whole set of other commemorative holidays, clearly not dealing with Jesus' birth, but rather with his death on Good Friday and his resurrection on Easter Sunday.

Not all commemorative holidays focus on a founder, however. We find that Judaism, for example, puts a strong emphasis on the Exodus, the deliverance of the Jewish people from slavery in Egypt some time—perhaps—in the thirteenth century BCE. God, the Jewish scriptures declare, performed a series of dramatic miracles that forced the leader of this powerful empire to release his slaves. In particular, the story says, God finally sent an "angel of death" through Egypt, such that the firstborn child of every family died. But the people of Israel were protected when they prepared a special meal and put the blood of the slaughtered lamb on the doorposts of their homes. The angel of death then "passed over" the Jews' homes, and the next day, the chaos of death throughout the land of Egypt finally made the Pharaoh let the slaves go free. To this day, Jews follow God's command to celebrate this event as Passover, an annual holiday in which they remember, with a ritual meal, ritual readings, and actions, how the Lord God brought them out of Egypt "with a strong hand and an outstretched arm."[4]

We see in these examples a strong connection between an annual holiday and specific historical—or purportedly historical—events. Thus we can expect a relationship of such

Figure 7.1   A Jewish family gathered for the seder meal, a commemorative ritual celebrating the Passover.

rituals to the stories of their founders, as noted in Chapter 3, and to specifically historical narrative, as noted in Chapter 5. There are other annual religious holidays, however, often associated not with historical events but with cycles of natural events. Thus a neo-pagan religion, like Wicca, might urge its followers to celebrate the solstices and equinoxes of the solar cycle, as well as the lunar phases. Here in a religion that focuses less on a transcendent God and more on the spirits and powers of nature, we find, quite reasonably, that the events celebrated are not those intrusions of God into history or the events of a founder's life, but the events of nature. Some Native American traditions, like those of the Pueblo Indians, recognize the power of *katchina* spirits that preside over various stages in the year's agricultural cycle. Thus special rituals associated with different *katchina* deities are

Figure 7.2   Ahola Kachina represents the beginning of the agricultural cycle. The ritual impersonation of these Ahola includes the blessing of homes and seeds around the time of the winter solstice.

performed at various times of the year to help ensure the spirits' cooperation in the success of planting, growth, and harvest of crops.[5] Here, perhaps, the annual rituals are not really commemorative, in the usual sense of the word, and the language of religion associated with the ritual practices will be less historical than mythic. Nevertheless, it becomes easy to confuse commemorative rituals with what we might call "**seasonal**" **rituals**, since both tend to come around on an annual cycle. Indeed, we find upon examination that the two are often mixed. It is perhaps no surprise that late December was chosen by early Christians for the celebration of Jesus' birth, for it coincided with the celebration of the winter solstice. In a similar way, celebrations of Christian Easter are easily mixed with celebrations of the change of seasons from winter to spring. This helps explain the strange addition of bunny rabbits and colored eggs to the celebration of Jesus' death and resurrection.

Returning to the discussion of more strictly commemorative rituals, we should add that not all are attached to annual holidays. The Eucharist, or Lord's Supper, of Christianity is a ritual in which Christians eat bread and wine that in some way represent Jesus' "body and blood." Like God speaking to the Jews after the Passover, Jesus speaks to his disciples during his last meal, telling them to eat the bread and drink the wine "in remembrance of me." Thus most Christians eat the bread and drink the wine regularly: some monthly, some weekly, some daily. Celebrating Jesus' "last supper" on Maundy Thursday, the night of Holy Week in which he is said to have taken this meal with his followers, is the annual celebration of the event, but clearly most Christians perform this commemoration much more often.

In the end, we might want to describe the irregular celebration of the Eucharist, along with the annual celebration of the Passover "Seder" meal, as a kind of re-enactment. That is, we find in such cases that the commemoration is celebrated especially by recreating something like the original event, acting out a series of prescribed behaviors that repeat the way the holiday was founded. The ritual dances of the Australian Aborigines are also re-enactments, though not of historical events but of the supposed dance and song of the original creator ancestors of the ancient "Dreamtime." These reenactments, the dance and call that supposedly follow the creative movements of ancient ancestors, are perhaps not truly commemorative, but not simply because the stories behind the rituals are mythic. Rather, it seems the aboriginal people see in these reenactments the literal re-creation of their world, a renaming and rebalancing of nature as the ancestors did it long ago. The dance, then, does not merely "remember" the ancient acts of creation; it continues that creation and heals the brokenness of nature. Thus these rituals are more like effective magic, which we consider in the next section.

EFFECTIVE RITUAL: MAGIC AND TRANSFORMATION

"Magic" might seem a trivializing term to use with respect to religious ritual, if we only think of magic shows and tricks done on a Las Vegas stage. In fact, however, I use this term to emphasize that in much religious ritual, it is believed that there is real magic going on. That is, many people believe that, when a religious ritual is properly performed, there is a genuine change or transformation that occurs in the world that is the effect of the ritual action itself. Thus we can use the general term "**effective ritual**" to describe religious rituals performed in the hopes that the actions actually change reality and do so with a kind of supernatural power. It is magic.

The dance of the Aborigines, mentioned before, is a case of what is sometimes called "imitative magic," or **mimetic ritual**. It accomplishes its purpose by intentionally imitating some other event, specifically the mythic creation act itself. When the natives dance, they literally enact the balance and wholeness of nature and thus bring about the desired effect, a kind of re-creation of nature as it was intended to be. Other native traditions, like rain dances or enacting a hunt, are similar cases of imitative magic. As one dancer appears as hunter and another appears as prey, they act out a successful hunt and hope thereby to make it occur. To speak more religiously, we might say that the imitative actions appeal to the spirits themselves and enlist the spirits of the deer and the buffalo to cooperate in the hunt. Or, at the very least, the ritual works as a kind of apology and statement of respect to the living spirits that dwell near at hand in the objects of nature. Animistic spirits can be changed with our words and actions, perhaps like an estranged friend can be reconciled with a gift of chocolate and words of kindness.

In a similar way, sacrifices are effective rituals. Offerings made to God or to the gods are thought to prove devotion or to recognize the sovereignty of the deity and, in a way, gain the gods' favor. In the Biblical traditions of Judaism, sacrifices made for sin and for thanksgiving involved the giving up of the "first fruits" of one's agricultural labor or indeed the killing of animals and pouring the blood upon an altar. Especially notable was the animal sacrifice for atonement, which involved the placing of the sins of the people upon two animals. Then, one of the animals was killed and the other was abandoned into the wilderness. These sacrifices were thought to atone, or make amends, for the sins of the people of Israel, making them and their worship holy in God's sight.[6]

In Christianity, we can note, this idea of a sacrifice that effects the forgiveness of sins was superseded by the sacrifice of Jesus in his death by crucifixion. Thus, for Christians, the ritual "payment for sin" was ultimately and finally done by God himself in the person of Jesus. Nevertheless, in the Catholic branch of Christianity the ritual of the Mass, especially in the Eucharist's bread and wine, the sacrifice of Jesus is reenacted and the magic of atonement is accomplished. Indeed, for Catholics the bread and wine are themselves literally transformed into the flesh and blood of Jesus when the priest raises these elements at the altar, and thus the sacrifice of Jesus as "the Lamb of God who takes away the sins of the world" is accomplished over and over through ritual.

We might note that many Protestant Christians have some trouble with this Catholic interpretation of the Lord's Supper. As we noted earlier, on one level this ritual is only commemorative, simply a symbolic remembrance of Jesus' atoning death. It is clearly not the purpose of this text to try to settle a centuries-old—and at times bloody—dispute within the Christian faith. For us, however, it might be useful simply to see that the vocabulary we develop here has some advantage for at least understanding religious viewpoints, even where they disagree. Is the Eucharist purely commemorative, or is it effective? Perhaps it is both. And perhaps it is for the Christian to decide what he or she believes about this central, sacred ritual.

Meanwhile, a very different and more general criticism of effective magic might be considered. For if we imagine a human ritual that performs a kind of spiritual magic, we might be suggesting that effective ritual places the power to manipulate God (or gods or spirits) into the hands of people and thus make the Ultimate Being seem less than ultimate. If one can change the gods' attitudes and intentions by performing rituals, it may seem that the gods are themselves subject to human mechanics: They are the effect, and humans are the cause.

For many Christians—not only Catholics—some of their special rituals are indeed effective, and yet they would maintain that God is not changed by human actions. Instead, they would say that God has given human beings these rituals as a means for changing their own spiritual state. Thus many of the Christian **sacraments**—a term that refers especially to rituals rooted in the authority of Jesus and taken to be especially effective—are a "means of grace," a way that God has given his followers to receive mercy. Perhaps it is paradoxical to suggest that humans can make God have mercy through the enactment of a prescribed ritual, but, again especially for Catholics, it is a great act of God's mercy that he put the power of these rituals into the hands of his Church.

Perhaps one way to avoid the paradox of seeing effective ritual as a way that humans control gods is to think of some effective rituals not as divine manipulations but as personal transformations. "**Transformative rituals**," then, would be less about how rituals change gods and more about how they change us.

A good example of transformative ritual can be found in a wide array of practices called **rites of passage**. This term refers to rituals that mark and sanctify changes in the stages of one's life. These major events of life—especially birth, death, and puberty—require, it seems, the presence of the holy. We have noted how rituals provide a sense of security and a marker of community, and so it is no surprise that one of the functions of these rites is to provide a sense of security in times of life that are potentially dangerous, almost certainly a little frightening, as well as full of hope and possibility. Certainly we see it in birth, and thus we find infant baptism in some forms of Christianity to be a means of preserving the baby's soul against original sin, and in Judaism the circumcision of boys on the eighth day of life marks the Jewish male as a member of the People of Israel, God's chosen people. Perhaps we see more fear and less possibility in death, but given a religious context, the end of life, too, is perhaps more like opening a door than closing down a life. Thus funeral rituals of many kinds populate the religious world and make it possible for disembodied souls to find a cleansing from life and, perhaps, a better transition to what waits beyond.

Least evident to many of us in the West, perhaps, is the initiatory rite of passage that accompanies puberty. Many indigenous cultures especially mark the transition of a boy into manhood with rituals that involve blood-letting, such as circumcision or, as with a small New Guinea tribe, the marking of the body with scars to match the bumps on the back of a crocodile.[7] Less painful, perhaps, but not less challenging, would be the "vision quest" of Native Americans, where a boy is left in the woods to go without food and with little sleep for several days. With this ritual, the hope is that he will meet spirit beings that will guide him on through life. Even in religions closer to city life, we find the Confirmation rituals of many Christians and the Bar Mitzvah of Judaism. In the latter, boys—and in more liberal Reform Judaism, girls, too—are taken aside in the early teenage years and taught Hebrew, the language of the scriptures, and then called upon to read scriptures in a public meeting. In passing this test, a boy is declared to be a man, now to be counted among those who must be present to have a fully authorized synagogue. The boy, in this rite of passage, ceases to be the child of his parents and becomes instead a "son of the commandments of God," which is the literal meaning of "Bar Mitzvah."

These rites of passage do not seem to be "magic," inasmuch as they do not seem to effect some change in nature or in the gods; but they do effect a change in the person, or at least in his or her status in the community. For Catholics, both the baptism of infants and the confirmation of adolescents are "sacraments" along with the Eucharist and are, in a similar way, "means of grace." That is, these rituals bring about forgiveness of sin. Marriage, too, is a sacramental rite of passage for Catholics, as it changes the status of the bride and groom in society and sanctifies sexuality.

Besides such rites of passage, with all their effective power, there are other common rituals that are "magic" insofar as they are personally transformative. Again, perhaps "magic" is not the best word to use, but in Hindu and Buddhist practices of meditation there is certainly expected a transformative power that can change the practitioner deeply and permanently. We should expect that such rituals, connected as they are to concepts of Brahman or Void, rather than to a god, do not work as changing one's relation to Ultimate Being through some forgiveness of sin. Nor does meditation really change the person's individual social status from child to man or from non-member to member. Rather, meditation is considered a practice of concentration and mental control that eventually helps one see into the mysterious nature of Ultimate Being itself. We discuss more thoroughly in Chapter 10 the nature of the enlightenment experience and its variations; for now, the point is only to note that the process of gaining such experience is a regular and formal kind of exercise. Indeed, like physical exercises, whose goal ultimately is a stronger body and greater physical health, these mental exercises are thought to be the slow, step-by-step cultivation of wisdom and insight.

As we might expect, Islam does not generally contain a ritualized form of meditation (though see the additional point, later in this chapter, about Islamic mysticism), precisely because the Islamic concept of Ultimate Being is more theistic than monistic. Nevertheless, within Islam a major ritual practice is the transformative ritual of fasting. During the month of Ramadan, Muslims all over the world refrain from eating, drinking, smoking, and sex from dawn to sunset, and, like meditation, fasting requires great self-discipline. But unlike meditation, the result is not really expected to be some new insight into the true nature of reality, some vision of Void or Brahman akin to enlightenment. Rather, the result of fasting is meant to be growth in character and, we might hope, a kind of sympathy for the poor.

Notably, the kind of self-transformation that one might hope to gain from fasting seems hardly different from any other kind of self-discipline. Setting aside a special time to study, or simply dieting, can be matters of trying to change one's habits for the benefit of better grades or better health. But from the beginning of this text, we have noted that the difference between a religion and non-religion is the presence of a transmundane Ultimate Being, and if fasting is meaningful when done to practice self-discipline or to gain sympathy for the poor, it is yet something more when it is done as an act of obedience to God. Thus fasting for the Muslim is an act of submission to God, not merely a matter of moral self-improvement. And ultimately, like meditation, its personal purpose might be the way it leads to harmony with the holy. Such ultimate purposes are considered in Chapter 12.

WORSHIP RITUALS

We noted earlier in this chapter that there may be some problems with considering rituals of magic and transformation to be effective, if indeed such power to transform reality and ourselves seems to belie the absolute and ultimate nature of the transmundane power. There may be other problems with such rituals if they seem to be selfish in their focus on personal change and development, more like a self-help method than religious devotion. We consider such problems again at the end of this chapter, but if one is looking for religious ritual that seems purely to be about the greatness of Ultimate Being itself, perhaps the best examples will be rituals of **worship**.

The English word "worship" is related to the word "worth," and at its most basic, it means that when one is worshiping, one is simply declaring the worthiness of God. We find this direct linguistic connection in the last part of the Christian scriptures, where, in the closing book of the New Testament, Chapters 4 and 5, the great crowds of heaven declare that God and the Lamb are "worthy to receive honor and glory and praise." Similarly, in their church services, Christians "praise the Lord," and in their Old Testament the Psalms regularly "tell of God's greatness." All this suggests that worship is perhaps a uniquely religious ritual, inasmuch as it is focused on the Ultimate Being itself and its (or His) qualities.

Worship can take place in a number of contexts. For Christians, Sunday became the primary day of worship early in the Common Era as a weekly commemoration of the resurrection of Jesus. That is, every Sunday is, in a way, a celebration of Easter.

That is why Sunday became "the Lord's day." Worship on Sunday probably gained much of its form from the Jewish celebration of the Sabbath, the day Jews have set aside for worship and the celebration of life. In church specifically, Christians, like Jews, often use music and scripture reading as ways of declaring the greatness of God and gaining instruction in religion. When Christians and Jews develop a relatively formal and structured system of prayers and songs and readings, the order of such practices is called "**liturgy**." And with liturgy, one finds a regularity and consistency in worship that people can find familiar and comfortable all over the world. Thus the Catholic Mass will be roughly the same format whether one goes to church in America or Italy or China; and prior to 1963, every service would have been in Latin, no matter what country one came from.

This normalization and familiarity of structure, including the universal use of one language, is still evident in Islam. All over the world, Muslims go through a series of regular steps in the prayer ritual called "***salat***" or "*namaz*," and for all of them the ritual declarations and the recitations of scripture are in Arabic. Thus Muslim men and women learn from an early age the regular process of bowing, kneeling, and touching the forehead to the ground as ways of physically demonstrating their submission to Allah. And though translated as "prayer," one should not think of this ritual as asking God for

Figure 7.3   A Muslim at prayer, following the ritual order of prayers and prostrations.

blessings or manipulating God into providing earthly goods. Rather, it is worship in the sense of essentially confessing God's greatness. That is why, throughout the ritual, the leader of the prayers intones "*Allahu Akhbar*," which simply asserts that "God is great."

Rituals of worship exist in other religions, such as in the Hindu rituals of *puja* and *darshan*. Less regularized than weekly liturgies, these Hindu rituals nonetheless emphasize the power and glory of the gods. In more festival contexts, this worship can include retelling the stories of the gods' deeds, not as a form of mimetic magic but as a recounting of divine heroism. In temples, the washing of images by the priests and the practice of leaving offerings before those images by laypersons are acts of devotion. Notably, the **petitionary prayers** and blessings of the devotees are also part of such rituals, and thus no doubt there are magical elements here as well. Yet the traditional Vedic rituals of an earlier phase of Hinduism are evidently more like effective ritual, such that various lines chanted from the Vedas literally are taken to be cures for snake-bite or magic words for preventing disease. But for Hindus devoted to a particular deity, the point of *puja* is *bhakti*, or loving devotion. As Krishna says to his devotee Arjuna in the *Bhagavad Gita,* "Whoever offers to me with loving devotion a leaf, a flower, fruit or water, I accept as from a pure-hearted being."[8]

All of this worship, we might note, seems most at home in the context of theism. That is, we do not find religious worship in the more philosophical elements of Daoism or Buddhism. Neither is there any place for worship in the more monistic ideas of Hinduism focused on Brahman. One does, of course, find that Buddhists honor and venerate the Buddha, as Confucians honor Confucius and Daoists venerate Laozi. Yet this "veneration" may not be worship, except insofar as, in all these religions, there may also be a tendency to deify these founders, as noted in Chapter 2. This makes sense, if we consider that veneration and worship are a lot like meeting or greeting God (recall the handshaking analogy presented at the beginning of this chapter), except that here we meet a Being or beings whose spiritual greatness must be acknowledge. When one greets God, therefore, one is interacting with a person, acknowledging God's greatness in a relational context. One might think that Brahman and the Void, too, are "great" in some sense, but there is no sense in telling them so. They aren't listening. Thus one does not find temples to Brahman in India among the thousands of temples dedicated to the thousands of gods, and one does not worship the Void in Buddhism. As we've seen, meditation in these contexts is a much more appropriate approach to these Ultimate Beings than is worship.

In a similar way, one does not offer petitionary prayers to Brahman or the Void or the Dao. Again, these notions of Ultimate Being simply are not relational, not responsive to greeting or praise or requests. It seems, then, that prayer, like worship, is more common for theism and is, perhaps, a sub-species of worship. I say "perhaps" because I've also noted in this section that much prayer can be more like effective ritual, an effort to intone the right words and perform the right actions so that God or the gods can be induced to respond to our requests. But it is also possible that religious theists do not see their prayers as inducing God to do anything. Prayers are perhaps more like requests, offered with a certain amount of "fear and trembling" before a mighty monarch who might choose to say no. When Christians add to their prayers—notably imitating Jesus himself—the phrase "Your will be done," they are saying to God that their prayers are ultimately not effective, but petitionary. They ask God for blessings, but the blessings do not happen because of the prayers. Thus, perhaps done with this careful awareness, theists recognize that even their petitionary prayers are really acknowledgments of God's power over all things. This is why, even in mundane planning, a devout Muslim will ritually add the word *inshallah* to his or her statements about the future. Thus you will receive blessings from God, and you will even get to the end of reading this chapter, only "if God wills": *inshallah*.

THE COMPLEXITY OF RELIGIOUS RITUAL

Much of the discussion in this chapter has been offered in order to help develop a vocabulary for naming and understanding religious ritual in its many forms. It might be helpful, for example, whether in studying someone else's religion or even in analyzing our own, to consider if we think the prayers are more like effective ritual or like worship. When I pray, do my prayers work to gain a result, or am I leaving the future to God in a kind of recognition of God's greatness? Trying to answer this question, we may discover something about our own rituals and about our concept of God, for, as we've seen throughout this text, each element interrelates with other elements, and some are more consistent with some concepts of Ultimate Being than others. Seeing such connections offers us a chance to think critically and logically about the complex phenomenon that is human religion.

At the same time, it might be evident in some of the examples already considered, as well as in many examples we might know personally, that much religious ritual is itself quite complex and likely includes several different qualities in a single ritual. We have seen, for example, that the Lord's Supper performed in the context of the Catholic Mass is at once commemorative and effective. When a Muslim goes on the pilgrimage to Mecca, he or she is connecting in a commemorative way with the places and events related to the founding of the religion, yet the rituals are also powerfully transformative and the inclusion of *salat* and the attitudes of devotion are evidently worshipful. We have also seen that rituals of many kinds have psychological and social functions, helping followers to feel comfortable and accepted in the presence of the community and of the Ultimate Being. Thus we should not expect simple one-to-one correspondences between specific rituals and their various types and purposes. Real life, and especially real religious life, is much more complicated than that.

At the same time, if we are thoughtful about these elements of religion, we do begin to see similarities and patterns that help us to understand the religions we study and the religions we practice. And these patterns can make a great deal of difference in what we think religion is. For example, in various mystical traditions within religions usually considered monotheistic, the practices of prayer and worship can become more like meditation and gnostic self-transformation. When the famous Sufis of Islam, the "Whirling Dervishes," dance their elegant flow of motion to the soft tunes of the Turkish flute, they are not doing *salat*, and the result of the ritual is not apparently worship in the same sense. They are perhaps cultivating a transformative experience, and the result of such mystical practices might be more aimed at a feeling of oneness with Allah than a relational "greeting" or distant acknowledgment of God's greatness. Subtly perhaps, this changes one's notion of God, slipping slightly from a monotheistic perspective toward a more monistic one, and we might therefore expect that some more traditional forms of Islam have been suspicious of these mystical practices. Indeed, we find this historically to be true.

We shall consider in Chapter 10 how rituals affect—and effect—religious experiences and how different religious experiences have their own consistency with Ultimate Being. For this chapter, we might end only by reiterating that the interwovenness of the religious elements is not random. Sometimes individuals find they are not fond of traditional rituals and might wish to change them or abandon them altogether. But one cannot do so without there being ripples of implication for one's beliefs about Ultimate Being, one's sense of the authority of founders and scriptures, and so on. There is more to religion than the acceptance or rejection of what we like or dislike, for there is logic and coherence in these traditions, perhaps whether we like it or not.

PROBLEMS OF RITUAL

We have seen in this chapter that ritual has the power to construct communities and to grant individuals a sense of security and normality within the context of religious belief. Thus we have seen that conformity to ritual is part of the way a person participates fully in his or her religion. That is, when one is willing to participate in a ritual, that action is related to participation in belief, and these two elements of religion, the behavioral and the cognitive, are therefore not separable. Just as there is orthodoxy in religion, such that having "straight doctrine" might make one an official believer in the religion, so is there a kind of **orthopraxis**, literally, "straight practice." It is no accident, in fact, that there are rituals in which one formally and precisely confesses belief, such as when Catholics recite the Apostle's Creed or Muslims declare their "witness" to the oneness of God and the prophethood of Muhammad. It might even be a kind of confession of faith when a Buddhist "takes refuge."[9]

In this connection between ritual and belief, we might be inclined to say that there are at least some central rituals which one must practice in order to be an orthodox follower. Of course, choosing this language somewhat confuses the "truth" and "goodness" elements of religion, but by and large it does accurately suggest the interwovenness of belief and action. We might consider, for example, the possibility that a Muslim could refuse to do the daily prayers or a Catholic refuse to take the Lord's Supper. In such cases, we might suspect that the person is not really "a good Muslim" or "a good Catholic." This is not, let us recall, to judge the person's goodness but to recognize what different religions declare to be central practices. For example, one could imagine a Catholic who decided that she would not baptize her newborn baby, but hoped instead that the child would choose to be baptized later in the child's life. In such a case, this person might have become more of a Baptist, and less of a Catholic, than she realizes. When the Guru Nanak declared that ritual pilgrimage was not required of his followers, knowing full well the importance in Islam of the pilgrimage to Mecca, he was essentially starting a new religion, whether that was his plan or not. And the result is Sikhism.

There are, however, other reasons that people sometimes find rituals to be problematic. We noted previously, for example, that there are some kinds of "magical" effective rituals that might seem to contradict the idea of the ultimacy of the Ultimate Being. If humans control the actions of the gods more than the gods control the actions of the humans, we might have an interesting philosophical and spiritual puzzle on our hands. A person might also find ritual troubling because it has the tendency to become dead and repetitive. The very power of habit that makes ritual something a person can count on to be right is the same power of habit that allows us to "go through the motions" of participating in a religion without feeling anything. Notably, we see here the intersection of the behavioral and the experiential elements of religion, and just as rituals ought, in some sense, to fit with a religion's beliefs, so we might expect that, when we participate in rituals we ought to feel something. But sometimes, instead of feeling the comfort and assurance that come with participating fully in a religious ritual, people only feel dull and bored. We might easily imagine someone reciting a creed or doing the prostrations of Islamic prayers or watching Hindu priests shine lighted flames upon the statues of the gods for the five hundredth time and having his or her mind entirely somewhere else.

For these and other reasons, we might find that some people will downplay the ritual aspects of religion in favor of some other element. Perhaps the ritual practices are not as important as the experiential. Or we might find that some will downplay the ritual in favor of some other behavioral element, especially morality, suggesting that going to church or meditating is meaningless unless one is also, in some sense, "a good person." In this text, it is not our job to determine which elements ought to take priority other than in recognizing that different religions tend to emphasize different elements. We might, however, note that it needn't be a zero-sum dichotomy, such that if one conforms to ritual orthopraxis, one is thereby less inclined to find deep religious experiences or more inclined to neglect morality. For Confucius, participation in ritual was a central part of the life of a noble person, inasmuch as ritual, or "propriety," as he called it, is as much an attitude of character as it is mere conformity to some system of bowing or giving sacrifices. Ritual propriety, he claimed, was ultimately a matter of the heart, a kind of willingness to be formal and polite and orderly in society. And when that willingness of heart becomes habitual, it is a moral virtue.[10]

So perhaps it is up to the religious follower to combine the elements in some appropriate way, cultivating perhaps the experiential along with the behavioral, mixing both the moral and the ritual. And we have already argued—and will see this again—that even when the doctrinal, cognitive elements of religion are de-emphasized, they still exist, hiding perhaps behind the definitions of which rituals and which moral behaviors are right. With ritual in particular, if one practices the rituals because of what the founder has taught or because of what is in scripture, or if one practices because of how ritual can help create religious experience, we can see how the three basic branches of religious elements—truth, goodness, and beauty—might be woven into a single thread.

KEY TERMS IN CHAPTER 7

commemorative ritual   The ritual "remembering" of a religiously significant event, thus the celebration or re-enactment of a legendary or historical event deemed central to a religion.

effective ritual   Religious rituals performed in the hopes that the actions actually change reality and do so with a kind of supernatural power.

kami   A god of Shinto, the native religion of Japan.

liturgy   A relatively formal and structured system of prayers and songs and readings performed in religious ritual, especially worship ritual.

mimetic ritual   Religious ritual that accomplishes its purpose by intentionally imitating some other event, either as desired in the world (e.g., mimetic hunting rituals) or as understood from myth (e.g., creation re-enactment).

orthopraxis   Literally, "straight practice," thus a set of prescribed specific practices that are required and proper, defining what does and does not fit into a specific religion.

petitionary prayer   Ritual speech to God or gods that make requests for blessing or protection, etc., acknowledging the prayer's dependence upon Ultimate Being to answer.

puja   In Hinduism, the ritual actions of worship directed at images of various gods.

rites of passage   Rituals that mark and sanctify changes in the stages of one's life, such as rituals performed at birth or puberty or death.

ritual   Any kind of formal, regularized behavior that is performed in accordance with specific occasions or conditions.

sacrament   Especially in Christianity, a set of rituals rooted in the authority of Jesus and taken to be especially effective.

salat   In Islam, the regular, structured prayers that include scriptural declarations and prostration, in order to physically enact submission to God.

seasonal ritual   Religious rituals associated with annual seasonal cycles, thus with planting or harvesting or solar cycles.

transformative ritual   Religious rituals whose effects are primarily on the person performing the ritual, in some way changing that person's spiritual state.

worship   The ritual act of declaring or acknowledging the greatness, or "worth," of the Ultimate Being in itself, thus like praise or veneration.

CHAPTER 8

MORAL ACTION

AT VARIOUS POINTS IN the discussion of religious ritual, it might be difficult to tell the difference between ritual and morality. As we saw, Muslims are required to pray five times a day—part of the famous Five Pillars of Islam—yet the same list of duties includes giving charity to the poor. In the case of the Jewish Sabbath, Jews are commanded to take a day off from work, and the traditions that unfold around that commandment include a ritual meal, special recitations of scripture, and synagogue worship. But this obligation in Judaism exists alongside other commands of God in the famous Ten Commandments that include the more obviously moral duties to refrain from killing and stealing. So where does ritual end and morality begin?

Perhaps we don't really need to answer this question. Let us simply admit that the line between the two is unclear, or, better, that the two circles—ritual and morality—overlap as in a Venn diagram. Morality can become ritualized; some rituals seem morally demanded. But both fit the second realm of the religious phenomenon called "Goodness," because both deal with behavior, or doing (in some sense) the right thing. And this may particularly be evident when we speak of morality.

"Morality" refers to our actions deemed right and wrong. It refers to the judgments we make about the good and bad of our behavior, such that when we do something moral, we think we have done what we should; when we do something we shouldn't do, it is immoral. A philosopher who talks about morality is said to be teaching "ethics," which might be called the science or the theory of morality. When one tries to explain why some action is moral and another is not, one is discussing ethics. For our purposes, this is not so crucial a distinction, except perhaps to say that, in a way,

118

the connection between morality and religion is like that between morality and ethics: Often religion is the reason given for the content and the justification of moral ideals.

OBLIGATION AND THE "QUEERNESS" OF MORALITY

When philosophers speak of the "queerness" of morality, they mean that moral language is kind of strange. It may be all the stranger because we use it every day, multiple times a day, but often really don't know what we mean. When we say people ought to do something or they shouldn't do something else, we don't really describe what they do or even what they will do. It is a statement about the value of what they might do. We say this moral language of "should" and "ought" is not descriptive, but prescriptive.

When we make a moral claim—which is, as I'll re-emphasize later, a kind of truth claim—we are saying that one action is better than another and that is why it is something we should do. Alternatively, of course, we might be saying one action is worse than another and that's why we shouldn't do it. But it is very hard in an explanation of morality to get outside this little circle: We use "should" to describe the better action and use "good" to explain "should." That's what makes moral discussions so difficult, so "queer." Morality is, in that sense, like talking about why one likes or dislikes a piece of music: We may easily say something is "good music," but it is difficult to say why.

Speaking of morality is different from speaking of popular music, however, because it carries with it a kind of seriousness we can call "obligation." That is, when we say one ought to be good to the poor or shouldn't hurt innocent people, we don't merely mean we like one thing and dislike another. We mean in a way that if someone, in fact, likes hurting innocent people, he or she is wrong. He or she shouldn't like hurting innocent people—and there we are again with "should." **Obligatoriness** is like a kind of force that morality has, a kind of demand it makes. In fact, it is not accidental that the word "demand" has the same root as "command" or "commandment."

It is from this sense of value and obligation that we get to the idea of moral authority. A moral claim—a sentence like "You should be generous to the poor"—is more than a suggestion; it is a command. And as such, we might ask where the authority for such a command comes from. If a general in the army issues a command, the command has force because the general has authority. The same command issued by some bystander or average citizen just isn't a command. So when we offer moral commands, where does the authority come from?

This is the basic question of ethics. Philosophers have developed a number of ethical theories that try to establish the authority of moral claims based on reason or social conformity. Some have argued that because pleasure is inherently "good," we "ought" to do the deeds that maximize pleasure and minimize pain. For our purposes here, we only need to note that this quest for the authority of moral commands is what frequently connects morality and religion. As we've seen, there is often a kind of logic in religion that connects its various elements back to Ultimate Being, a final reality that "just is." And the same goes for morality. You might imagine that a Christian preacher would say we ought to be generous to the poor, but he says this not on his own authority. He may make moral commands, but only because of his role as minister. And that role, in turn, has authority only because he quotes the Bible, which has its authority from the Apostles, who have their authority from Jesus, who has His authority from God. And God's authority? It "just is."

Precisely what religions add to moral claims, then, is a sense that their power and obligatoriness go beyond mere human invention. Morality seems to be in need of authority—that is its queerness—and religion provides it. That is not to say there is no non-religious morality; we've already noted the existence of various philosophical theories. But we can see why so often morality and religion are linked by this concept of authority. For, if I announce that I want you to be good to the poor, that may be a quaint self-assertion; but if God himself commands you to do so, then morality gains the obligatoriness and authority it seeks.

We shall see in the next section that there are various ways that religion provides the authority behind morality, and we shall have to consider some of the problems that arise from this connection. That is, the same philosophers that try to find non-religious moral systems often argue that religious moral systems have particular difficulties, both logically and practically. But for now, let us only try to examine the force that religion adds to moral claims to see the ways religion so commonly and naturally includes morality as one of its key elements.

MONOTHEISM AND DIVINE COMMANDS

Perhaps the most obvious connection between morality and religion is the one we've already been assuming: God gives moral commands. Because of the cultural context of the European and American audience, most of us have heard of the Ten Commandments, maybe even had to memorize them as a child. Certainly they give us a paradigm case of a religious morality, with the rules of "Don't steal," "Don't murder," and "Don't commit adultery." We shouldn't forget that this list includes the commandment to keep the Sabbath Day holy and to worship no other gods. Recall that ritual and morality are difficult to distinguish at times, and for us in this chapter perhaps only the last six commandments seem most like "morality," as they deal with our interactions with other people. Perhaps we also don't particularly like the prohibition against extra-marital sex and think the commandment against adultery is outdated. But we should see that these famous ten moral rules come, so to speak, as a set. If the command against murder has divine authority, so does the command against adultery and the command to keep a day "holy." Divine authority is not overruled by our personal tastes, or else it is not divine authority.

In general, when we speak of morality like a list of moral rules, we speak of morals as **deontology**. This word means that the rules as such carry authority and we are discouraged from questioning some ulterior purpose or hoped-for result of our moral action. We should obey moral rules because they are the rules, and that means that adultery and murder are wrong even if they might seem justified by some other end. For example, it might seem justified to condemn an innocent person in order to quell an angry mob, if sacrificing one person would protect hundreds. But the deontological view of morality would say no. We will speak of morals as **teleology** later, where the moral ideals are justified more by what they accomplish than by their status as moral rules.

Figure 8.1   The Ten Commandments as traditionally depicted, written in Hebrew on tablets of stone.

Other deontological ethical lists can be found in the world's religions besides the Ten Commandments of Judaism and Christianity. Even in Judaism, the "law" of God is much broader than these ten rules, and traditionally the developments of Rabbinical Judaism have shown that, if you read the books of Moses for all of their rules of behavior, there are not just ten commandments, but 613. These rules are further detailed in the writings of the Rabbis called the Talmud, in which the law of God tells us not only when and with whom one can have sex, but even the kind of material one can use in the wicks of the candles lit on the Sabbath Day.[1]

Similarly, Islam has a detailed list of moral rules called Shariah, or Islamic Law, given by God and exemplified in the life of the prophet Muhammad. Included are the rules and procedures for ritual actions like the pilgrimage and prayers, but also the rules for what constitutes theft, how to divide up property among heirs, and how to establish what one owes in charity to the poor. On a less detailed level, one sees quickly in a good Muslim society that people don't eat pork or drink alcohol, don't gamble, may not lend or borrow money at interest, and should dress modestly. All this is in addition to what we might expect as the moral laws of God, with prohibitions of murder and sex outside of marriage.

If it seemed to us that deontological lists of moral rules go logically well with notions of prophets and monotheism, we'd be right. That is not to say that other lists don't exist, and indeed there is an interestingly recognizable list of moral rules in the so-called Five Precepts of the Buddha. In this list, along with rules against killing and the misuse of sex, one also finds the prohibition of intoxicants. For monks, the list of moral rules is much longer, with "Ten Precepts" that include the prohibition of touching money or attending entertainment shows. Beyond even these ten precepts, there are full books of *vinaya* rules, rules for making the monasteries run properly and smoothly. Even with all this rule-making, however, we might see in Buddhist teaching that much of the moral instruction is not deontological. The monastic rules, for example, are meant to make it more possible for monks to achieve enlightenment, and even the basic moral precepts are not about being "good" or "bad." Moral actions, rather, are said to be "skillful," that is, more or less conducive to a way of life that can result in awakening and liberation. In that sense, the Buddhist precepts are more teleological than deontological.

The easiest connection, then, between a deontological morality and religious authority remains in the basic logic that connects morality to scripture and prophets, and from there to God. As usual, we should not expect that there are no exceptions to this logic, but we can also begin to understand the relation of moral authority and "what God has said," so that we understand why people quote the Bible or the Quran and use these texts as moral rulebooks. Again, we can like or dislike this connection, believe in it ourselves or not, but in any case we should be able to understand why people speak of "obeying God's word," or why they might want the Ten Commandments on the courthouse lawn.

THE VIRTUE OF THE SAGES

Confucianism and Daoism represent for us interesting examples of religious moralities that are not deontological or teleological. They are something more like an approach to ethics that philosophers call "**virtue theory**." Especially in Confucius we find an emphasis on virtue, but the appeal to religion—if indeed we should call Confucianism "religion"—is clearly not in any appeal to the authority of God. We have already had our discussion about whether Confucianism should be called "religion," and we noted back in Chapters 1 and 2 that there is in the Confucian philosophy an appeal to the Dao of Heaven that may ultimately be analogous to the Ultimate Being of monotheism. Yet for many scholars, the entire focus of Confucius' writing is on morality and social order, not on worship or any relation to spirits. And they are right. Even so, I suggest here that it is precisely the religious element in Confucianism that makes it more than moral philosophy by giving morality a kind of higher authority.

We should begin to see that the word "authority" does not have to refer to some law-giving God. At the same time, we saw that in the monotheistic religions moral authority cannot rest merely in human assertion. And this is the case with Confucius, too. That is, Confucius insisted that he was inventing no new ideas, but was, he believed, merely transmitting the wisdom of mythic Sage Kings. Thus the wisdom he appealed to was that of sages who had finally and firmly understood the moral order of the universe—the Dao of Heaven—and managed to implement it for human society. Education, moral self-cultivation, and ultimately the whole order of Chinese society was therefore a matter of conformity to our own true nature, the order of human relationships given in the Dao.

For Confucius, then, the logic of religious morality is not from God through prophets, but from the true nature of reality as understood by sages. And the ideal result is that we who follow their wisdom begin to practice the kind of life-habits that make us more truly human and make society more naturally harmonious. These life-habits are virtues: benevolence and wisdom, respect and humility, obedience to authority, and honoring of one's parents. As the Confucian philosopher Mencius said, everyone who is human is naturally born with the basic seeds of these virtues, and the moral work of all people is simply to become what we naturally should be.[2]

The point to consider is how a different concept of Ultimate Being leads us to a kind of moral wisdom different from monotheistic deontology, even as the Dao is manifested to humanity through a sage, not through a prophet. We saw in the previous chapter that this idea of proper behavior is followed for Confucius in elaborate rituals, and yet even these rituals—or at least the willingness to devote ourselves to ritual propriety—is a virtue. It is ritually proper to say "please" and "thank you," but it is morally virtuous to become a polite and honorable person.

Ironically, perhaps, the difficulty for Confucian thought comes from within its own logic. If those who understand the Dao can tell us how to behave in accordance with our own natures, it is obviously important that those who claim to understand the Dao are not mistaken. For Confucius, the Dao was best understood in terms of human relationships and the reciprocal honor shown between fathers and sons, rulers and subjects. But at the same time, Daoism in China arose and claimed that the Dao was best understood in terms of the constant flow and changes of nature, summer to winter, day to night. Consequently, the appropriate "virtue" for the wise Daoist was *wu-wei*, "non-action," a kind of wise and willing acceptance of things as they are and non-resistance to change. Thus for the Daoists, morality in terms of Confucian virtue was a rather silly distraction, trying to put a human face on the Way of Nature when in fact there is no face. "Leave off, teaching men virtue!" cries a character in one of Zhuangzi's parables.[3] All the ritual, the benevolence, the honor and order of government—all this, say the Daoists, is futile. Replace it instead with the virtue of non-action, letting the changes of nature come and go without resistance. Thus to the Daoists, Confucians were stuffy and foolish; to the Confucians the Daoists were lazy and self-indulgent.

This disagreement between Chinese philosophies should alert us to the fact that understanding the Dao and seeing clearly the virtues that we should therefore cultivate is not as easy as it may seem. The Dao does not reveal its will and moral order through prophets, as we know, and so "human nature" as our natural "way" may not be easy to define. Nevertheless, we see in both Confucianism and Daoism a kind of logic we should recognize. Morality is not merely the suggestion of a man, not even a very wise man. Morality, the right kind of human action, is a way of life that copies an even greater Way. The authority of virtue morality is in the authority of the sage, and the authority of the sage is in the Dao, the Way of Heaven.

MONISM AND TELEOLOGICAL MORALITY

When we turn to religions whose Ultimate Being is more monistic than theistic, and thus perhaps more world-denying than world-affirming, we find another kind of religious ethics. The religions of India in general, it seems, have a tendency to be suspicious about involvement in the world, and that includes involvement in the world's social morality. And thus, where Brahman is the Ultimate Being in the more philosophical, less polytheistic versions of Hinduism, we discover the ideal of the *sannyasi*, the world-renouncer, and thus a moral ideal more like the Daoist than the Confucian or the theist. When a Hindu man renounces the world, he gives up his name and social status, relationships and duties, entering a period of instruction under a guru in a kind of school called an *ashram*. The literal meaning of *ashram* is "no work."

Though not Hindu, the example of the Buddha himself is instructive. Born a prince in luxury and comfort, the legend says, the Buddha had reached the age of twenty-nine when he saw the three great visions of sickness, old age, and death. With these sights, he was inspired to renounce his princely life and seek release from the cycle of rebirth. In these ways, he is a paradigm of all monks that follow and a kind of model for much Indian religious pursuit. Less noted in the story, however, is that he leaves behind a wife and newborn son, an act morally problematic in some religious (and non-religious) views, but wholly expected and even ideal in India. The founder of Jainism, Mahavira, follows a similar path.

The point to see in these examples is that the action of **renunciation** is wholly consistent with a worldview that emphasizes the illusional nature of this world and sees all possession and sensuality as a kind of trap. In the case of Hinduism, we can see clearly how this is consistent with Brahman as Ultimate Being. Brahman is the one reality, the single substance of all that exists, including one's own soul, the Atman. Thus this life, this ego, and these relationships are all *maya*, or illusion, and participation in this illusion only binds one more deeply to karma and rebirth. To escape this world and find liberation from rebirth, one must renounce normal life, including its normal obligations and duties.

In the last chapter of this book, we discuss these concepts of liberation, and later in this chapter we discuss religious antinomianism, the religious denial of common morality. Here, we only want to note the logic of how an idea of Ultimate Being can in fact seem to suggest morality that is contrary to social duty, yet consistent with the idea of there being a kind of ideal behavior grounded in the nature of Ultimate Being.

At the same time, it would be clearly wrong to suggest that Hinduism or Buddhism is an amoral system. For it is well known that, from these same world-renouncing religions come important constructs of morality emphasizing karma. Karma literally means "action," and it refers to the assumption that the deeds we do in this life have automatic repercussions in our future rebirths. We noted in Chapter 6 the story of the Buddhist monk Mogallana and his fate of being murdered in future lifetimes because he had killed his own parents in a previous life. Clearly, this is not amoral. In fact, the Buddha himself, in clarifying the Noble Eightfold Path toward liberation, includes the important ideals of "right action," "right livelihood," and "right speech." And we saw earlier that the Buddha enumerated sets of precepts for his monks and for the lay community: Don't kill, don't steal, don't misuse sex, don't lie, and don't use intoxicants. Except for the last, perhaps, the moral rules in this list are pretty standard.

In Hinduism, the actual moral duties of this world are clearly outlined in *The Laws of Manu*, a text emphasizing caste and gender roles and the moral duties that go with each. Appearing in Hinduism after the traditions of renunciation had become strong, this text tries to find the right place in a social system for the re-nouncers and give equal place to the "householders" who continue to live in the world of moral duty. Jainism, perhaps most famously, develops within its world-renouncing tradition the emphatic morality of *ahimsa*, or non-violence. Based upon the ideal that all living things have eternal and impersonal souls, it fol-lows that one should not do violence to any animal, and the moral implications

Figure 8.2   A Jain monk, traditionally dressed in the white robes of the Svetambara sect, his mouth covered in case he accidentally inhales and thus harms an insect.

range from the insistence on a vegetarian diet to monks sweeping the path they walk on in order to avoid accidentally stepping on a bug.

Perhaps what we note in the strong moral teachings of these world-renouncing reli-gions is that they function in a society that also creates a relatively strong monk–laity social division. We talk more about such social divisions in the next chapter; here we need only note that a society made up entirely of renouncers would clearly collapse, and therefore the social order requires still a morality that functions in a worldly manner. For the monks themselves, however, morality might be better understood teleologically than deontologically. That is, as noted previously, in teleological morality the purpose of good deeds is not obedience to a divine being, nor the value of morality in itself, since these religions focus neither on God nor on the illusory world. Rather, morality is part of a process of enlightenment that is more the ultimate goal of religious practice than is social order. In Hinduism, it may be important for the laity to practice the duties appropriate to caste and gender, but it is not valuable for the renouncer. Indeed, it is for the renouncer something that must in fact be renounced. Yet morality is not therefore abandoned. As Sankara, the great eighth-century Hindu philosopher, noted, one can only become a renouncer if one is of good character and "from a good family." High caste and good moral behavior are presumed.[4] As noted earlier in this chapter, the moral precepts of Buddhism imply that immoral action is "unskillful": One simply will never find enlightenment if one does not act morally. And yet, once one has cultivated the necessary character that leads to renunciation and, ultimately, purity of mind, morality has fulfilled its teleological purpose. Renunciation then remains the ideal.

RELIGIOUS EXEMPLARS

A final way to look at morality that is neither deontological nor teleological is to consider the moral exemplar. Even in secular morality, it is sometimes suggested that moral decision-making can appeal, as Aristotle said, to the kind of actions a man of wisdom would perform. When Christians ask, "What would Jesus do?" they are making the same kind of logical move, although on a different level. For Jesus, to the Christians, is not merely "a man of practical wisdom" but the Son of God, and thus Jesus is an example of moral behavior above all others.

Back in Chapter 4, we saw how religious founders are the source of religious authority in matters of "truth," often indeed the source of scripture, whether or not they wrote it themselves. Similarly, here in the context of "goodness," the founders are often taken as sources of authority, functioning as moral models. Muhammad, we saw back in the discussion of scripture, was the source of the Quran in the sense that he was the conduit through whom Allah gave "Recitations" to mankind. At the same time, we saw that the words and actions of Muhammad himself became a kind of secondary scripture, the Hadith or Sunna literature, which, alongside the Quran, became the foundation of Islamic Law. Thus "What would Muhammad do?" is not merely some theoretical question but a very real part of the science of Islamic jurisprudence.

Confucius provides a similar model in China, yet, as we should predict by now, his position as moral exemplar is quite different from that of either Jesus or Muhammad. As a sage—neither a prophet of God nor divine incarnation—Confucius is even more a model of human nature, an idealized image of what every one of us can be if we just know how to cultivate virtue. Interestingly, as we saw, Confucius himself did not claim to have any special abilities or insights, but only to be copying the great sages of the past. Even so, it might not surprise us to find out that, in popular Chinese culture, Confucius is eventually divinized, declared a kind of divine ancestor. One wonders if Confucius himself would approve.

One may, of course, challenge in general the idea of appealing to human models as the basis of human morality. There may seem to be a kind of ungrounded presumption in claiming a "mere human" as the foundation of virtue, as if a boy wanting to "be like Dad" when he grows up is anything more than a bit naive and childlike. But for religion, of course, the foundation is deeper. These human models are merely human models, perhaps, but we have been stressing from the beginning that it is their connection with

Ultimate Being that gives them their authority. And in the case of a divine incarnation, like Jesus or the Hindu god Rama, the model to the believer is God himself. Thus Jesus, after washing the feet of his disciples, tells them that he is indeed their "Lord and teacher," and yet this act of service is something they must go on to emulate. "Now that you have seen me do this," he says, "blessed are you if you do it, too."[5]

PROBLEMS OF RELIGIOUS MORALITY

It would be almost dishonest to finish this chapter without noting the kind of objections raised against religious morality, both from within religion and from without. From within religion, we have already noted the example of Daoists criticizing Confucian morality for having failed to see the true nature of the Dao and, consequently, having "taught men virtue" in conflict with man's own true nature. From the Confucian perspective, we noted, Daoists seem to misunderstand the Dao and thus encourage an easy simplicity of life that just avoids one's moral duties to family and to society. Thus the Daoists may be guilty of religious antinomianism.

"**Antinomianism**" literally means "against the rules," and it suggests that there are philosophies that seem to make it acceptable, even better in some way, to break the rules of what most of us would consider common morality. This is not merely a matter of having rules different from those of society or the state, as when early Christians refused to recant their faith in the midst of persecution, insisting that they had to obey God even against the orders of Rome. The devout Quaker pacifist that refuses to go to war even if drafted is not antinomian. But Christians have been guilty of antinomianism at times, and indeed it seems there has been a temptation to that fault from the beginnings of the faith. This is evident in the letters of Saint Paul where, by emphasizing that one need only appeal to Jesus as savior in order to go to heaven, he invites the critique that this implies one can live as sinfully as one pleases without repercussions. "Shall we sin all the more so that forgiveness may abound?" he asks. That would indeed be antinomian thinking. But to his own question he quickly replies, "Of course not!" Yet the fact that he had to raise the question shows the danger inherent in Christian salvation, that, being "saved by grace," one needn't care about morality.[6]

Another case of apparent antinomianism can be found in some practices of Buddhism. In one famous parable, two traveling monks meet a woman standing at the edge of a stream, and without pause, one of the monks carries her across the water and puts her down on dry ground. A mile later in the walk, the second monks risks the question of how the first monk could break his monastic vow not to touch a woman. And in pithy Buddhist style, the first monk answers, "I put the woman down on the opposite shore, but you are still carrying her." The implication: If you have no attachments, then the rules don't matter.

In Zen and other forms of Mahayana Buddhism, there are more stories of masters and teachers who break the rules, insulting the Buddha and beating their students in order to help them achieve the awakening of enlightenment. "If you meet the Buddha on the road," says one famous Zen *koan*, "kill him!" The point, of course, would be that one shouldn't get hung up on the role or even the teaching of the historical Buddha himself, since in the end the important thing is to awaken the Buddha Mind within yourself. More recently, and more notoriously, the Tibetan Buddhist teacher Chogyam Trungpa of Boulder, Colorado, was found to be having various sexual affairs with his students, male and female, and when the behaviors came to light, it was noted by his defenders that this, too, can be a teaching about how to transcend the burdens of the world. After all, the use of sexual imagery in Tibetan Buddhism is historically common, and it has always been acknowledged that there are numerous pitfalls for interpreting such acts and images wrongly. Of course, not all of the students of Chogyam Trungpa accepted such antinomian explanations; the master's alcohol and drug use perhaps made such excuses even less believable.

Perhaps it is possible to find a response to the challenge of religious antinomianism in our broader discussion of the religious elements of beauty, truth, and goodness. For we can see that the emphasis we are now making on goodness, especially moral goodness, does not necessarily deny any prior emphasis on the centrality of religious belief or religious experience. Interestingly, in the two examples here, we might suggest that Saint Paul was so intent on the claims of religious belief that it seemed as if he had undermined religious morality. And analogously, it might seem that the focus in Buddhism on religious experience could make religious morality pointless. But we have seen already that neither Christianity nor Buddhism is without its moral focus, though for both religions moral goodness may not be the most important focus.

A different kind of challenge to religious morality comes from the outside, from secular moralists who find appeals to God and prophets to be both unnecessary and dangerous. Whether it is unnecessary—that is, whether one can establish a sufficient basis for moral authority without some appeal to Ultimate Being—is beyond the scope of this book, but it is a fine issue to discuss in an Ethics course. Whether religious morality is "dangerous," however, is something we should consider.

Secular moralists like John Stuart Mill have admitted—perhaps grudgingly—that Western culture owes something to religion in the evolution of our moral sensitivities. But at the same time, he says, the same authority with which religion teaches, say, the Ten Commandments makes it difficult for religion to change with the times. Commandments that are, so to speak, "written in stone" not only claim to have the authority of God, but claim that authority for all time and for all people. Thus religious moralities, Mill argues, tend to look poorly on challenge and questioning, failing, he would say, to acknowledge the need for societies to change along with social needs.[7]

A similar challenge appears when two moral ideals are both supported by the appeal to religion, even though we might like one of them and dislike the other. In his infamous critique of Mother Theresa, atheist Christopher Hitchens criticizes the apparent saint for mixing into her care for the poor of India a firm stance against abortion and a tendency to encourage conversion to Christianity. But it would be clear to any good Catholic that these positions are not so separable: One cannot remove Jesus from Mother Theresa's view of abortion any more than one can remove him from her compassion for the sick. Religious morality tends to come in packages.

Of course it is not obvious that these critiques settle the argument; it would certainly be a bit presumptuous to assume that Mother Theresa is wrong, and Hitchens is right, about abortion or religious conversion. Other examples might be mustered, however, drawn from scriptural verses that seem to command the extermination of one's enemies (as one can find in Jewish and Christian scriptures) or that seem to allow for a man to hit his wife (as one can find in the Quran).[8] And if such verses are to be taken as divine authority, the religious believer is in a difficult position, trying to decide how to assert that authority when it suits him or her and ignore it when it doesn't. Such a strategy is really just to replace divine authority with one's own opinions, undermining the whole force and purpose of religious morality.

MOTIVATION FOR MORALITY

We have spent a great deal of time in this chapter dealing with the question of moral authority and the content of moral claims. "What is the right thing to do, and on what authority does this moral directive rest?" we have asked, and we have seen how religion in reply lends force and content to morality. Yet perhaps we have been overlooking—or merely presuming—another aspect of ethical thought: the motivation for morality. That is, it is one thing to agree that giving money to the poor is the right thing to do, but one still may simply choose not to do it. We can know that the speed limit on the street is 40 miles per hour and know the basic legal authority behind the law, and we may still choose to drive 50.

Perhaps the most obvious addition of religion to the motivation for moral behavior is that we presume one cannot "get away with it." Most likely, those who drive 50 in a 40 zone do so simply because they think they won't get caught, and if they suddenly see a police car at the next corner, no doubt they suddenly are motivated to obey the law. If we presume a kind of monotheistic view, and add that God is all-knowing, there is clearly no such thing as not getting caught. The Quran makes clear, for example, its repeated warnings that God knows what we do and knows what is in our hearts. This is why the recitations of the words of Allah are a constant "warning" to those who think there is no God and no day of judgment.

Karma can similarly work as a motivator for morality. Although karma does not presume monotheism, nor is karma "omniscient" in any sense, karma is nonetheless relentlessly threatening. In fact, karma is arguably more of a threat, inasmuch as karma cannot choose to forgive or be merciful. Karma is not, after all, a divine mind suggesting moral rules, getting angry, or being merciful as it pleases. Karma is more like causation: If you jump off a cliff, you will smash on the rocks below. Neither the cliff nor the rocks get angry or punish you for jumping; neither the cliff nor the rocks can have mercy.

But all of this suggests that the primary reason for morality is fear, and while that may be true in many cases in religion, it does not seem to be the sole or even first motivator. On the opposite side of the same coin from fear of punishment, for example, is hope of reward; the fear of hell is not necessarily more prominent or even conscious in the believer's mind than the hope of heaven. One needn't be particularly afraid of failing a class or of being unemployed in the future to be motivated to study in college. One can hope that there are benefits and indeed can trust that the economic system adequately rewards those that work hard and honestly. Similarly, religion offers people a great hope for hard and honest work far beyond a college degree and a good job. And to insist that this is merely a different shade of fear is simply cynical.

We shall consider in the last chapter the question about salvation and ultimate beatitude, particularly looking at this connection between morality and final reward. We shall note there, however, that there is much more to religious views of salvation than the overused claim that "If you're good, you go to heaven." This may indeed sometimes be a motivation for being good, but we will see in Chapter 12 that this particular notion of salvation is not really as common as we might imagine. Even so, religion motivates morality in other, less direct ways, by promising benefits to life and a greater chance for enlightenment. That is, much more "this-worldly" goals can be found in religious calls to morality, from the way Buddhist precepts help clear the mind to the way Confucian virtues help one simply live well and prosper.

In all these ways, religion can motivate morality with hope, even as the college student can be motivated to study. The difference, of course, is that, with the uncertainty of the economy and the burden of student loans, the unhappy college student might well give up in despair. Given the omniscience of God, the all-pervasiveness of Karma, and the wisdom of Confucius or the Buddha, however, the hope for final justice and reward can be deeper and more certain. The job market may fluctuate, but God and the Dao of Heaven do not.

In all these examples, we seem only to be concerned about our own well-being, whether in this world or in the next, and for some critics of religious morality, this may seem to make religious moral action ultimately selfish. Perhaps it often is. But there are other ways that religion enhances moral motivation, both through the recognition of the greatness of the source and through a greater appreciation for the object of our moral action. That is, we can see that religion also encourages moral action by encouraging the love of God and the love of others.

For Christians who would insist that morality is not the primary means of achieving a blissful afterlife, the motivation for morality may lie neither in the hope of heaven nor the fear of hell. When the Christian receives salvation through Jesus, morality is no longer the means of gaining heaven, but is rather a response to God's goodness. To contrast again the speeding example, we might imagine that someone obeys civil law not because he or she is afraid of being caught but out of a kind of respect for law. Not fear, but patriotism, can inspire one to be a good citizen. Similarly, those who see God as the source of moral authority may choose to obey God's law simply for the sake of God's own greatness. The love of God motivates the believer's action, not just fear or the hope for personal benefits.

In another way, religion can enhance moral motivation by offering rationale that explains the value and importance of the object of moral effort. In the previous example regarding the Jain doctrine of *ahimsa*, we noted that the ideal of non-violence toward all living things is rooted not in a command of God but in the belief that all living things have a certain kind of soul. The mosquitoes we swat as well as the humans we serve are beings with *jiva*, a soul that is impersonal and perfect, pure and omniscient, even if neither the human nor the mosquito realizes it. Similarly, as noted in Chapter 5, human beings are described in the Judaic religions as being created in the divine image. There is more to the person and to the mosquito, we might say, than science alone can reveal, and that is why they deserve our love and respect. Religion has taught us so.

None of this is to deny that there are, perhaps, other, non-religious ways to assert the value and dignity of the human person or the annoying mosquito, but these are noted here to suggest that, once again, religion supplies something in our moral world that is both reasonable and powerful. Whatever human rights might be declared in the constitution of any particular government, it is perhaps all the more forceful if we can suggest, as the U.S. Declaration of Independence does, that human rights are "endowed by the creator." Of course, whether or not the United States, or any other government, has been particularly good at fulfilling the promises of equal rights and the dignity of the person is another question. That governments often have relied upon religious ideals to establish basic precepts is evident; whether governments still should rely upon religious ideals is a much more problematic consideration. And that is the topic of the next chapter.

KEY TERMS IN CHAPTER 8

ahimsa   The ideal moral notion of non-violence, especially derived from Jainism and the belief that all living things have an inviolable soul.

antinomianism   Literally "against the rules," suggesting a philosophical or religious view that may justify breaking or disregarding common morality.

deontology   A conception of morality primarily in terms of rules, so that the rules as such carry authority, in contrast to stressing the value of the end or result of the action.

Laws of Manu   A Hindu text that reasserts the value of participation in social life by clarifying the duties of persons according to class and gender.

obligatoriness (of morality)   A kind of force that morality has, such that moral statements are not merely suggestions but have the feel of a demand.

renunciation   The religious ideal of leaving the common world of relationships and possessions, thus refusing to participate in common duties of social life.

teleology   A conception of morality that primarily justifies moral claims in terms of what they accomplish, the value of the achieved ends.

virtue theory   A focus of moral thinking on character traits and the cultivation of behavioral habits, rather than on moral rules or achieved ends.

wu-wei   Literally "non-action"; in Daoism, the virtue of wise and willing acceptance of things as they are and non-resistance to change.

CHAPTER 9

SOCIAL ORDER
AND GOVERNMENT

IN OUR DISCUSSION OF religious morality, it might already have been evident that there is no clear line between personal morality and social structure. Not only is murder immoral, it is also against the law. But even moral concerns about sex, a topic that many of us Westerners take for granted as being personal and private, has implications for the structure of families and economics and, therefore, the greater society. When we observe the second table of the Ten Commandments, it is interesting to note that they are often worded in terms of relationship to one's neighbor.

One implication of this is that the so-called separation of church and state is not as simple as we might like to believe. For this text, the term "church" is clearly problematic, since that is a term specifically for a Christian institution, so we might want to replace it with other terms, suggesting a "separation of mosque and state" or of "temple and state." But just for convenience, perhaps, "church and state" can be retained. Yet the concept of their separation is problematic for another reason: We cannot take it for granted that all religions share this idea of the separation of the religious institution and the larger social order.

Richard Niebuhr, in his book *Christ and Culture*, suggests a typology for describing how a religion can be related to the larger society in a variety of ways. Of course, here again, using the Christian term alone—Christ—makes us focus only on how Christianity is related to the surrounding social order, so, again, we could speak in larger terms of "Allah and Culture" or "Buddha and Culture." But the useful point about Niebuhr's descriptions is noting that sometimes the religious ideals function quite in harmony with the social order, but sometimes rather contrary to it. Thus we have "Christ of Culture" and "Christ Against Culture," as well as a number of other, more nuanced descriptions.[1] We see in such a list that there are many ways in which a religion interacts with the larger society, and we find this to be true especially as we look across the different religions of the world. Yet we also see in Niebuhr's analysis that even within one religion, Christianity in his case, there may not be a single, normative way in which the religion works within society. Even so, we shall see in what follows that different religions generally do represent specific patters of interaction with their larger society, developing beyond ritual and personal morality the way that religions define the "good" for humanity.

RELIGION AND SOCIAL ORDER

I have already spoken a great deal in this chapter about "social order," but I have not paused to define the term. Generally, "**social order**" refers to the organization of people in a society according to various ranks and privileges. The social order can define for people how they are to behave and what roles they play in life, what kind of jobs they can have, and what property they can own. These distinctions are sometimes made along lines of gender, sometimes along lines of religion itself, sometimes along more mysterious lines. Sometimes we say there are no "lines," which is to suggest that everyone is equal, and this, too, is a kind of "social order." For the purposes of this chapter, the way religion defines social order will also include how people are organized within the religion itself, in terms of leadership and authority.

As a major example, perhaps one of the ways religion most evidently constructs social order is evident in the **caste system** of Hinduism. Traditionally, the caste system divides Hindus into four major groups called *varnas*, which literally means "colors." From top to bottom, they are usually designated as the castes of Priests (*Brahmins*), Warriors (*Kshatriyas*), Merchants (*Vaisyas*), and Servants (*Sudras*). These titles seem simply to define people by their jobs, and indeed there are many sub-castes that define jobs more strictly and in more detail, including the designation of the lowest sub-class of the *Sudra*, the so-called Untouchables. Yet these names do not define jobs simplistically, since not all *Brahmins* are in fact priests, and it isn't as though all members of India's military are somehow *Kshatriya*. Instead, these titles designate certain privileges of social status. In fact, part of the point is that these "levels" are less about the jobs and more about religious purity and ritual practices. For traditionally, to be born into one of the three upper castes, the so-called twice-born, allowed one to undergo specific rituals of purification and education, such as the sacred-thread ceremony, a Hindu rite of passage that moves a boy from the status of a child to that of a young man ready to study the Vedas. *Sudras*, by religious law, were not allowed to read the Vedas.

In a society like ours, where theoretical equality and upward mobility are ideals, this idea of caste can seem harsh. Notably, even between castes there is a kind of upward mobility but only when tied to other Hindu beliefs, especially karma and

Figure 9.1   The Untouchables or Dalits of India represent the lowest of the social classes, usually associated with socially and ritually unclean jobs.

reincarnation. It is interesting to note, making a connection to Chapter 6, that the ideas of karma, reincarnation, and caste actually function together, inasmuch as those who are born as a *Brahmin* or as a *Sudra* are believed to have earned those places in the social order by virtue of behavior in a previous life. By the same token, adherence to one's caste and one's social role as defined by that caste helps to accrue the good karmic merit that will help one advance in the next life.

Nowadays, the caste system in India is problematic and has technically been outlawed, at least as any criterion for giving jobs or economic benefits. There are, in fact, affirmative action programs to benefit the low castes, in recognition of how this system has historically led to oppression. Yet it remains true that dirty jobs, for example dealing with trash and animal carcasses, are relegated to the Untouchables, and on a personal level, especially outside the main urban centers, it remains very unlikely that anyone would marry outside of his or her social class. The caste order, in fact, has at times been considered racist, since, in its origins, the *Sudra* status was given to the darker-skinned native people whose culture was changed and "Brahminized" by the lighter-skinned "noble" classes that migrated into India over 3,000 years ago. Yet, even if it is problematic, this system of social order is not easily abandoned, precisely because it has its roots in ancient religious tradition, even in the Vedic scriptures.[2] And, as we've seen, part of the point of scriptures, for good or ill, is that they establish a strong and relatively stable authority. In this case, that authority extends into social order.

Another case of religion defining social order that is similar to how Hinduism develops the caste system is evident in the social hierarchies of Confucius. Yet because Confucianism takes as its Ultimate Being the Dao of Heaven, the social order of Chinese philosophy tends to see the social structures as part of the natural "Way" things are. Indeed, as discussed in Chapter 8, the Confucian ideal of religion is heavily ethical and social, claiming that the Dao, the order of harmony in the world, is reflected in natural social relationships, especially those of parent to child, husband to wife, elder to junior sibling, elder to junior friends, and king to subjects. These relationships are, moreover, inherently hierarchical. That is, the first person named in each pair exercises a kind of natural authority over the second, being primarily the leader, mentor, and teacher. Yet this natural hierarchy is not at all abusive, the Confucian would say, since the primary point of this natural order is that the person in each social role must cultivate the virtues proper to that role. Thus, while children and wives and subjects must be obedient and submissive, the parents and husbands and kings must be wise and benevolent. And when each person virtuously lives out his or her role, society runs smoothly and coherently. We should note that this listing here of social roles is not quite Confucian, since it speaks of "parents" and "siblings," when, in fact, the Confucian hierarchy explicitly states these roles as those of "fathers" and "brothers." For the social order of Confucius was undoubtedly patriarchal, and in that sense it may seem to violate our expectations for gender equality. But the Confucian ideal is unashamedly hierarchical in nature, and the harmony of society is not dependent on some construct of equality but on the virtue of those who fulfill their place in society. And ultimately, this image of society is not merely a suggestion or experiment; it is the Dao of Heaven, the Way things are, and the Way they should be.

Besides a natural social order like that of China or a system of social castes like in India, we can find another form of religiously defined social structure by drawing social lines simply by the religion itself. For example, it was common during the early centuries of Islam that, as new lands were conquered, members of other religions—especially Jews and Christians—were given a special status as *dhimmi*, or "protected people." That meant they could continue to practice their religions, but they did not have equal status as citizens within Muslim society. For example, they had to pay a special tax and could not serve in the military.

Another example, in some ways in between the Muslim and the Hindu examples, is the basic case of being Jewish. Clearly, when we speak of being ethnically Jewish, this is a designation into which one is simply born. Traditionally, one is Jewish if one's mother is Jewish, period. And from earliest times, this has meant being a descendent of the Patriarch Abraham by his wife Sarah, hence through the line of Isaac and Jacob (alternatively called Israel). Thus all Jews are, literally and biologically, "children of Israel," and everyone else is a **Gentile**. Yet, historically speaking, this has not tended to give the Jews special social privileges; quite the opposite, as Jews have often been persecuted throughout their 3,000-year history. And yet, Jews do have a special religious status: to be a "righteous Gentile," one must obey seven moral laws, but to be a righteous Jew, there are 613 moral laws. Also, it is actually possible for a Gentile to become a Jew, though this is difficult, especially for men who would have to undergo ritual circumcision. Or, more strictly, an adult Gentile can become a "convert" to Judaism; then his or her children will be Jewish.

Another major line along which religion divides society is gender. The distinction between men and women is perhaps even more obvious than racial or ethnic boundaries, and religions all over the world have often given precise statements about the ways that men and women are to live. A full discussion of the place of women in the world's religions is clearly impossible here, and indeed there are ample books written on this topic precisely because it is such a significant factor in how religions function in society. Generally, women are traditionally honored in religions though often given a lower social status. In some extreme cases, such as the Digambara sect of Jainism, it has been declared that women cannot achieve salvation—largely because salvation can be achieved only by becoming a naked ascetic, which women may not attempt—and therefore a woman must accept her social status as a woman and be reincarnated as a man in order to improve spiritually. In Islam and Christianity, women are said to be equal to men in all spiritual ways, and in some Christian sects, women these days can become ministers and perform all religious duties alongside men. But it is still true, for example within Catholicism, that there simply are no women priests and there has never been a female Pope. In Islam, because the Quran explicitly makes men the head of the household, women cannot inherit property at the same rate as men, nor is their witness in religious law courts equal to that of men. And a woman can never lead the prayers in front of men, though she may lead prayers in front of other women.

In reaction to such social structures, the modern religion of Wicca has tended to emphasize the female aspects of nature and of "the Goddess." Sometimes, she is depicted as "triple goddess," given the specific honorifics of Maiden, Mother, and Crone, to emphasize the value of being a woman at all stages of life. In many other modern religious sects, including the liberal versions of Christianity and Judaism, female leaders—preachers, rabbis, and ministers of various kinds—are common.

The social divisions noted here are all only exemplary and admit to wide variations. But part of the point is that much of this division is rather deeply traditional, sometimes even rooted in scriptures that are not easy to transcend. Thus we who often think of ourselves as egalitarian might find these social divisions a troubling aspect of religion. But it should be noted that various ideals of equality are also given religious basis. Certainly when Islam began, it elevated the status of women above what Arabian society accepted at the time, whether or not we think it egalitarian by our standards. And whether or not we think Christians have lived up to the ideals of equality, it is often noted that, at least theoretically, Saint Paul was making a radical statement of equality when he wrote that for Christians "there is neither Jew or Gentile, slave or free, male and female. For you are all one in Christ Jesus."[3] And we should acknowledge the religious justification, even from the rather un-religious Thomas Jefferson, who declared it a self-evident truth that we are all "created equal."

RELIGION AND RELIGIOUS ORDER

Not only do religions justify structures of social organization that can create levels of social distinction for a whole nation, but they also create hierarchies and social structures within the religion itself. That is, religions—like all human societies, perhaps—tend to organize, and therefore tend to elaborate on roles for specific individuals and groups that will have authority explicitly pertaining to the religious ideas and practices themselves. For example, we all likely know that the Catholic branch of the Christian church has a pope who is not, in our earlier sense, a prophet or a founder, and yet who has authority to state doctrine and to give direction to the entire Catholic Church. The actual organization of the Catholic Church continues through a complex system of bishops and priests, monastic orders, and educational institutions that have authority in various relations to one another and to the Pope himself. All the way down to the level of the local parish, leaders are appointed according to various hierarchical systems, and the local priest alone—as opposed to the laity—has the authority to administer the ritual of the Lord's Supper.

In such an example, we might want to emphasize the complexity of the system of authority, or we might want to emphasize the authority itself. Certainly it is not as simple as, say, a business model that has a CEO, three vice presidents, twenty-five managers, and a few hundred laborers. But like such a model, it is indeed hierarchical, as some persons have authority over others. We might also note—as noted briefly before—that most of these authoritative roles are reserved for men.

We can note that Christian sects or denominations differ over the issue of authority within the religion. Indeed, it was almost unavoidable that when Martin Luther and the Protestant branch of Christianity began to emerge, disputes with Catholic doctrine were also disputes with the authority of the Pope. One sees in Luther's Ninety-Five Theses, for example, not only his challenge to selling indulgences, but also challenges to the Pope's authority to offer such bits of forgiveness-for-sale. Today, some denominations carry names that describe their form of church government, such that Congregationalists traditionally place authority in a kind of democratic appeal to the laity, while Presbyterians place authority in the elders (presbyters). Neither of these groups would accept the authority of a pope.

Other religions have hierarchical forms of religious organization that can seem authoritarian and male-dominated. Islam—at least the majority Sunni branch—has no pope, but historically the Islamic empire was to be ruled by a **caliph**, literally a "successor" to the political authority of Muhammad, a "Commander of the Faithful."

This was apparently a position of political power, although not a position of religious authority, and within a generation of the Prophet's death, Islam was fighting civil wars over who would rule the expanding empire. For religious authority, Islam, as we have seen, denies that there can be any new prophet, and as time passed the authority of interpreting and applying the teachings of the Quran and the Hadith fell, therefore, to scholars. As with the "sages" of Judaism's Talmud, authority here was less institutionalized, more a matter of proving to the community one's ability to understand and teach the contents of the holy texts. Even so, the role of such teachers has overwhelmingly, if not exclusively, been reserved for men.

The authority to teach and guide within a religion based upon the achievements of one's scholarship has also long been the tradition of Chinese Confucianism. At least theoretically, the Confucian idea of a civil service exam in which anyone could study and excel and, based upon his achievement, rise to a position of authority, was perhaps the world's first experiment in social upward mobility. Even so, such social achievement was largely disdained by the Daoist sage who preferred simplicity and ignorance, becoming a teacher of the religion only insofar as people around him recognized his home-spun wisdom and Daoist insights. Indeed, given their preference for "free and easy wandering," it is difficult to say whether the Daoist example offered much social organization at all.

As usual, we see in such examples that the kind of authority structure a religion exhibits, as well as how one achieves that authority, can be quite variable. The role of the shaman, as mentioned in Chapter 3, can be authoritative in the sense that he or she is needed in the general society as a person to mediate between spiritual beings and the responses of the people. Sometimes the role of shaman is hereditary, so that a tribal shaman may pass on that role to a son. In some cultures the shamanic role has been largely reserved for women, as we find, for example, such a role given primarily to blind girls among indigenous peoples of Okinawa. Temple priesthood at some shrines in Japanese Shinto is also hereditary, as the temple functions as a kind of family business. Perhaps most unusually, we find in Tibetan Buddhism that many sects see the authority of the **lama** passed on by reincarnation. That is, the greatest spiritual teachers are said to be reincarnations of earlier generations of spiritual teachers. When the current Dalai Lama dies, therefore, his colleagues and mentors will make a diligent search for a small child who will pass a series of tests to show that he is, in fact, the earlier lama reborn into a new identity. Thus the spiritual authority of the lamas of Tibet is taken to reside, in some sense, in the same person lifetime after lifetime.

In all these ways we see the variety in how religious authority is transferred and even in how much religious authority the authority has. As the reincarnation of a great enlightened being, the Dalia Lama could be seen as having even more spiritual authority than the Pope, who is merely a representative, or "vicar," of Christ. Yet clearly the Pope's authority was much too strong for Luther and remains a problem for many non-Catholic Christians. Muslim scholars to this day may have some authority in declaring official rulings of Islamic Law for the less educated public, but clearly scholars disagree and they are, after all, fallible humans. The "imam," the man who leads the prayers in front of a male or mixed-gender congregation of Muslims, has no real authority at all, but is only leading the prayers to keep everyone together.

In spite of this variety, some of us in Western, egalitarian societies might find uncomfortable the notion that one religious person has any kind of authority over another. Yet religions do seem generally to need scholars and teachers, leaders who perhaps preside over ritual, and some whose spiritual achievements are models for the rest of us, so that we, "the rest of us," may be guided in truth, goodness, and beauty. This notion of "the rest of us" roughly corresponds to the term "laity" used often in this chapter. The **laity**, or lay-persons, are those who do not take on any role of religious professional, and yet definitely count themselves as full participants in the traditions. In the Catholic Church, the laity counts as all those who are not monks or nuns or priests of any kind, even though there may be "lay leaders" and "lay helpers" in teaching and ritual practice. In religions of India that produced a strong renunciant movement, such as early Buddhism and the less theistic forms of Hinduism, it became clear that some men and women will renounce worldly life to seek salvation from reincarnation, while most of the people, "the rest of us," will perhaps have to be content with gaining good karmic merit for a better rebirth. This division might seem too harsh for those of us that think salvation should somehow be universally accessible, but for much South Asian culture, the monk/laity division allows the former to truly renounce possessions and worldliness, as they beg for food and receive gifts of clothing, while the laity genuinely need the monks for blessings, instruction, the magic of chanted scripture, and the opportunity to gain good karma.

Does it seem "unfair" that religions construct systems of order that seem to give some people power over others, or that some will seem closer to salvation than others? Perhaps. Certainly, in his reaction against the authority of the Pope and against the supposed holiness of monks and priests, Luther thought it necessary to assert "the priesthood of all believers." People coming to God should not depend, he thought, on any humanly constructed system of authority. Yet even the modern Lutheran Church has pastors, men and women who have been educated in scriptures and history and then have been "ordained," recognized ritually within the church as having the authority to teach and preach and give out the ritual sacraments. Perhaps we can understand the threat of authority and the ideal equality of all under the roof of temple, mosque, and church; yet we may also see a natural tendency to construct systems of order and authority, if only so that the organizations run well. In any case, we should also be wary of merely assuming that some recent, Western ideal of equality is somehow right, or indeed that we ourselves are truly egalitarian. Even the classrooms we sit in have authority structures in place, perhaps whether we like our professors or not.

RELIGION AND ECONOMIC EQUALITY

Wealth is clearly another important part of any social structure, at least as soon as a society is developed enough to make private ownership of property an understood concept. As soon as a social order makes it possible to own something, it seems almost inevitable that some people will own more than others. Thus we once again face issues of equality within the structures of society that, again, are often a matter of religious concern.

We already noticed in the preceding chapter on morality that, when we consider religious views of wealth and poverty, we often find important emphases on the duty of those with property to care for the poor. From the beginnings of Islam in Mecca, we find that Muhammad often spoke out against two practices: polytheism and the pride of wealth. We find it unsurprising that the one God, Allah, inveighs against the worship of other gods, but perhaps we should not take it for granted that God also challenges wealth. Is there anything intrinsically wrong with having wealth? How much wealth? Perhaps the problem with wealth is the same as the problem with idolatry: we humans perhaps have a tendency to place our confidence in things less than Allah. Jesus, after all, in a similar vein, tells a parable about the rich man who, as he amassed his wealth and settled down to a comfortable life, suddenly dies. "Fool!" God says to him, "Now who is going to own all your wealth?" Or to quote a more memorable phrase of Jesus: "You cannot serve both God and money."

At the same time, there are hints in Judaism, the mother religion of both Jesus and Muhammad, that wealth can also be seen as a sign of God's blessing. Abraham, the great Patriarch of Judaism, was very wealthy, the Bible says, and some day, the promise of God to the Jews declares, the people of Israel shall be blessed with the wealth of the world. "The wealth of the nations shall come to you," says the prophet Isaiah, "your sons shall come from afar, their silver and their gold with them."[4] Even Job, whom we met in Chapter 6 as the victim in a classic story of suffering, was blessed by God after his trials, so that he was twice as wealthy as he was before the test.

Of course, we have known since Chapter 5 that we shouldn't read these stories simplistically. Even as myths or parables, however, we see that religions can interpret wealth in a very positive way, seeing it as a blessing or a reward from God or due to the "good karma" of a previous life. In a classic sociological study of religion and economics focused on the culture of the early Protestant Church, the German sociologist Max Weber noted how belief in God in Europe after the Reformation helped Protestant Christians emphasize the value of hard work and frugality. In his book, *The Protestant Ethic and the Spirit of Capitalism*, he points out how economic success was seen as a sign that one had done the honest work God requires.[5] In a more seedy way, perhaps, modern television preachers to this day, from Kenneth Copeland to Joel Osteen, preach a "prosperity gospel," insisting that God wants us to be rich, and that if we pray and have faith, we will find salvation at the end of life and a great deal of wealth and prosperity along the way.[6]

Perhaps these religious views of wealth are not entirely contradictory. Perhaps it can be argued that God does indeed sometimes bless people with wealth—though perhaps not as mechanically as "Word of Faith" teachers suggest—and the wealthy are then called to beware of trusting in that wealth. They are then called, moreover, to be generous to the poor. The moral call to charity, indeed, seems a common theme throughout the Abrahamic religions, from the laws of Moses to the prescribed alms (called *zakat*) of Muhammad. In the latter case, it seems that, in fact, the careful calculation of 2.5 percent of one's wealth given to the poor acts to "purify" (the literal meaning of *zakat*) the rest of one's wealth. That is, having wealth is justified by the willingness to give at least some of it away.

Explicit care for the poor or the justification of wealth is more difficult to find in the religions of India. This might be expected. For, as we've seen, the religions of India tend to have a more critical view of individual ego and of the physical world in general, and this extends to a strong mistrust of property overall. Indeed, we have seen in the historical founders of religions like Buddhism and Jainism that wealth is ultimately renounced by the holiest of people, and that some kind of monastic life, without family and without possessions, is spiritually ideal. And as monks and ascetics of Buddhism, Jainism, and Hinduism own nothing, they must be supported by the lay people, even if those people do not themselves have much in the way of wealth. We noted previously that the presence of monks in one's community is a necessity for the laity, so that, by giving food, clothing, and other goods to the monks, the people have the opportunity to earn good karma. For the monks and *sadhus* themselves, however, wealth is a trap and must be avoided. In the founding stories, both Siddhartha Gautama (later, the Buddha) and Nataputta Vardhamana (later, Mahavira) were born into luxurious wealth and gave it away, not because of an explicit concern for the poor, but because of the inherent selfishness involved in ownership of property. Mahavira eventually gave away even his clothes and spent the rest of his life naked.

In our time, the arguments of political economics will find the forces of different religions arrayed on all sides. For the most part, however, it seems religions will often at least note the dangers of wealth and some need to be concerned for the poor. Pope Francis has recently spoken out against the inherently corrupting and acquisitive nature of capitalistic economics, and it is no accident that there are thousands of shelters and food banks all over the country associated with churches and religious groups like the Salvation Army. Perhaps the political arguments of our day are not about whether religion advocates for the poor and against selfish wealth; the question is often whether charity should be a private phenomenon or something run by the state. In his book *From Sacred to Profane America*, author William Clebsch notes how often in the United States there were institutions originally handled by Christian organizations that eventually became the proper work of the government. Nationwide charity, he notes in particular, urged as a kind of moral reform by the Christian preachers of the "social gospel" in the late nineteenth century, "became profane achievements in the reform programs legislated under the administrations of the Roosevelts, Wilson, Truman, and L. B. Johnson."[7]

"CHURCH AND STATE"

The example just given, noting how charity as the voluntary giving associated with religious morality can become an institution of the government, brings us back to the concept of the relation between church and state. We have already noted the problem with the word "church"' in this context, but even more, at this point, we must remember that the much-touted ideal of the separation of religion and government is not something we should take for granted. It is a common notion for many modern Europeans and North Americans, but in many other religious cultures, there is no obvious reason why the state should be independent of the "church." Indeed, it is arguable that divine law is exactly what we need to guide civil law.

One sees this especially in Islam. We see even today in the Middle East, as Islam-majority countries liberate themselves from secular and sometimes oppressive governments in Egypt, Libya, Afghanistan, and Iraq, that there is still the need to decide how much of that "secular" state should in fact be under the control of Islamic law, or Shariah. We find here not some new oppressive intrusion into personal freedom but a logical extension of Islam's own history, inasmuch as Muhammad, the founding prophet of the religion, was himself both religious and secular authority. That is, as the fledgling Muslim community grew in the city of Medina, Muhammad took on more and more political and military authority. Then, after Muhammad's death, it was generally agreed that there could be no new prophets to take Muhammad's place; however, the struggle over the role of caliph began almost immediately. Islam, therefore, from its beginnings, was not merely a religion for personal piety and private devotion; Muhammad would never say, as Jesus did, "My kingdom is not of this world." The Islamic "kingdom" is very much of this world, and this helps us understand why modern Islam-dominated nations struggle with how much a secular constitution should be based on Islamic law.

The overlap of religion and state government, in fact, is not as unusual as we might think. In China, the "religion" of Confucius was clearly intended to be the model for how to run an empire, and many of his teachings about virtue and the Way of Heaven were especially intended to be read and followed by kings. That is why we find that the Confucian idea of salvation, if we are to use the term at all, is much more this-worldly than the salvation of, for example, Christianity. For the king to be wise and virtuous earned him "the **mandate of Heaven**," and to rule China with that authority meant bringing the entire nation into harmony with the Way. I speak more of this idea of "salvation" in the final chapter, but we can note here the somewhat religion-based nature of Confucian society. We should also note, of course, that there is an internal consistency within this religion that connects founders and social order and the religion's concept of Ultimate Being.

As usual, along with the internal coherence of a single religion like Confucianism, we should expect quite a variety of positions on the relation between religion and government, and some of them might be quite surprising. Even though Jesus said that his kingdom was "not of this world," we witness in Christianity since Emperor Constantine a tendency to link governments to the authority of the church. From the developments of Canon Law in Medieval Europe to the constitution of the city of Geneva under John Calvin in the sixteenth century, it has often been understood that Christian morality could be, and should be, adopted by those in civil authority and instituted politically "for the common good." Even in the United States, there were lingering laws against blasphemy until the U.S. courts overturned a New York State law in 1952.

Another interesting example is Tibet. Here, ever since the rise to power of the 5th Dalai Lama, supported by military troops of Mongolia, the Yellow Hat sect of Tibetan Buddhism has been acknowledged as having both religious and state authority. That is why the current Dalai Lama must be in exile outside of Tibet: His sheer presence in Tibet as a claimant of political authority is a threat to the secular claim of authority by the Chinese government that insists Tibet is only a semi-autonomous state of China. It is notable that the 14th Dalai Lama has questioned whether the political authority

Figure 9.2   The Dalai Lama is historically both the religious and political leader of Tibet.

of his office should be maintained in the modern world, but he by no means thinks the Chinese government should exercise authority in Tibet. He has already stated unequivocally that he will choose to be reincarnated outside of Tibet, and that the Chinese government should not be trusted to find the 15th Dalai Lama.

Perhaps the point of these many examples is that we should not take it for granted that there needs to be a separation of church and state. How involved a religion may be in the social order and social government is quite variable and depends, not on our modern notion of the modern secular state, but on the religions' own understanding of their history and the nature of Ultimate Being. Just as we should not assume that all religions share a notion of God or common concept of the soul, we should not assume that all religions share our modern and very Western concept of secular government.

RELIGION AND WAR

Before ending this discussion of the relation of religion to social structure and government, we should consider one more controversial issue: the relation between religion and war. In our time, this issue has become prominent largely because of a common opinion that war and violence are especially associated with Islam and religiously inspired terrorism. Given the prominence in the news of stories of "Islamic jihad," from the terror of 9/11 to the suicide bombers in Baghdad more recently, it is easy to associate Islam with violence to the extent of seeing such acts as somehow intrinsic to the religion itself. And in response to the mass of rather poor writing about how Islam is inherently violent, there is an equally large mass of equally poor writing about Islam as a "religion of peace." The truth is almost certainly somewhere in the middle.

There is no hope that this oversimplified dispute about Islam can be solved in this book, but for our purposes we note that the complexity of the problem goes back—as we might expect—to the founder of Islam, the prophet Muhammad. It seems clear from the earliest records that Muhammad himself engaged in warfare, justifying it explicitly in terms of self-defense and retaliation. One the one hand, Muhammad himself notoriously had a whole village of enemies beheaded, while on the other hand he proclaimed a general amnesty to his enemies upon conquering the city of Mecca. Moreover, upon Muhammad's death, it is clear that his followers found it possible to justify the re-conquest of Arabia and the military expansion of Islamic empire, following the revelations and the example of Muhammad. Thus the very roots of Islam give us a complex picture of this religion's understanding of war and violence, and that complexity is evident in the relation between Islam and war today.

Other religions are certainly more intrinsically pacifistic. Just as we saw that the religions of India were suspicious of worldly wealth and possessions, so were they also suspicious of any form of violence and political power. And because of their belief in reincarnation, it is understood that violence, even toward non-human beings, was immoral. Thus the famous Jain ideal of *ahimsa*, noted in Chapter 8, emphasizes a diligent non-violence, and for us it is unsurprising that this non-violence is consistent with the more general attitude of distancing oneself from the illusion and distraction of the world.

Even so, neither Hinduism nor Buddhism has kept itself from involvement with the politics of empire and the use of warfare. Ironically perhaps, the very same equanimity and calmness of meditation that allows the Buddhist to achieve nirvana also gives the Samurai warrior the clarity of mind and calmness of purpose necessary to cut an opponent in half with a sword. In China and Japan, the art of purifying the mind is part of the art of military success; thus the development of the "martial arts." There is a certain irony in finding poorly done, but thoroughly entertaining, movies with titles like *The Buddhist Fist*. It seems unlikely the Buddha himself would approve.

Yet religions in many ways become involved with government and social structures so that, when those systems of social order themselves become violent, the religions can be made to fit in. Thus the decades-long civil war in Sri Lanka saw the Buddhist Sinhalese fighting against the Hindu Tamils, even though both religions could be interpreted as inherently pacifistic on some ideal level. On the practical level, however, kings may support Buddhism but still find it necessary to go to war. And even Krishna in his teachings to Arjuna in the great Hindu classic, *Bhagavad Gita*, is encouraging the warrior to fight in battle. Indeed, in his argument he quotes the earlier scriptures declaring that, since the finite self is an illusion, it is a mistake to think there is really a killer or a victim.[8] Ironically, perhaps, the same illusory nature of the world that makes it a mistake to be violent and to have possessions also makes it permissible to go to war.

So in the end, it is again a common mistake to take simply the relationship between religion and violence. It seems we can neither point to Saint Francis and declare religion peaceful nor assert that "religions cause wars," pointing to the Crusades. We should probably instead look at the philosophies and the founders of religions— realizing here, for example, that Francis is probably more like Jesus than was Richard I—to see what we think might be the most consistent view of warfare given within the religion itself. At the same time, as we consider ensuing history of a religion's development, we can see how its own saints and authorities have interpreted war and violence, how it can or can't be justified. In the case of Christianity, we see how, with the merging of the pacifistic faith and the political power of the Roman Empire, it became necessary for the great theologian Saint Augustine to consider carefully how war should be waged, what are its limits, and what are its proper motivations. And with that consideration, we begin to see in Western philosophy the development of what becomes "**just war theory**." Thinking carefully about what constitutes a "just war" might be a valuable ethical study for any of us, religious or not, as we seek to live morally and consistently in a world of governments and social order, with all their capacity for political violence.

KEY TERMS IN CHAPTER 9

caliph In Islam, literally a "successor" to the political authority of Muhammad.

caste system Hindu class structure, organization of levels of religious and social privilege based on birth family, or, religiously, on reincarnation determined by past karma.

dhimmi In Islam, the traditional distinction of non-Muslim people, especially Christians and Jews, under the "protection" of an Islamic state.

Gentile Literally, "nations," the term within Judaism for anyone not born into the people of Israel, thus not ethnically Jewish.

Just war theory In Western philosophy, the systematic effort to consider how war should be waged, what are its limits, and what are its proper motivations.

laity The people of a religion who do not take on any role of religious professional, and yet definitely count themselves as full participants in the traditions. Also "layman," "laywoman," and "laypersons."

lama In Tibetan Buddhism, a teacher and leader, sometimes both with spiritual and secular authority, taken to be a reincarnation of earlier generations of spiritual teachers.

Mandate of Heaven In Confucian thought, the idea that a king has the authority to rule because of his virtue and wisdom, guiding the entire nation into harmony with the Way.

social order The organization of people in a society according to various ranks and privileges.

zakat In Islam, the moral requirement to give 2.5 percent of one's wealth to the poor; charity or alms-giving that acts to "purify" (the literal meaning of *zakat*) the rest of one's wealth.

EPILOGUE TO PART II:
The Promise and the Problems of Religious Goodness

It is evident in this section of the book that religions all over the world concern themselves not only with what people believe but also with what they do. There are things we should do and things we shouldn't do, and religion tends to support these moral claims with a sense of authority that outstrips mere human assertion. This can be a good thing or it can be a bad thing, inasmuch as the same Power and Authority that can require me to give to the poor may also tell me to sacrifice my child in His name.

Even so, there are some theologians and philosophers of our time that have hoped that a focus on religious practice instead of on religious truth claims can help us to create a more peaceful world. Perhaps, we might say, if religions could focus on shared ideals that emphasize working for justice or working to end poverty, we could let our disagreements about God and salvation sit in the background. Perhaps, as we saw in the Epilogue to Part I, it is not really possible that all religions can be "true," but perhaps religions that contradict one another philosophically could nevertheless all be "good."

Some writers have in fact tried to encourage a kind of religious harmony or even religious pluralism by trying to emphasize the good over the true. Practical efforts like those of Eboo Patel and his "Interfaith Youth Core" have been organized to try to get people of different faiths to work together on social projects. Thus, for example, we can find Hindus and Christians and Muslims all working on environmental cleanup or disaster relief, and in the process we might find that, doctrines aside, they can agree on what we ought to be doing for the good of others.[9]

On a more grandly philosophical scale, writers on religious pluralism like Paul Knitter have argued that we can find in genuine religions a parallel focus on "liberative praxis." This term is used to name very generally the sense that religions are all trying to give people some kind of practical freedom, whether it be freeing people from poverty or oppression, or giving them a sense of freedom from guilt or hopelessness. Love and compassion and social concerns can be found in all major religions, Knitter claims, and consequently there is a unity of these religions, not around what they believe, but around what they tell us to do.[10]

There is evidently some truth to this, and we noted at the outset of Part II that there can be good reasons for people wanting to downplay "orthodoxy" and emphasize "orthopraxis" in its place. At the same time, we have seen in these last three chapters that there are different views of goodness in the world's religions, and even if it were

continued . . .

continued...

possible to claim that, for example, working at a homeless shelter is something that Hindus, Christians, and Muslims could agree to do together, it is not at all evident that such a practice is very consistent with all three systems. We have noted, for example, that the caste structure of Hinduism is given in their basic scriptures, and we can add that that same caste structure is explicitly denied in India by Buddhism and Sikhism, which also explicitly deny the authority of those Hindu scriptures. So while there may be good deeds we think we all can work on together, it is not obvious that we can do so without emphasizing one religion's ideals over another's, or perhaps rather asserting certain modern ideals as "good" no matter what the religions say.

The irony of the search for religious unity in orthopraxis rather than orthodoxy is that, to a great extent, the former is dependent on the latter. This means that, when religions make statements about what a person ought to do, how he or she should behave in society, and what rituals he or she should perform, these moral claims are also truth claims. Thus we have noted often in the materials of the last three chapters that the directions for practical action often have their roots in the religions' scriptures, in the models of their founders' lives, and in their fundamental notions of Ultimate Being. And we have been trying to argue that this internal logic of religion is a good thing, part of how the devotees live coherent lives and part of how we, from the outside, can understand their way of life. For this reason, it is somewhat artificial and, arguably, illogical to try to divide out the good from the true. We might still want to try, arguing perhaps that interfaith social action and interfaith harmony are, after all, good things, though again this evidently requires us to make some important assumptions about which things truly are "good." But in the end, trying to separate the ritual, moral, and social ideals from the sources of authority and belief may leave us less able to understand what religion really is. ❀

PART III

BEAUTY, OR WHAT RELIGION WOULD HAVE US FEEL

THIS TEXT IS ORGANIZED around three basic elements of human life that are particularly prominent in religion: Truth, Goodness, and Beauty. Since Chapter 1, we have seen how these elements, so fundamental and, arguably, irreducible in specific areas of life, are interwoven and mutually dependent, even though we have attempted to address these elements in distinct units. Thus we addressed religious doctrine and teaching, the great breadth of ideas and beliefs that religions to various extents claim to be true; and we have considered the rituals and morals and social structures that religions construct as "good" for a whole and healthy human life and for a proper relation to Ultimate Being. So now we turn to Beauty.

In some ways, beauty is the most curious and overlooked part of religion in many Introduction to Religion studies. Some texts literally say nothing about it. Perhaps calling the topic "Beauty" makes it more mysterious than it needs to be; if instead we were to speak of "religious experience," we might find textbook chapters and even whole books on the subject. Even so, it is difficult to know what to say about religious experience, partly because we are considering those elements of religion that do not easily lend themselves to description. And yet, all the way back to Chapter 1, we have seen how references to religious feeling and experience are a fundamental aspect of religion according to some of the definitions we considered. Religion is "a feeling of absolute dependence," said Schleiermacher, or religion is a "sense of the numinous," said Otto. When we spoke of the Problem of Evil in Chapter 6, we noted how Peter Berger thought religion perhaps springs from a feeling that the world is not as it should be. Some have spoken of how standing in the presence of a lightning storm can inspire a sense of awe and, by extension, a feeling of religiousness.[1] All of this recognizes how important religious feelings, or a sense of beauty, can be to the basic nature of religion, and thus we come to a consideration of religion as "beauty."

But what do religious feelings mean? What is this idea of beauty, and what does it do in the ways of life called religions? Ironically, perhaps, when we ask questions like this, we are already mingling the sense of the beautiful with the elements of truth and goodness. That is, if we have some sense that something is wrong with the world and we begin to ask why, we find ourselves connecting our experience of suffering with our ideas of Ultimate Being and constructing theodicy. If we think that somehow religion is about love or compassion, we might quickly see that these words suggest both feelings and actions. There are—as we shall see below—very specific things that a religion teaches us to do in order to cultivate the kinds of experiences we are supposed to feel. Back in Chapter 7, we saw how some kinds of worship and, especially, meditation rituals are teleological practices, actions done for some extrinsic end, and sometimes that end is a feeling. Thus religious experiences, religious actions, and religious truth claims are interwoven. By now, this should not be a surprise.

In this third part of the text, therefore, we consider various aspects of religious beauty, specifically ideas of religious experience, the religious use of art, and the religious concept of beatitude, or ultimate happiness and fulfillment. There are, of course, connections to previous chapters and discussions of action and belief, but we will also see that there are religious views that would isolate and raise to prominence especially this aesthetic part of religion. Perhaps, indeed, all this focus on religious ideas and beliefs, with all its doctrinal disagreements and disputes, along with our focus on religious actions, perhaps so burdensome in the emphasis on morality and ritual, has been more trouble than help. Perhaps we find a more peaceful and less conflicting view of religion if we leave these behind and focus only on the aesthetic. Perhaps we can find a unity of religions, not in their doctrines or in their rituals, but in their feelings. Perhaps. But this, too, is something that must be discussed in the text, and in the process of discussion, inevitably and perhaps ironically, people's religious feelings must be translated into words and ideas. We have seen before that, where some religions might resist the use of text or ritual, nonetheless text and ritual remain. And here, even our discussion of religious experience and feeling will be, rather obviously, discussion. For those who would prefer not to read or analyze, but more simply to rest in religious peace or float from the floor in religious ecstasy, this book will not help. But we can talk about it.

CHAPTER 10

RELIGIOUS EXPERIENCE

THERE ARE MANY KINDS of religious experience; this should not surprise us. But, as I've already noted, there is not a great deal of discussion about religious experience in many Introduction to Religion textbooks, even though religious experiences are in many ways central to what it means to be religious. Inasmuch as we want to understand the religious phenomenon, therefore, we ought to try to understand the various kinds of religious experiences, perhaps develop a vocabulary for describing these experiences, and begin to see how they, like the other elements of religion, can be related to the central religious focus on some Ultimate Being.

Before we begin trying to develop this vocabulary, it would be useful to define what we're talking about. **Religious experiences** are feelings and emotions, or the more affective and aesthetic feelings one has, particularly in connection with some supernatural reality. We can speak in our mundane world of our feelings of love or fear or happiness or comfort, but we should note that these same experiences and feelings are often associated with one's relation to God or Brahman. Similarly, we can all relate to the "aha" experience when one suddenly understands a difficult math problem, but in religion this might be compared to the remarkable and definitive Buddhist experience of enlightenment. Of course, the Buddhist would say the enlightenment experience is absolutely unique, a far greater awareness than getting a math problem. But then it is probably also true that those who speak of their peace or joy or happiness with God would insist this experience is far more than feeling quiet and peaceful on a sunny summer afternoon. Yet on one level, we can all understand what religious people mean when they describe religious experiences, even if we have never had one, although on another level, the religious person would almost certainly insist that we would be mistaken to think their experiences of the presence of the Holy is but one more version of something normal and mundane. And given our definitions of these phenomena, the religious person would be right.

So we are going to discuss inner experiences, feelings, and emotions that express or represent one's particular relation to the divine. In a way, this is like talking about miracles, as it refers not just to events in the world but events that religious people think are specific acts of God. Yet religious experiences are unlike miracles, because the experiences are personal and interior. Presumably, if we had been standing at the shore of the Red Sea when Moses came, parted the waters, and went through "as on dry land,"[2] we could have seen the event ourselves; when a religious friend says he feels the presence of Jesus, there is no external event to evaluate. These experiences are **subjective** rather than objective; they are events in the person's inner life rather than in the observable world. And that makes these experiences all the more difficult to talk about. All we have to go on are the descriptions the religious people themselves give us of their experiences, and sometimes they would rather be silent. Yet we will find patterns and forms that are often consistent, relative to specific religious beliefs and actions, and this will yield some tentative vocabulary for describing and thinking critically about religious experience in general. For religious experience, in this way, is like the other elements of religion we study, as we see how it interacts with ideas and practices.

THE VARIETIES OF RELIGIOUS EXPERIENCE

One way to begin this discussion is to note a study by William James rather conveniently titled *The Varieties of Religious Experience*. Even in the context primarily of Christianity, James—something of a mix between philosopher and psychologist—collected many stories that begin to show how religious feelings and emotions can be described in numerous ways. He noted, for example, that some religious emotions are positive and pleasant, like feelings of peace and acceptance, a sense that God is nearby, that God loves us. That God "loves the world" is, of course, a Christian doctrine, but the feeling that God loves "me," the individual, and that I am whole and happy in God's presence is something else, something more. This positive feeling James calls the "healthy soul."[3]

There is also, however, the "sick soul." One might think that religious emotions always should be positive and happy, but one doesn't have to look far into Christian stories, or even the Christian scriptures, to see otherwise. For we also see expressions of alienation and loneliness, a sense of being separated from God and in need of forgiveness. Thus the writer of Psalm 13 cries, "How long, O Lord? Will you forget me forever?" and even the greatest of the saints have described what is sometimes called a "dark night," when it seems God has left them.[4]

Yet in all this mixture of religious feeling, there is also the experience of changing from "sick" to "healthy," an experience of transformation that has, perhaps, its most dramatic form in the religious experience of being "born again." The term comes from the Christian Gospel of John (3:1–8), in which Jesus tells a visiting Jewish teacher that one must be born both "of flesh" and "of spirit," and some Christians have understood this to mean that there should be in an individual's life an experience of change, a moment perhaps when one "becomes a Christian" or "gives his life to Jesus." As the famous song, "Amazing Grace," says it, "I once was lost, but now I'm found; was blind but now I see."

From this brief list of religious experiences, we quickly learn a couple of things. First we see variety, as James emphasizes, and this particular variety all appears within one religion. At the same time, we find that these experiences have a particular theological, and sometimes scriptural, foundation. The ideas—the "truths"—of sin and separation, then redemption and renewal, are found in Christian doctrine, so it is not surprising that we also find them in Christian experience. That is not to say that all Christians speak of these experiences in these words, or that no other religions have analogous experiences. But it does mean that we can use the terms we develop for understanding religious experience in the context of religious ideas. Beauty and truth are connected.

VISIONS, VOICES, AND THE PROPHETIC CALL

The story is told of how Moses was in the wilderness watching sheep when he saw from a distance a bush that was burning and yet not burning up. He was curious about this phenomenon and so approached the bush, whereupon a voice called him by name and told him he was in the presence of the Holy. The culmination of this experience was that Moses became for all of the Abrahamic religions a prophet, chosen, here in this experience, to carry God's words and carry out His will.

It is difficult to say, had we been nearby when Moses had this experience, if we would have seen the bush burning or heard the voice. Was this miracle or subjective experience? Speaking phenomenologically, we need only note that this experience of Moses was powerful enough to change him and lead to the development of scriptures, rituals, and morals that have in turn changed the world we all know. Such an experience is sometimes called a **commissioning experience**, a supernatural encounter that calls a person to special service to God. Note here that I say "God" and not "Ultimate Being." For it might be clear that such an experience goes rather directly with a concept of Ultimate Being interpreted theistically rather than, say, monistically. That is, Moses—I might add other prophets, from Isaiah and Ezekiel to Islam's Muhammad— is called to be a prophet, and we have already seen since Chapter 4 that the concept of prophet is logically related to monotheism in a way it is not related to monism. More concretely, Moses' experience calls him to be a prophet, but Laozi or the Buddha could have no such experience, simply because neither the Dao nor the Void can "call" anyone.

Here, as we've often seen, is the logic of religion. Of course, we might see this as interesting enough but rather irrelevant for most of us, since most of us will never experience a prophetic commissioning. Yet the general kind of experience Moses had might be more common than we think. That is, on a rather less dramatic level we can find people who do think God has spoken to them. Famous visions and visitations by saints, such as the visit of the Virgin Mary at Medjugorje or Guadalupe, have become the basis for important movements within the Catholic Church, but, much more commonly, average people can feel God's guidance and hear what the Prophet Isaiah called "a still, small voice." Such a voice from God, though not enough to start a new religion, is still an important part of religious experience and fits especially into religions that think of Ultimate Being as both a transcendent God and a loving Father.

Let us note here that there are in fact "voices" and "visions" that do start new religions. That is, if a call from God seems to occur within a specific religion, yet violates in some way that religion's views of how God speaks or what God says, then we have a problem. When Baha'u'llah founded the relatively new religion of Baha'i in nineteenth-century Persia, it was for him a dramatic enough experience that he became a new prophet, leading to new scriptures and a new faith. This call is all the more dramatic because it happened in the context of Islam, where it was immediately seen as heresy. All revelation from Allah, according to Islam, ends with Muhammad; thus, Baha'u'llah, they reasonably concluded, could not succeed in being merely a continuation of revelation. In this way Baha'i becomes a new religion. A similar argument might be made about Joseph Smith and Mormonism.

For our purposes it is perhaps enough to see that all of these "prophetic" experiences are consistent with some view of prophets, which in turn conforms best to a view of Ultimate Being like theism. The commissioning of prophets appears as a dramatic experience at the beginning of many of these prophetic faiths, but a similar, if very subdued version of the experience can still be recounted by many people who seem to hear God speak. For the Greek Orthodox Christians, for example, one might claim that they hear Christ speak to them regularly in the Divine Liturgy. Hieromonk Gregorios claims indeed that "the Divine Liturgy is Christ in our midst."[5] And thus on a regular basis average people experience the Ultimate Being speaking into their lives.

Yet one must be careful. If God "speaks into one's life," we should see how the speaking fits into and conforms with already established aspects of the religion. We can note in the case of the Eastern Orthodox tradition that the experience is tied into an established ritual practice—a connection we consider again later. But if we find that the divine power speaking "in our midst" contradicts the more foundational

Figure 10.1   The drama and beauty of the Divine Liturgy, the worship service of the Eastern Orthodox Church of Christianity, may be a profound way to inspire religious experience.

message of the earlier prophets, then one is in danger of being a heretic. And unless one is willing to claim to be a founder of a new religion, perhaps the experience needs to be challenged by the belief. Does this mean beauty must follow truth?

We consider this question more directly later in this chapter. For now, let us consider the relation of truth to beauty by introducing a new term: **orthopathos**. Clearly meant to be parallel to the terms "orthodoxy" and "orthopraxis," the new term is offered to suggest that even mysterious and subjective religious experiences will find a certain consistency with claims of religious truth and directions for religious practice. Just as there is "straight doctrine" and "straight practice," so is there "straight feelings" that belong, so to speak, within the larger phenomenon that we call a specific religion. And we can understand the variety of the world's religions better when we see how these elements are woven together.

ENLIGHTENMENT

If the prophetic vision is the foundational commissioning experience for a prophet, the analogous experience for a sage might be enlightenment. Indeed, as we see in the case of the Buddha, this is precisely what his title means: The Buddha is, by definition, the one who awoke. Thus, as we saw back in Chapter 4, the Buddha becomes through his sermons and other teachings the source of authority and the content of what becomes the earliest Buddhist scriptures. It would be wrong to call him a prophet, of course, but as with a prophet, the very foundations of the religion begin with a powerful experience that few people have had.

At the same time, for some sects of Buddhism, this emphasis on the experience of enlightenment potentially extends to everyone. In Zen, for example, we have already seen a certain disdain for doctrine and belief, and the alternative to orthodoxy is experience. Do not try to explain BuddhaNature, the Zen master might be saying, but experience it in yourself, for you, too, are an "enlightened one," in your "true nature." All you have to do is see it.

Not all sects of Buddhism think everyone is a Buddha, but there remains in other Buddhist sects an emphasis on a kind of insight experience that can and should apply to everyone. Just as we saw that a variety of weaker experiences of "God speaking" can appear in theistic religions, a variety of "awakening" experiences appear in many forms of Buddhism, as well as in other religions with a Gnostic quality. The term **"Gnostic"** is a Greek word from which we get the word "knowledge" and refers to a special kind of transcendent insight gained through special spiritual experience. Within Buddhism, then, as well as in some other religions where "awakening" is emphasized, not only is there a perfect enlightenment of the founder but there is also some kind of awakening experience that is the ideal for us all. "Do not simply believe my words," the Buddha said, "but verify for yourselves what I'm teaching." And that verification is essentially the Gnostic experience of insight.

At its most basic level, Buddhism—along with other religions that emphasize meditation and concentration techniques—can be verified rather easily. When you're angry, count to ten and take a long slow breath and you'll feel calmer. When under stress, sit quietly and count your breaths, feeling the center of breathing in the lower abdomen rather than the upper chest, and you'll find your stress somewhat relieved. In this way, we can all understand the experience of the Buddha on some level, perhaps. At the same time, we can also begin to see how meditation and relaxation techniques can lose any connection with Ultimate Being, as we see various yogas and meditation methods touted in utterly non-religious contexts and taught, apparently without challenge, in public schools where a class on praying to God would be unacceptable.

Later we shall have to consider what, in fact, is verified by the experience of calmness when one meditates. For now, perhaps, the point is simply that we can understand on different levels the experiences of sages, at least insofar as we know what it is to relax and quiet our minds. We can also, to some extent, understand that the Gnostic element of enlightenment, the awakening to some mystery beyond the mundane, is, for some religions, possible for us all. As the Zen scholar D. T. Suzuki has said, there must be some genuine awakening to reality, a greater reality beyond what we know through the senses, or else meditation is merely "quietism." [6] Perhaps trying too hard to sound

Zen-like, we might say that *shikantaza*, "just sitting" in meditation, must yield some experience of *kensho*, seeing, or it is just sitting.

In the case of other sages, such as Confucius, it is perhaps more difficult to see what religious experience might be prominent. There doesn't seem to be any need for a breakthrough kind of awakening, though certainly in Confucius himself one gets the impression that he has an insight into the Way of Heaven that most people do not have. In his famous, short "autobiography," he said that at age 14 his mind was set on learning, and by age 30 his path was set. By the time he was 70, the story declares, his desires and his character were in complete peace. Yet it was somewhere in between, around age 50, he says, that he understood the will of Heaven.[7]

Perhaps we see here—though it may be a stretch to apply James' language—that there exists, even in the case of the more Gnostic experience of sages, something analogous to the sick soul and the healthy soul. We find, for example, in Suzuki's Zen, an emphasis on mental tension and dissatisfaction to the point at which the **satori** or awakening experience is a dramatic realignment of self, reminiscent of the Christian singing, "was blind, but now I see." In the case of Confucius, no such dramatic change is needed. Instead, one conforms slowly and carefully, through ritual and study, to the virtues of character that align one with the Dao. Perhaps even among the sages there are some that must be "born again," while for others it is evidently unnecessary.

However risky this comparison might be, it is clear that the experience of the sage and that of the prophet are different. The coherence of religious elements helps us understand why prophets have a "call from God," whereas sages do not, and why, on a more common level, theists might say they feel God's presence or hear his voice, but the Buddhist does not. That is, we see here a certain orthopathos in the way a specifiable religious experience fits into a known religion. And we can come to understand those religions better by developing a vocabulary to help us name and explain the different experiences.

To further understand the experiences of prophets and sages, then, we can follow the lead of Mircea Eliade, one of the great fathers of the scholarly study of religion, and suggest that some people have a religious experience we can call "ecstatic," while for others the experience is "enstatic." The former literally means to stand outside oneself, absorbed in the presence of some sacred power; the latter suggests a deeper experience inside oneself, absorbed perhaps in one's own contemplations. As usual, we should not say that theistic religions have only "ecstatic" and never "enstatic" experiences, or that monistic religions have the opposite.

Nevertheless, the logic of religion does suggest the general alignment of the ecstatic sense of an external Presence with theism and the inner-looking, enstatic sense of calmness with a more immanent Ultimate Being. Indeed, to press the generalization further, we begin to understand how some religions have been troubled and split by the failure to conform religious experience to orthopathos. We find, for example, that when some early Christians were developing a Gnostic interpretation of

Christianity, suggesting we should become Christs through Gnostic awakening rather than worship Christ himself, the more orthodox "apostolic" church declared them heretics.

MYSTICAL EXPERIENCE

The double reference in the previous section to being "absorbed" can lead us to a discussion of a particularly interesting area of religious experience that we call **mysticism**. For some scholars, the mystical experience is a profound and powerful experience of Ultimate Being that can be found all over the world's religions, and as such it holds the promise of being a kind of unifying thread in the many different faiths. "Absorption," to continue using the word, can suggest, at a deeper religious level, that many people find a kind of movement away from themselves, as they get lost in that Greater Reality that religions generally seek to describe. The ego, or the individual self, becomes "extinguished," say some of the mystics of Islam; "I become nothing," say some Zen Buddhists. And in this process of absorption, it is said, the individual "becomes one with the Absolute."

In the context of religions that focus on a more monistic notion of Ultimate Being, this mystical experience may seem most at home. In the philosophical schools of Hinduism, for example, where the Ultimate Being is Brahman, the "one without a second," we ourselves are most essentially Atman, the deeper, truer self that is ontologically equal to Brahman. My individual identity, say these Vedantist philosophers, is a kind of error, an illusion that keeps me from realizing that my true identity is the identity of the Ultimate Being, and the great liberating experience is to feel that you are "one with the One."

With theistic religions, the issue is more complicated. Mystics in the Jewish and Islamic faiths do speak of "union with God," and in some cases that experience of oneness with God is so powerful that the worshiper's identity seems to melt away and all that remains is the presence of God. We have already noted that there can be a certain preference for the experiential over the doctrinal, and for some writers, like Juan Mascaro[8] or even Aldous Huxley,[9] the mystical experience of oneness with the Ultimate and the corresponding loss of individual identity is "Perennial Philosophy," the great experience that unites all faiths.

However, insofar as the denial of individuality corresponds best with monistic, not theistic religions, the "union" of the self with God in theistic faiths has sometimes been problematic. The famous Islamic mystic Mansur al-Hallaj once, in mystic rapture, declared himself al-Haqq, the True One, an epithet of God.[10] In the Christian context, the mystic Meister Eckhart, having detached his soul from all worldliness, could experience "the birth of the Son in the soul" and thus declare that his own soul was the same as "the only begotten Son of God."[11] There is some logic to this announcement of equality with God, given the power of the experience, but in these

Figure 10.2   Famous sculpture of Benini, "The Ecstasy of Saint Teresa."

cases, the implications of the experience were unacceptable. We have already spoken of the necessary relationship between truth claims and other parts of the religious phenomenon, and we see that connection here again. We shall discuss later in the chapter the struggle between "truth" and "beauty."

Of course when mystics speak of "union" with Ultimate Being, there may be variations on exactly what this means. We've seen that literal absorption of self into Brahman—a literal oneness of being, like a glass of water poured into a lake—is consistent with philosophical Hindu thinking. We can call this ontological union, as the very being (*ontos*) of the self and the Ultimate are one. For a Taoist, the Tao is less like a lake than a river, not a single substance, but nature's all-pervasive pattern and flow of change. Thus, when the Taoist speaks of becoming "one with the Tao," he means something more like a perfect cooperation, a fluid movement of change discussed in Chapter 8 as *wu-wei*, "action-less action." This state of union we might call harmonious union, like a stick floating on the stream or like a singer in a great choir. Within theistic traditions like Christianity, one sees a third alternative that we might call relational union. Here, as with mystics like Teresa of Avila or John of the Cross, the "union" is analogous to a love relationship so complete that the individual feels lost in love of the Other. Here, marital and love language become prominent.

In all these cases, the religious experiences described by famous mystics are powerful and evocative. Yet we might suggest, as we did earlier regarding the prophetic call, that average people also have "mystical experiences" on a less grand scale and expressed less poetically. Many religious people feel the presence of God or can meditate and practice breathing exercises to feel "at one" with their surroundings, even if for only a moment. Average Christians might tell you of their "personal relationship with Jesus," and describe it in terms of love. Thus, even in the more mundane cases, and even though some scholars might find the more dramatic mystical experiences to suggest a unity of religions that transcends orthodoxy, there is a variety of religious experiences. Yet it is a variety to a great extent consistent with ideas, and when it fails to be consistent, there can be problems. This is another indication of what we've been calling "orthopathos." We wrestle more with this term in the next section.

THE EPISTEMOLOGY OF RELIGIOUS EXPERIENCES

In discussing the varieties of religious experiences, we have noted both the dramatic and the commonplace, experiences of prophets and sages, visions of God and the awakening of enlightenment. For many people, a simple peace of mind, a sense of the presence of the holy, or a moment of meditative calmness can be central to their religious life, as indeed can negative experiences of moral guilt or a sense of "waiting for the Lord." In Hindu temple ritual mentioned briefly in Chapter 7, *darshan* occurs, which is seeing and being seen by the god. We can imagine as the doors of the sanctum are opened and the image appears that worshipers experience a sense of awe and excitement, especially then as the image is illuminated by the smoky flames of burning wax. Imagine this ritual done in thousands of Hindu temples long before electric lights, and one might almost feel with the worshipers the presence of a deity. Imagine native peoples standing before relentless storms or Christians on a Sunday morning singing hymns in harmony. These are the simple yet life-changing experiences of literally billions of people all over the world for most of human history. The feeling—perhaps equally an "experience"—that the world around us is nothing more than molecules obeying mechanical laws is a relatively rare feeling.

That, of course, does not make it false. And by the same token, having religious experiences does not make religion true. Indeed, we have been noting throughout this text that the good, the true, and the beautiful are different categories of human value, though aspects clearly interwoven in normal life, perhaps especially so in religion. Yet "feeling the presence of God" is not exactly the same as saying that God is in fact present or philosophically proving the existence of God. Many an adolescent has felt profoundly the experience of being in love, only to smile years or days later with the equal assurance that it was merely infatuation. These feelings are, after all, merely subjective.

We noted at the outset of the chapter this "subjective" quality, seeing that the religious experience is internal to the individual and therefore not easily verified or even believed by another. And yet, when a Zen Buddhist has the experience of *satori*, he or she is certain that something has been genuinely seen. That is, as D. T. Suzuki claims, the enlightenment experience is noetic, it has content that teaches us something about reality, and indeed he insists that what we see in this experience is more certainly true than anything we can talk about or experience with our senses. Similarly, when Christians say they have been "born again," they think that some change in reality has occurred. If we were to smile and nod and emphasize that these experiences are, like adolescent love, merely subjective, we would fail to see that religious experiences are more than experiences alone. They have direct connections to religious truth claims.

The relationship between experience and truth claims is called "**epistemology**." Even when we consider how our senses work—what we see and touch—then reality, as Morpheus pointed out to Neo in the *Matrix* movie, "is only electrical signals interpreted by our brain." We make assumptions about how much and how accurately our senses give us true information about the world, and we recognize that different animals with different sensory apparatus will see and hear the world differently. When we ask in religious contexts how much and how accurately these experiences give us true information about God or Emptiness, we are asking an analogous question. And with religious experiences, we are often much more skeptical. With our eyes, "seeing is believing," but with religious experience, we might say that *satori* or "the presence of God" is merely a feeling.

The epistemology of religious experience can seem all the more problematic when we recognize that some religions have intentionally used hallucinogenic drugs to induce visions and other dramatic experiences. Back in the earliest Hindu scriptures, known as the Vedas, there are many references to Soma, a deity himself who gives his juice as a drink to other gods and to human priests to manifest power and divinity. Though still uncertain what kind of "juice" this was—some have suspected a kind of mushroom extract—there is little question that we are dealing here with psychotropic drugs. We can also note the use of peyote in some Native American religious traditions and even the famous "Good Friday Experiment" of Walter Pahnke, in which a group of theology students used psychotropic drugs to see how it enhanced their religious experiences in a Christian worship service.[12]

In defense, religious people might note that these drug-induced religious experiences are both rare and unnecessary. After all, most of the religious experiences described in this chapter have nothing to do with altered states of consciousness. Or do they? When the Buddhist meditates, even calming his mind for a few minutes and practicing breath control, this is a brain-altering practice. When the Charismatic Christian dances and sings and claps in church, or when the "Whirling Dervish" spins, they change their heart rates and brain chemistry and thereby, arguably, induce religious experiences analogous to those who take drugs. Muslims and penitents of many religions fast for extended periods of time and feel closer to the divine, yet Bertrand Russell, in his insightful if occasionally unkind criticisms of religion, has said, "From a scientific point of view, we can make no distinction between the man who eats little and sees heaven and the man who drinks much and sees snakes."[13]

Arguably, Russell's "scientific" viewpoint is too reductionistic. Certainly William James noted that for many calm and average people the religious experience is very much like sensory experience. And if we are going to doubt somehow the value of religious experiences, shall we also doubt the value of artistic experience, the sense of beauty of a sunset or, indeed, falling in love? Aldous Huxley, whose famous experiment using mescaline brought him to a kind of religious insight into the Perennial Philosophy, declared that the drugs did not alter normal consciousness so much as open up a new consciousness. That is, perhaps the religious use of drugs does not distort consciousness so much as clear away the obstructions of normal seeing, giving us new and better eyes to see reality. If I have a telescope and can see the moons of Jupiter while you, without the instrument, cannot see them, that only means that I have a way of seeing that you do not. And if it takes a certain attitude of faith or meditation or, indeed, mescaline, to see Ultimate Being, then so much the worse for Russell's "science."

But this only brings us back to where we started: What, then, do people see in their religious experiences, and how does it relate to religious truth claims? We have already seen that there is a tremendous variety in religious experiences, so how can all of them be true? Perhaps they can't. But we have been suggesting throughout this text that the experiences and the doctrines—beauty and truth—are not the same thing, so perhaps it makes no sense to ask if a religious experience is true. But at the same time, it makes a great deal of sense, and is indeed necessary, to ask how the "beauty" of a religious experience is interwoven with religious truth claims and, indeed, becomes dependent on them.

An interesting case to study in this regard is the comparison between two Christians of the fourteenth century, Meister Eckhart and Julian of Norwich. I already mentioned the first of these previously where I noted his powerful experience of Jesus and his dangerously heretical conclusion that he himself had become "the Son in the soul." Similarly, Lady Julian's visions so emphasized Jesus' love and forgiveness that she felt totally pure and that indeed she herself had never been a sinner. But upon reflection, she confessed that this was clearly contradicted by the truth of Christianity and, therefore, that she had to reinterpret her experience. Thus, instead of saying she was not a sinner, she chose to say that forgiveness was so complete, it was *as if* she had never sinned at all.

The point of this comparison is to note how doctrine informs experience, or at least its meaning. Religious experience tells people something about reality because they have beliefs about reality that the experience can refer to. As we've seen, religious experiences happen to people who are already in the context of religious ideas and their related religious practices. We've noted since Part II that prayer and meditation, though arguably similar, are not the same practice, and that their differences can be traced back to what people think about Ultimate Being. Similarly, we should expect that the experience of relatedness, the feelings of love or communication with God, are more common in the context of prayer than meditation and more common in the context of theism than monism. Also, when one has a religious experience, there are already interpretations of that experience in the context of the religious tradition, already a terminology of *satori* or being born again, that can be used to interpret what the experience means. And for the most part, the experience fits into those interpretations, as it fits into the context of prior truth claims. This, at last, seems to be the connection between orthodoxy in belief, orthopraxis in behavior, and orthopathos in religious experience. In an interesting way, Meister Eckhart's experience was the wrong kind; Lady Julian's was right.

It may seem uncomfortable, even bad, to say any religious experience is the wrong kind, but arguably such evaluation of religious experience within a specific religious context is not avoidable. It is interesting, for example, that the Zen Buddhist tradition, as we've seen, would stress a direct "pointing to the mind" that is somehow independent of words and rational thought. Yet even here, we find that the tradition has within it the acknowledged possibility that the student of Zen can be deceived and needs to be guided, even in experience, by a master. Thus the Zen tradition constructs the ritual of *dokusan*, the examination of the student by the master, not to see if he has the right doctrine, but to see if he has had the right experience.

From this phenomenological point of view, the point is not to judge anyone's "spirituality," let alone their eternal value. We are only looking at the phenomena of religion and noting that the pieces are interwoven, and those pieces include the nature and interpretation of religious experiences. Having suggested the notion of orthopathos, noting that emotions and feelings of religion must fit into the interwoven nexus of goodness, truth, and beauty that religions embody, we are not saying

Figure 10.3   The *dokusan* ritual is an examination of the Zen student by the master to determine the student's progress in achieving *satori*.

that it is impossible or evil if an experience fails to fit the expected model. We are only noting that, like problems of the rejection of ritual or the denial of standard beliefs, one who has a religious experience that he or she interprets outside the common context of a religion risks the charge of "heresy" from within that religion. Of course, if the person is bold enough, he or she might start a challenging new sect of an established religion, like Mirza Ahmad did in Islam or Joseph Smith in Christianity. At its most challenging, a new and powerful religious experience can start a new religion that will develop with more or less clarity its own expectations of orthodoxy, orthopraxis, and orthopathos.

CONCLUSION

Religious experiences are powerful. They can be the very beginning of a major religion of the world or the beginning of an individual's personal journey into faith. Religious experiences challenge and confirm beliefs, inspire and thwart our practices.

Overall, then, we need to take religious experiences seriously and consider how they are interwoven into the system that is religious life. In the process of taking religious experiences seriously, we must acknowledge their intensely personal and subjective character, but at the same time see how religions presume aspects of the experiences' interpretation and context. Thus we shouldn't demand too much of the relationship between truth and beauty, but neither can we ignore it.

We might, in the end, hope to dismiss all religious experience as self-deception, as perhaps Bertrand Russell would advise. Or we might rather wish to assert the pure and powerful unity of religious experience as the advocates of Perennial Philosophy seem to do. But perhaps the importance of religious experiences in general requires us to accept the value of such experiences and to be thoughtful about how they are interpreted in all their variety. As usual, the study of the phenomenon of religion, including religious experiences, is more difficult than either acceptance or denial. It requires us to think.

KEY TERMS IN CHAPTER 10

commissioning experience   A supernatural encounter that calls a person to special service to God.

ecstatic (religious experience)   Literally, to "stand outside oneself," having an experience of absorption in a sacred power outside oneself.

enstatic (religious experience)   Literally, to "stand inside oneself," having an experience of absorption in a deeper experience inside oneself, absorbed perhaps in one's own contemplations.

epistemology (of religious experience)   Generally, an analysis of the relation between experience and truth claims. In religion, the concern may be with the relation between religious experience and claims about Ultimate Being, generally whether religious experiences yield any information about the truth of religious beliefs.

Gnostic   Relating to a special kind of insight gained through religious experience.

mysticism, or mystical experience   A powerful religious experience in many faiths that is described as a deep absorption into the Ultimate and a corresponding loss of identity. Generally, a deep sense of "oneness" with Ultimate Being.

orthopathos   Literally, "straight feelings," the suggestion that even subjective religious experiences will display a certain consistency with claims of religious truth and directions for religious practice.

Perennial Philosophy   An interpretation of religion that views all religions as fundamentally built on the same mystical experience of oneness with higher reality.

religious experience   Feelings, emotions, and the more affective and aesthetic experiences one has, particularly in connection with some supernatural reality.

satori   In Japanese Zen Buddhism, the sudden, breakthrough experience of enlightenment.

subjectivity (of religious experience)   Experiences characterized as events in the person's inner life rather than in the observable world, that is, in contrast to objectivity.

CHAPTER 11

RELIGION AND ART

RELIGIOUS EXPERIENCE IS QUITE fundamental to the religious human phenomenon, and yet it is an element of religion that is particularly difficult to clarify. We are, after all, trying to discuss the ineffable within religious feelings and trying to bring into a systematic worldview the part that seems most resistant to being systematized. Perhaps it is like trying to talk about being in love: We might intuitively resist seeking an understanding of love in some psychological or brain-neuro-scientific analysis. Even if it's true that "being in love" corresponds to certain chemical markers in the brain, the neuroscientist's explanation is not what we're talking about when we talk about love. Reminiscent of our discussion of "language" in Chapter 5, perhaps what we need is not an analysis of emotion; what we need is a love song.

In fact, it is quite common to try to add expressions of art to our feelings in religion, just as it is common to make that addition when we add the song to the feeling of love. In a way, the addition of poetry and music to emotion brings the feeling out, moving it into the world for all to see, or, rather, for all to feel. That is, there is something about the music and the poem that take our emotions and share them. "I am in love," one might want to say, or "I stand in awe of the majesty of God," and by writing a poem or creating music or making stained glass, we are telling others about the feeling. Moreover, we succeed at this communication, perhaps, by creating a hint of that same emotion in others. The love song not only tells people how much we are in love, but it also can evoke feelings in others and even back in ourselves. Similarly, the dramatic architecture of a Gothic cathedral not only expresses the grandeur of God; it conveys that expression by helping the visitor or the architect feel it himself or herself.

All of this suggests that there may be a kind of natural connection between our inner experiences and expressions of art, especially in religion. Indeed, the oldest forms of art we know may well be the expression of religious experience, with ancient cave paintings hinting perhaps of animistic spirits. Art in its various forms brings out and shares with others the mystery of religion—the *mysterium tremendum et fascinans*—and quite naturally becomes for us in this text a straightforward extension of the discussion of "beauty" as the third dimension of the religious phenomenon.

At the same time, we should expect by now that no discussion of any one aspect of religion is straightforward, for different religions' uses of art can vary quite dramatically. Pictorial art may be quite common and quite beautiful in some religious contexts but resisted or even prohibited in others. It is interesting to note that calligraphy finds special prominence in Chinese and Japanese Buddhism, but it also appears dramatically in Islam. There are some religious people who resist artistic expression altogether, perhaps recognizing the inherent danger in the power to express and evoke religious emotion. And there are reasons for these uses and rejections of art as, once again, we see that, by and large, religions maintain a reasonable relationship between their elements, even when we are talking about elements that are, in themselves, not really about words and reasons.

In this chapter, then, we extend our discussion of beauty into more concrete forms than we considered abstractly in the previous chapter. For whatever religious experiences we might or might not have had, many of us can stand before a painting or listen to a song and recognize beauty. Like the first examples in Chapter 10, noting the spiritual experience of standing before a sunset or watching lighting in the night sky, the appreciation of art in connection with religion can help us understand what religion feels like, whether we are religious or not. The difference, of course, is that our appreciation of sunsets and lightning evokes the wonder we feel at nature; art is the aesthetic wonder we create ourselves.

PICTORIAL ART

There are many different kinds of art, of course: painting and sculpture, music and poetry, dance, architecture, and calligraphy. We could start with any of these examples. But religious pictorial art—the drawing and painting of depictions that represent sacred beings or sacred stories—is, for some of us, particularly evident. Of course, instead of merely painting the images of spiritual beings on a cave wall, one could actually carve those images in the stone itself, so there is a natural extension of painting into sculpture. Other media are possible, too, such as the use of stained glass or mosaic tiles. But in all these ways, it seems that the artist is trying literally to show us something about what is holy.

One might, for instance, try directly to depict the Ultimate Being. There are very common iconographic depictions of the many Hindu gods, each with his or her recognizable symbols and forms. One almost always, for example, sees Krishna with a flute, even when he is depicted as a cute baby playing in the milk curds. Shiva is the wild man on the mountain, deep in meditation, sitting on a tiger skin, the Ganges River flowing from his hair. Kali is black, as her name suggests, and she is depicted horrifically, with a necklace of severed heads and a skirt made of severed arms. All such images, with all their minute details, contain references to classical stories of the gods, as well as standard symbols of power (like multiple arms) and supernatural wisdom (like multiple faces). And it is no surprise that we find such standard art in endless amounts in Hinduism. For we have seen that popular Hinduism understands there to have been many, many gods incarnated into the world, and thus depicting them in the details of their lives is common. Indeed, it is practically necessary.

At the same time, we see no depiction of Brahman, the more abstract Hindu concept of Ultimate Being. The reason is clear: Brahman itself is formless, the inexpressible "One without a second" that, for the more mystical side of Hinduism, is the great ocean in which our souls are but single drops. When the Hindu artist desires to express Brahman, therefore, he or she uses an equally abstract symbol, the *Om*. Yet even this symbol can be presented with power and beauty: It can be drawn in bold colors and outlines, or shown with radiant light emerging from its boundaries (see Figure 2.2).

We find similar forms of symbolism used for "depictions" of what cannot be depicted, such as the Dao (with the famous *yinyang* symbol) or the *enso*, the "empty circle" used as a symbol in Zen Buddhism for the pure mind. The case of Islam is particularly instructive because Muslims have always quite consciously rejected depictive art, partly due to its association with the worship of other gods in pre-Islamic Arabia. Thus when a Muslim wants to represent artistically the beauty of Allah, he or she will often turn to calligraphy, the writing of the name of God in beautiful, flowing Arabic letters. We will talk more about calligraphy later.

In the use of images, Christianity is an interesting case study. Christians, like Muslims and Jews, believe in a God that is ultimately non-corporeal and incapable of being depicted, and like the other Abrahamic religions, Christianity strongly prohibits idolatry. And yet, clearly, Christian history is full of images, scenes from Jesus' life, depictions of Jesus in glory, images of saints, even depictions of God the Father, as in Michelangelo's famous frescoes in the Sistine Chapel. Why would Christians do this?

The answer, interestingly, is that Christianity is similar to Hinduism in this regard: God, they believe, has chosen to become physically incarnate. "The Word became flesh and dwelt among us," their scriptures say, and thus the depiction of Jesus is technically not idolatry at all. But what of saints? We can note in reply that, precisely because Christianity is focused on the historical manifestation of God in Jesus, the religion is also strongly focused on its historical narratives. Thus the stories of the Bible, the lives of saints, characters from the Old Testament, and more have always been used in

Christianity for teaching. Especially when very few people could actually read the Bible, the use of pictures and sculpture and stained glass became primary teaching tools.

Buddhists often have a similar use of art as instruction. In almost any Buddhist temple, one finds a series of depictions of the life of the Buddha, from his birth, through his enlightenment, to his passing into Final Nirvana. And even though, as we saw in the second chapter, the Buddha is not himself technically the object of worship, still he is the greatest example of Buddhahood and the perfection of mind, and thus is an inspiration to monks and laity alike.

So depictive art teaches and inspires. It often uses standard images, like halos and multiple arms, to suggest power and glory that we attribute to the holy, radiances we wouldn't see with our own eyes if we were standing there beside the saints and the Buddhas. If we understand the power of art and the importance of beauty in religion, we understand why so much art is religious art, and why religious art is appreciated all over the world. But we also see why some art, perhaps especially depictive art, is problematic. For if images of gods with multiple faces, glories, or radiance and symbols of power can inspire our feelings of awe, then art can inspire those feelings even if the gods are "false gods." That is, the feeling of worship may be inspired not by the Ultimate Being but by the artists, and if one's religion emphasizes the uniqueness of God and the strict prohibition of worshiping anything besides God—as in the case of Islam—it is only reasonable that Muslims would be strongly against any depictions that inspire worship. That does not mean, of course, that Islam is against art; it is only against images. It is, as we say, not anti-art, but **aniconic**. Islam has its own forms of beauty, but these will have to be addressed under other categories.

OTHER VISUAL ARTS: CALLIGRAPHY AND ARCHITECTURE

We can easily find on the Internet some of Michelangelo's pictures of God from the ceiling of the Sistine Chapel (see Figure 6.1), in which God seems to be a sort of dour-faced old man, white haired, afloat in the sky, surrounded by baby-like angels. And although such art is arguably quite beautiful, it is also arguably quite wrong: God is not a big, white-haired man, and in the creation myth of the Christians there is no reason God must seem so serious and grim. And that is at least part of the problem with religious pictorial art: It does help us see and feel and learn of religious ideas, but it may also misguide us. And for that reason, some religions would rather avoid it.

In its place, Islam famously has developed calligraphy to great levels. Many manuscripts of the Quran give us the text not merely to be read and understood but to be enjoyed visually, with the words of the Quran written in beautifully flowing, interwoven letters. Similarly, one finds in many mosques and Islamic shrines elaborate pictures, not of persons or animals or God, but of words, where various architectural features are covered with the swirling, decorative poetry of the scriptures. The term **"calligraphy"**

Figure 11.1   Page of the Quran with text in beautiful calligraphy.

itself means beautiful writing, and we can understand why Islam in particular holds this art form in such high esteem. For, as we've seen, Muslims believe that the Quran is the direct and perfect word of God, delivered to and received by Muhammad perfectly, therefore the most perfect manifestation of God's mind in the world. Thus the words are already divine; how right then to make them visually beautiful as well.

Arabic writing, with its fluid forms and interspersed dots, may be particularly appropriate for calligraphy. Chinese writing is, too. In the Chinese language, of course, one does not write letters that phonetically make up words; rather one writes entire words as single symbols, some very simple and others quite complex. As we might see the symbol "$" and know it means "dollar," so the Chinese would see the symbol 禮 and know it means "propriety" (*li*). And we can therefore imagine that if one wanted to elaborate the word with meaning beyond its prosaic vocabulary, we could develop the symbol itself until the symbol says more than the word alone. Thus the word is also a picture, a beautiful work of art.

We shall see in this chapter that in many practices of Chinese and Japanese Buddhism calligraphy takes on a special artistic status, not only because of the meaning of the word drawn, but because of how it is drawn. That is, the word itself may be less important than the clarity of mind that goes into writing it. Calligraphy in Chinese and Japanese traditions, therefore, becomes artistic as the perfection of the lines, the spread of the ink, and the smoothness of the brush strokes themselves represent Enlightenment. In *A First Zen Reader*, Trevor Leggett gives an example of calligraphy in which the perfect form of the writing itself is said to show the writer's purity of mind, and the word being written is simply a single horizontal line that is the figure for the number 1.[1]

Another way to portray religious beauty visually but not pictorially is through architecture. It is often noted that the glory of a Gothic cathedral lies in its power to pull the eyes upward into the sweeping vault of the sky. The architectural discovery of the flying buttress allowed builders to carry much of the weight of the stone room in the pillars outside the church, and thus the pillars inside could be taller and thinner, allowing people to experience a grandeur of size and scale as never before. Even the walls could be higher and thinner, allowing more room for windows and thus more light. All in all, these churches could help visitors feel the presence of God in a way that the spoken word, perhaps, could not.

One can have a similar aesthetic experience in some of the great mosques of the world. Taking clues from the great Hagia Sophia of Constantinople, Muslims saw the aesthetic power of the high, sweeping dome and the glittering mosaics that decorated those domes like the night sky. Rejecting, of course, the murals and paintings that covered the inside of many Byzantine churches, Muslims nonetheless took the glorious architecture and developed it further into the multi-domed wonders of the great mosques of the world. In such mosques there are, of course, no pictures of God, but the glorious architecture can help one feel God's presence, and the beautiful calligraphy can inspire one to read God's words.

In India, one fascinating example of architectural wonder is the Kailasa temple in the Ellora cave complex. Here, over centuries of labor, Buddhist and Hindu and Jain monks lived in caves and carved the rock to make rooms and temples. The Kailasa temple in particular is a multi-storied building carved entirely below ground level—carved, that is, down into the rock beneath one's feet, such that the temple, rather than being built from stone, literally *is* the stone of the mountain. And the name, Kailasa, refers to a central Himalayan mountain that was believed in India to represent the *axis mundi*, the center of the world. It is from this mountain that the springs of major rivers of India flow, and to this mountain pilgrims walk to prove their devotion to various gods. The temple, therefore, is a representation of the grandeur of the mountain of the gods, and architecturally is one of the wonders of India.

One can argue, of course, that the architectural glory of these buildings is a great waste of time and money. One can belittle the fulsome ostentation of such architectural glory and wish instead that the resources had been spent on practical things, like care for the poor or the building of a hospital. But of course this is largely to assume that the good should take precedence over the beautiful. More generally, we have seen that the aesthetic is as intrinsic to religion as the behavioral, though we can also imagine the two in conflict, just as we've seen how religious art can seem in conflict with

Figure 11.2 Kailasa Temple at the Ellora caves, central India, a temple carved entirely into the mountain.

religious belief. Even so, we can understand with the power of calligraphy and architecture why religions want to create, and even should create, such beauty.

POETRY AND MUSIC

In Chapter 5 we noted that there are many different languages that religions speak, from history to myth to parables and instruction. Poetry was one of the "languages" common in religion, and in that chapter we noted several examples. The Psalms in the Jewish/Christian Bible are often well known, and people sometimes memorize these poems precisely because they seem to convey an idea at once true and beautiful. That is, the doctrinal notion that the Ultimate Being is the kind of god who cares about and nurtures people is a truth of those religions that see the Creator as a God of love, but it sounds so much greater to say, "The Lord is my shepherd, I shall lack nothing/ He leads me into green pastures and makes me lie down beside still waters."

We have already noted that the Quran is written in a kind of rhyming prose that, to its contemporaries, was one of the marks of this being a divine text. Indeed, in the story of Muhammad's prophetic call, he is told by the angel to "recite," yet he denies that he can. The context of Arabian culture of the time suggests that he thought he was being asked to invent poetry, the kind that was common among the caravan drivers and horse-men who sang of their women and horses and praised one another for the best poems. Yet Muhammad, we are told, was no poet—God, in the Quran, tells him explicitly to say so—and therefore, if what comes from Muhammad turns out to be glorious poetry, it can only be because it is the work of God, not the work of a man. Here, art proves holiness.

Less well known than the poetry of the Quran, perhaps, is the massive poetry of the great Hindu epics. The Mahabharata is arguably the longest poem in the world, con-sisting of nearly 100,000 verses, thus longer than the *Iliad* and the *Odyssey* put together. Of course, as epic literature, it is essentially mythic language, and translations of the Mahabharata often are reproduced simply in prosaic, storytelling form. Yet we who can only read a prose translation might be missing a powerful aspect of the original text if we miss its meter and rhyme. With poetry, there is more to a story than the story.

Noting that the poem of the Mahabharata is also a myth might remind us again of Chapter 5 and the discussion of the complexity of religious language. Indeed, as we've noted already, the strength of art in religion is also, in some ways, its weakness, for the artistic quality of poetry's images and metaphors can also make it difficult to interpret. Poetry can indeed be powerful, but it can also deceive us if we fail to under-stand what is poetry and what is doctrine, what is imagery and what is instruction. Recall the imagery of Psalm 137 that expresses the desire to smash one's enemy's chil-dren against a rock!

Just as powerful as poetry—and just as problematic—is religious music. Indeed, perhaps the only thing that can make the beauty of poetic language more beautiful is when the words are set to beautiful music. Notably, it is evident in the Psalms of the Bible that are quoted as poetry that much of it was set to music. Several Psalms tell us that they were meant to be sung to particular tunes, even though we no longer know what those tunes are.[2] When Jesus had eaten his "last supper" with his disciples and just before they went out to the Garden of Gethsemane, the narrative says they sang a hymn, and later when the first Christians were being guided in their beliefs by the letters of St. Paul, they were urged to "sing songs and hymns and spiritual songs" (Col 3:16). And Jews and Christians have been singing ever since.

Christianity is perhaps one of the most musical of religions, and within that faith, perhaps the most famous example of a religious musician is Johann S. Bach. It is often noted that Bach, working as a church organist and choirmaster, composed new music every week, with full orchestration for multiple instruments and parts for choir. Fa-mously, he noted on most of his works the letters "SDG," standing for the Latin words "*soli deo gloria*," meaning "for the glory of God alone." G. F. Handel also declared his work to be for God and became famous for his spiritual works, including the well-known "Messiah" with its "Hallelujah Chorus." The work of Christian composers like Bach and Handel have been sung throughout the whole world, and clearly one does not have to be Christian to enjoy the beauty of such works of art. But there is no ques-tion that its origins and its meaning are explicitly Christian. As one writer puts it, the

Figure 11.3   Christian church in England, with choir.

complexity and beauty of these men's music "were intended to draw the mind of the listener not to the cleverness of the composer but to the divine Beauty itself."[3]

Besides Christianity and Judaism, Sikhism is a very musical religion. We might remember that its founder, the Guru Nanak, emerged in India in the context of spiritual poets of Hinduism and Islam, and we would find in his biography that, after his call to teach the message of God, he traveled throughout India reciting his poems and singing. In fact, in his travels he was usually accompanied by a musician, so that his poems were not merely read or recited, but sung. To this day, any visitor to a *gurdwara* will witness Sikh styles of worship that begin and end with accompanied singing.

One might find other musical examples in the world's religions down to the simplest forms of chanting. At some point, however, it becomes a bit less clear if we are dealing with music at all. And this is not meant to be an artistic evaluation; this is not a question of whether we like or dislike a particular style of music. It is, rather, a fact that in some cases, such as Islam, it is quite common to hear the Quran chanted, and yet Islam retains a certain mistrust of music. That is, while the call to prayer and the recitation of the holy scriptures can sound very musical, Muslims themselves will often insist that this is not singing, for the holy words of God need no human singing to be the most glorious and powerful art in the world. Similarly, much of the chanting of scripture that one finds in various schools of Buddhism is not evidently meant to be art at all. It is, rather, a way of memorizing and standardizing the text, so that prayers and teachings could be saved orally long before they were written down. The chanting of texts and holy words, therefore, is sometimes "art" and sometimes not. How can we tell which is which? From a phenomenological point of view, we basically have to ask the chanters themselves. From our more systematic study, we might also ask what kinds of art seem most consistent with what kinds of founders and what notion of Ultimate Being. Jesus apparently sang hymns; it seems unlikely the Buddha ever did.

Before we end this discussion of religious music, we might note once again that there are also dangers in religious art. It may be difficult to see any possible harm in hymns and chanting, but there have always been examples in different religious traditions that show a certain mistrust of the power of art precisely because it is so powerful. We have already noted how there can be a certain mistrust of music added to the Quran in Islam, perhaps because the music actually distracts one from the words of God. In Christianity, as early as the fifth century, Saint Augustine voiced his concern that "when I find the singing itself more moving than the truth which it conveys, I confess that this is a grievous sin."[4] And we must admit that, when it comes down to simply popular music, probably fewer people can sing along with a Bach cantata than have sung along with John Lennon's "Imagine there's no heaven." Mozart, who wrote some of the most glorious sacred music of the world, also wrote a great deal of very secular music which is equally, or perhaps even more beautiful than his religious work. The German theologian Karl Barth once said, "When the angels sing for God, they sing Bach; when they sing for themselves, they sing Mozart, and God listens in." As with other forms of art, the addition of its powerful aesthetic feel to the powerful ideas of religion can be a glorious combination, but the power of musical beauty left to itself has the potential to become idolatrous.

ART AS PERFORMANCE

There are, of course, other arts besides the visual and the aural, and it is perhaps easy to forget those arts that are especially **performative**. We mean by this term those artistic practices that are active, like dance or drama, and it is perhaps especially easy to overlook these arts in the context of religion. After all, while it seems we often encounter the vast world of religious music and religious painting, we do not often bump into something like religious dance. Yet one famous example of inspired dance is found in King David, the great and devout king of Israel, who, the Bible says, "danced before the Lord with all his might." And in today's Pentecostal churches, Christians can be found jumping and dancing as they sing to God their praises. To a lesser degree, one sees "dance" in the clapping and swaying of a Christian choir singing their worship songs, especially in African American churches.

Yet it is not clear that these examples represent the use of art in religion. The "dance" of King David or of modern Pentecostals may be more about the spontaneous reactions of religious ecstasy, less like an artistic dance (say, ballet) than like jumping up and down when one sees an old friend. It seems, in fact, that while we might generally speak of "religious dance," it sounds incongruous to speak of "religious ballet." Is there in religion the kind of dancing that seeks to express or represent beauty the way, for example, Bach tried to represent the glory of God in his music?

Perhaps. In modern times, certainly, there have appeared Christian ballet companies and, with them, explicit efforts to explain and explore dance as a religious art. More historically, it might be fair to say the closest thing to "religious ballet" would be the movement of priests and acolytes in religious procession. It may not be ballet, nor is it ecstatic dance; yet it is an intentionally solemn and graceful movement, the flowing of human figures toward the front of the church, that could be called a kind of performative art, meant to inspire worshipers and to reflect beauty in the ritualized worship of God. More dramatically, there are also the dances of Taoist priests in China or Tibetan shamans, whose footsteps trace out mysterious interactions with spirits. Here, too, no doubt, the performance can be powerful and moving for the audience, though perhaps one does not tend to think of priests and shamans as dancers.

The difficulty in some of these cases, however, might be in trying to distinguish the artistic from the ritual elements. We noted in Chapter 7 how some kinds of ritual are "mimetic" and magical. That is, we noted, for example in Native Religions, how masks and dance could be used to imitate the actions of spiritual beings whose aid and cooperation were solicited by the tribe. Through performance, one enacts the movements of the hunt, and the value of the dance lies, therefore, not in its beauty, but in its efficacy. In the case of the Australian Aborigines' ritual dance called "corroboree," we noted how the dance imitates the creative acts of ancient ancestors, marking out the patters of creation itself and re-establishing the harmonies of nature. We wonder, therefore, if the purpose of the movement is really to be artistic in some aesthetic sense or to produce spiritual effects in the physical world.

Similarly, we might note the importance of dance in the mystical practice of Sufi groups like the famous "Whirling Dervishes." These Muslim mystics, since the era of their Turkish founder Mevlana Rumi in the thirteenth century, have incorporated into their mystical practices the soft and haunting music of wooden flutes and a remarkable spinning dance. This is unquestionably religious dancing, and yet its original purpose was not evidently aesthetic in a simply artistic sense. Indeed, it seems the primary purpose of the spinning motion is to produce particular states of consciousness and, ultimately, mystical experience. That is not to say the dance is not beautiful or artistic. But we might be asking whether the dance is more like the transformative ritual of meditation or like a Bach composition. Is the purpose of the graceful dance to be beautiful *per se*, or is it to induce religious experience? Such concerns raise for us an interesting question of whether the artistic and the mystical aspects for the Sufi Dervishes, like the artistic and the mimetic aspects of the corroboree, are fundamentally lost in the modern phenomenon of having these "dances" performed for paying tourists.

These questions about the actual purpose of performative art can also be raised in other cases where it seems the actions are more about the state of mind of the performer

Figure 11.4   A performance of "Whirling Dervishes," the mystical practice of Muslims from the Mevlana order.

than about the art itself. An interesting example can be found in the construction—and destruction—of **mandalas** in Tibetan Buddhism. These detailed and colorful artworks are, in one sense, like pictorial art, representing the dwelling of an enlightened being or perhaps a map of the cosmos itself. The lines and figures are meticulous and vibrant, beautiful to look at. And yet the point of the mandala is not to be beautiful; indeed, in a way, it is quite the opposite. For the focus of the construction of the mandala is not on the art, but on the *process* of carefully scraping bits of colored wax or sawdust into the tiny lines and figures. The concentration of the artist is really a form of meditation, and this pictorial art is more truly a performative art. Moreover, when the mandala is finished, there is generally the expectation that it will be destroyed, the dust swept up and the messy pile of colors cast upon running water. Thus it is explicitly the impermanence of the art—the fact that it disappears and is nothing but tiny pieces of color swept away on the stream—that is the lesson of the mandala. To keep the mandala around and to admire its beauty is to fail to understand it.

All of this seems to indicate that there is a complex and problematic relationship between performative art, on the one hand, and ritual magic or transformative rituals on the other. We noted in Chapter 10 how physical practices, including dance, can be used to induce religious experience, but upon analysis we considered

Figure 11.5   Tibetan Buddhist monks working over the elaborate and colorful mandala, which is said to represent the abode of enlightenment. When complete, the mandala is swept away and the multicolored dust thrown onto moving water.

whether such a practice might be like "seeing God" on drugs. In Chapter 7, we noted how ritual magic can be performed so as to move gods and spirits, thus accomplishing our own purposes in a way that seems to challenge the very ultimacy of the Ultimate Beings. Those same issues might be troubling to some processes of performative art, inasmuch as such art has purposes quite different, it seems, from the creation of beauty that points us to Beauty. At the same time, there is no doubt that the spinning of the Dervishes and the stamping of the corroboree, along with Native American powwow dances, have become for our time a lot like the singing of a Bach cantata: All can become forms of art utterly detached from their religious meaning, while people appreciate the art simply for the art itself. *Ars gratia artis.*

SUMMATION

It might be quite a task to consider other forms of art even more difficult to attach to religion than dance. Is there, for example, specifically religious art of clothing design or landscape architecture? Well, yes, inasmuch as priests' vestments and the grounds around a Baha'i temple are understood to be particularly attractive and symbolically meaningful. Is there a religious art of cooking, religious chefs analogous to religious music composers? That is less evident. Even so, there's no reason to think it impossible that this can happen, and that people in a variety of ways can be attracted to the visual, aural, tactile, and, yes, gustatory experiences of beauty that are thought to draw us toward, and even represent in a finite way, the beauty of Ultimate Being. It is the strength of religious art of all kinds that people find delight, pleasure, and beauty through our senses, and that sensory objects can be created by humans to point beyond themselves to Beauty itself. Thus art is almost naturally religious.

At the same time, we saw that this power of art, the value of beauty in itself, can also attract people away from religion, recalling how Islam prohibits the use of images, no matter how beautiful they might be. Indeed, the more beautiful the art, the more idolatrous it threatens to be, precisely because it awes and thrills us quite apart from any proper religious implication. Thus a beautiful image or a glorious temple can inspire the viewer, beautiful music can thrill the listener, and that beauty could be the tool of a "false religion" or of no religion at all. Even if art is often or naturally the companion of religious feeling, it is clear that the two do not always go together: Religion sometimes resists art, and art can break free of its religious source. This explains why many people who have no religious intentions may still love the music of Bach, just as people may still love to celebrate Christmas quite apart from its obvious religious meaning. In Chapter 7, we saw how such holidays can lose their religious content, and, in Chapter 8, we saw how morality can become valued modes of behavior without their religious importance. Similarly, we can see here how religious art can be valued after losing its religious core. We may have to debate whether this is a good thing or a bad thing.

Even so, this chapter has shown that we can expect religion and art to be common companions, though exactly which kinds of art and which kinds of religion go together is not common. As usual, we see that there is a kind of logic that exists within religions, and that even how they use—or reject—art can make sense. At the same time, there is a great variety of things called religion, and there is a great variety of things called art. They do commonly have a relationship, but their relationship follows a broad yet understandable range of patterns.

KEY TERMS IN CHAPTER 11

aniconic   The characteristic of having no images (icons), or rejecting the use of images.

calligraphy   Literally "beautiful writing," thus the art of making letters (as in the Quran) or glyphs (as in Chinese), especially decorative or elaborate.

mandala   In Tibetan Buddhism, a detailed and colorful representation of, for example, the dwelling of an enlightened being. The artwork itself is meticulously and meditatively produced and then destroyed.

performative art   Those artistic practices that are active, like dance or drama.

CHAPTER 12

BEATITUDE, OR SALVATION RECONSIDERED

THE TERM "BEATITUDE" IS not very common in today's English-speaking world. It might have been easier to close this text with a chapter called "Salvation," inasmuch as that word is more common and has a kind of obvious religious ring to it. But we have already spoken of salvation in Chapter 6, where the context was stressing salvation as a kind of doctrine or belief, one logically connected to religious beliefs about suffering and the nature of our own being. When we speak of "beatitude," however, we are not speaking of salvation as a doctrine but, as its inclusion in Part III might suggest, as a kind of religious experience. It is, after all, not accidental that there is an evident relationship between the words "beatitude" and "beauty."

Thus when we reconsider salvation in terms of **beatitude**, we are trying to speak of what religions say about our ultimate experience, our ultimate fulfillment. For the term "beatitude" means something like happiness, or even blessedness. A dictionary might say beatitude is a sense of complete fulfillment, a final and total wholeness of existence, a completeness of who we are. For ancient Greek philosophers like Aristotle, the idea of beatitude was connected with an idea of human nature and the ultimate purpose of what it means to be human. Thus, when we complete ourselves, fulfill our deepest and most essential nature, we find that we are truly happy.

We modern speakers of English are unfortunately likely to misunderstand the term "happy," and thus misconstrue the meaning of beatitude. When we think of being happy, we might think of being in a good mood or having a nice day. As Aristotle would say, being happy for a day is not "happiness" in his sense, any more than seeing one robin makes it Spring. For we can well imagine a drug addict, ill and debilitated, unemployed and homeless, who nevertheless has found his hit for the moment and is therefore, in some sense, happy. But it is clear that such "happiness" is far from human fulfillment. Indeed, it is rather pitiful. Real happiness, therefore, is not some mood or artificial emotional state; it is a kind of fullness of life.

When we add Thomas Aquinas to Aristotle—Aquinas, whose thirteenth-century theology so evidently Christianized Aristotle's philosophy—we see that the religious addition to Greek ideas included the insistence that we are not truly fulfilled and complete until we return to the ideal for which God created us. We were created, Aquinas would say, for moral innocence and the presence of God, and we do not truly find our beatitude until we find ourselves innocent again in heaven. Or, to hear it from another great Christian theologian, Augustine, we can quote his prayer: "God, You have formed us for Yourself, and our hearts are restless until they rest in You."[1]

If the idea of ultimately "resting" with God sounds like the Christian concept of heaven, it probably is. We noted in Chapter 6 that the idea of heaven in the afterlife is a common notion of final purpose in the Judaic, monotheistic religions. There, we emphasized the internal coherence of the religions' truth claims, how ideas about Ultimate Being, about the nature of the self, and about salvation—not to mention morality, ritual, and more—fit together logically. Here, we shall try to discuss heaven as beatitude, what makes heaven heavenly, but we shall also have to discuss how heaven is gained. That is, we not only discuss the "what" of beatitude, as in what exactly religions tell us is our ultimate happiness, but also the "how" of beatitude, or, how we gain this blessed state.

We also, of course, have to recognize in our discussion of what constitutes ultimate human happiness the fact that there are ideas of beatitude in the world's religions that are quite unlike the idea of heaven. We have already seen this in Chapter 6, where we briefly noted that ideals of a kind of impersonal union with Ultimate Being may be more consistent with monistic ideas of the transmundane than is some notion of heaven. We shall note in this chapter, for example, the varying concepts of nirvana and enlightenment, not only as religious experiences, as noted in Chapter 10, but as ideas of final and ultimate fulfillment.

Overall, then, we shall see that religions promise us something glorious, some state of being that is our final fulfillment and is the result, in one way or another, of religious life. This state of being may be described as the *summum bonum*, the highest good. The "good" is not the goodness of Part II, for it is not about what we do; it is rather about the good we may experience. It is in some way the answer to questions about "the meaning of life." Most generally, we shall continue in this chapter to refer to beatitude: what it is and how we find it, according to various religious views that make these glorious promises. As usual, it should not surprise us that the complex ways of life we have come to see in the world's religions end with glorious hope, even as they began with a glorious notion of transmundane reality.

VARIETIES OF BEATITUDE

We have already mentioned the concepts of heaven and nirvana and noted that they are, in important ways, different. As noted in Chapter 6, the imagery of heaven, whether Christian or Islamic, is personal and sensual. We might want to take that imagery—especially, perhaps, the imagery of gardens and wine and sex in the Islamic scriptures—and interpret it more figuratively, but it is difficult to escape the idea that heaven in these religions is a kind of idealized worldly fulfillment. While for some the images of "streets of gold" or "almond-eyed houris" might seem too worldly to describe our ultimate joy, recall that the Judaic religions in general have a relatively positive view of creation. God created the world, they say, "and it was good." Banquets in heaven and wine under garden trees, therefore, suggest a kind of happiness congruent with what we know of happiness here on earth. As we were, according to the myth, created for life in the Garden of Eden, so we are promised a life after death described in terms of similar innocence and pleasure.

Even so, one gets the impression from these theistic religions that the ideal joy in heaven is not the pleasures themselves. As noted in Chapter 6, the last of the Christian scriptures describes the glory of heaven not merely in terms of personal pleasures, but more so in terms of the presence of God. But this, too, is consistent with the overall religious picture of Christianity. For Christianity—and, to a different extent, Islam—understands God to be relational, a God of love who chooses, in some sense, to dwell with humanity. "Behold," the angel cries in the Christian text, "the dwelling of God is with people." And thus the "New Jerusalem," it says, has no need of sun or moon, for the glory of God is the light of the city.[2]

Nirvana, we have already noted, is something different. In religions that are more suspicious of worldly pleasure and see the ideal human state as somehow transcending this world, a heaven of sensual delights cannot be the highest good. For early Buddhism and, in a different way, the other gnostic traditions of India, such as Jainism and Upanishadic Hinduism, the ideal state of being for humankind is a state of consciousness that harbors no desires, exhibiting instead a kind of absolute quiet and clarity of mind. We noted in Chapter 10 that the Enlightenment experience is said to be a kind of complete awakening of the mind, but not in a normal, worldly sense, like understanding a difficult math problem or seeing the solution of a murder mystery. Rather, there is a kind of insight into the true nature of reality (as in experiencing Emptiness for the Buddhist) or of ourselves (as in discovering the identity of Atman and Brahman in Hinduism), and the result is a perfect equanimity and peace of mind. This state of mind, then, and not some heavenly presence of God, is the state of human beatitude.

Neither a city nor a garden, the state of nirvana is described in early Buddhist texts like *The Questions of King Malinda* largely in metaphors and negations.[3] Vast as the ocean, the text says, and majestic as a mountain, still this quiet of mind is not an object, nor does it contain thoughts of objects or desires for objects. Like the Void itself, the ideal state of consciousness cannot be truly described in itself, but is known only through the gnostic insight of awakening. Yet for the Buddha, as for the Jain Tirthankaras, this state of consciousness is a kind of omniscience, perfect awareness of all reality. Nirvana, then, does not suggest community or worship or even pleasure; nirvana is more like being God than seeing God.

In examples like heaven and nirvana, we see important differences in the value and place of individuality, relationship, and pleasure. These values, so important in religions that focus on a Creator God who interacts with humans created "in God's image," are not only missing, but largely disdained in the Indian religions that are suspicious of rebirth in the physical world and that idealize gnostic awakening. Even so, we can see that both of these notions of beatitude focus in a sense on the individual. That is, when the Buddhist achieves nirvana, he does so alone. The awakening of the Zen student to the purity of his Buddha Nature in a way detaches him from ego and selfhood, and yet that detachment is purely his own. Even as the Buddha taught his followers to escape the trap of thinking of ego as any kind of permanent soul, he also emphasized that they had to achieve this goal all by themselves.

So heaven and nirvana, though alike in some ways as individual goals of ideal human beatitude, are importantly different in how they describe human fulfillment. They might also be importantly different insofar as nirvana may be an achievement of spiritual awakening even before death. That is, even though heaven can be described in terms analogous to earthly pleasure, the full reward of heaven does not take place in this life. For heaven to be the ideal place the monotheists suggest, it must be in another world, a world without injustice or suffering, a world remade by God after a final judgment. Nirvana, in contrast, might be a state of consciousness that can be achieved—and apparently was achieved by the Buddha—in this life. The awakened Buddhist may thus be said to enter the state of perfect equanimity and peace even before death, even if he or she is still to some extent shackled with all the impediments of birth in the realm of *samsara*.

At the same time, there is a kind of other-worldly aspect to Buddhist beatitude. The concept of *samsara*, just noted, describes the world of birth and rebirth, all the realms of existence, in fact, that are characterized by karma and suffering. Thus to find enlightenment, to achieve nirvana, is to find complete detachment from desire and thus to end suffering. It is also to end karma and thus rebirth, and so the final goal of early Buddhism, ultimately achieved when the enlightened person throws off the final shackle of bodily life, is called "Final Nirvana," or "nirvana without remainder." We can say, therefore, that the Buddha himself achieved his state of perfect calmness and clarity of mind at about age thirty-five, but when he died at age eighty he was done with *samsara* altogether. He had achieved *moksha*, or "liberation" from birth and rebirth. Given that there is no "I" in this afterlife, nor any value to ongoing experience, it is difficult to say what exactly the state of Final Nirvana is supposed to be. The Buddha himself didn't tell us; indeed, he made a point of not telling us.[4]

It should be evident in the comparison between heaven and nirvana that even ideals that seem alike in some ways are importantly different in others. We find further and even more drastic differences in religions for which the ultimate human beatitude is apparently neither otherworldly, like heaven, nor even individual, like nirvana. Confucius seems to

Figure 12.1 The Buddhist "Wheel of Life" depicts the various realms of rebirth (in the larger pie sections), as well as, in the center, three animals that represent greed, hatred, and delusion that drive reincarnation, keeping us trapped in samsara. The demon, Time, holds it all in his claws.

have thought that his ideas of virtue and ritual, if followed assiduously, would result not only in some valued personal peace, but in a kind of harmony for all society. We can recall that the generally Chinese idea of the Dao was itself this-worldly, an idea of harmony that exists in the balances of *yin* and *yang*, and in the natural harmony that exists within the common human relationships of the family. For Confucianism in particular, this latter familial harmony is achieved through virtue and ritual, such that the proper habits of human relationship develop the harmony that is somehow apparent in the Dao of Heaven. Thus it only makes sense that, if a human society could finally cultivate the virtues that Confucius taught, the harmony of society would be a perfect mirror reflecting of the harmony of the Dao. As a consequence, peace and order, prosperity and happiness would follow, not as the result of some judgment in the afterlife, but as the result of good living here in the world. And though there is here an individual achievement, the ideal of "The Gentleman," whose deeply habitual virtue and understanding of the true nature of things makes him whole and peaceful in himself, the final ideal is a social harmony, a nation with a virtuous king and virtuous subjects, where crime is unknown and natural disasters averted.

We might be surprised to find that a similar kind of group-oriented, this-worldly beatitude is also apparent in some forms of Judaism. Given that both Christianity and Islam focus so heavily on an individual, other-worldly heaven, we might expect their mother religion to have the same kind of ideal. In fact, in some teachings of Judaism, one does find some focus on "the world to come," but religious Jews are divided about what this means. We might note in the Christian New Testament that even at the time of Saint Paul the Jewish council was divided over whether or not there was a life after death.[5] Still today, one may find Jews who accept the idea of a resurrection and a Judgment Day, but one also finds many for whom "the world to come" refers more to a rebuilding of this world according to the laws and commandments of God. And if we go all the way back to the founding of Judaism, we find that the patriarch Abraham, when called to follow and obey God, was not promised heaven. Rather, he was promised a large family, prosperity, and a land to call his own.

In all these examples, we should see that it is simply not true that religions generally promise some afterlife as reward for faith or moral goodness. There are significant differences in the kind of ideal achievement that the religions of the world envision, and we shall see in the next section that there is also significant difference in exactly what one must do to achieve it. For now we need only recall the differences between individual and more group-focused ideals, some of which seem to be promises about what happens after death and some that seem very this-worldly. Some images seem to retain a strong sense of individual identity and relationship, even using sensual imagery of a blissful heaven, while others disdain identity, relationship, and sensuality and promise instead a kind of peaceful detachment. We have seen that the former is consistent with a religion like Islam or Christianity, while the latter is more at home with Buddhism. These connections, we hope, again help us to see the coherence of religious systems and to understand the various images of what accounts for humanity's ultimate hope.

"WHAT MUST I DO TO BE SAVED?"

It seems that many people who look and perhaps hope for some unity of religions think that all religions basically promise that "If you're good, you go to heaven when you die." We have already seen, however, that not all religions promise heaven as the ideal state of human beatitude, nor do they all seem to emphasize the achievement of this state after death. The same variety applies to the first half of the sentence, the part that expresses essentially how one achieves the ultimate state of beatitude. There are indeed religious ways of life that promise afterlife happiness based on moral deeds, but this view is actually relatively rare. Indeed, we might find that it does not really exist where we most expect it.

Even so, we can first look at this idea of "being good" as a means of achieving the ideal religious state of being. It is evident in such an idea that there is an expected connection between the active, especially moral dimension of religion and this final achievement of beatitude. We noted in Part II of this text, however, that the moral and the ritual dimensions of religion are sometimes not easily distinguished, so we might find here that "being good" will include more than just general moral goodness; it may also include active participation in important religious rituals. In Islam, for example, there is a strong emphasis on moral goodness as obedience "to Allah and to His messenger," but we noted in Chapter 8 that there is a difference between, say, giving money to the poor because one might care for others' suffering and giving money to the poor because it is commanded by God. Both might be good actions, but only the latter is submission to Allah, and, as the name of the religion indicates, being good is not only about conforming to some set of deeds but also about having the right attitude of submission to God. And we can note that doing the daily prayers is, along with giving charity, another of the famous "Five Pillars" of Islam, and as such it is also part of what it means to be good so that one goes to heaven. Consequently, the generous atheist is not in the same category of "good" as is the generous Muslim, and if we think we can judge otherwise, we perhaps fail to recognize the sovereignty of Allah who is, after all, the final judge.

In some ways, it should be evident that salvation based on "doing good" seems to fit best with a concept of Ultimate Being that involves God as a moral law-giver. We shall see later, however, that there are religious views that do focus on God in this way, but which do not suggest that one gets to heaven through good moral action. On the other hand, we will also find that there are religious views in which the ideal state is achieved through moral work, and yet they do not focus on a law-giving God. Confucianism is such a case. We have already noted that the ideal state of being for Confucius was not some heaven in the afterlife but an orderly and prosperous society made up of virtuous individuals in this life. Recall that the concept of the Dao in China was, for Confucians, a kind of moral social order (not so, however, for Daoists), and so we again find that there is a consistency between the religion's idea of Ultimate Being and the focus on moral virtue as the means of achieving the highest good. That is, for Confucianism human beings achieve the ideal state—individually as the Gentleman and collectively as a harmonious society—by, in a sense, enacting the Dao here in the world. As Confucius said, "Man can enlarge Dao, but Dao cannot enlarge Man,"[6] suggesting that the great order of being waits, so to speak, on human beings to make it real. Thus, for the ideal harmony of the Dao in this world to be realized, *we* must do it, and that "doing" is the hard work of moral self-cultivation.

If, however, we were to think that all religions emphasize morality and virtue—whether as obedience to God or as conformity to the ideal nature of Dao—as the means of realizing human perfection, we have only to reconsider the concept of nirvana for a counter-example. We noted back in Chapter 6 that the fundamental problem of humanity for the Buddha is suffering, and that suffering is caused by desire. But even farther back in the causal line is the root problem: ignorance. For if we fail to understand impermanence, what later Buddhists emphasize as the emptiness of things, the Void, we are doomed to attach value and desirability to the illusions of things around us and self within us. Thus, as ignorance is our fundamental problem, the solution is not virtue and moral goodness, but wisdom and insight. This is salvation, not by good deeds, but by gnosis.

As with Buddhism, we find in the mystical, philosophical schools of Hinduism an emphasis on awakening as the means of liberation (*moksha*). Trapped in the cycle of rebirth due to our "nescience" (or ignorance), according to the Vedantic philosopher

Sankara, the solution to our problem is the realization that our souls, the Atman, are in fact identical to the great substance of all existence, the Ultimate Being of Brahman. Sankara, in fact, is explicit in noting that deeds, whether acts of ritual or moral observance, cannot be an effective means of finding *moksha*, because moral actions are necessarily part of the world that is the illusion distracting us from the greater reality.[7] Thus moral and ritual actions are not only unhelpful, they are a distraction from the real goal of seeking our unity with Brahman.

This is not to say that moral action is irrelevant in the Hindu philosophy of Sankara. As Mayeda points out, moral cultivation is presumed by Sankara as a necessary preparation for the kind of mental discipline and meditation practices that ultimately lead to enlightenment. Similarly, we find in the Buddha's Eightfold path, the disciplined system of actions and meditation he prescribes for finally achieving the liberating insight, elements of moral self-control that include "right action" and "right speech." We noted this teleological role of religious morality back in Chapter 8, and it is useful here to restate it. Yet it is clear that enlightenment, not good deeds as such, is what finally liberates one from rebirth. It is good to be able to hold oneself back from the desire to steal a cell phone, but it is ultimately the realization that the cell phone is nothing but a collection of "empty" parts that finally liberates one from desire itself.

Besides the idea that one achieves heaven through moral effort or that one achieves nirvana through enlightenment, some religions suggest that one cannot achieve the ideal state of being at all. That is, some religions emphasize that one must receive salvation as a gift of God's grace and forgiveness. This is especially evident in Christianity. Early in Christian thought, Saint Paul very explicitly argues that no one can be righteous before a perfect God by virtue of some list of moral good deeds. Also, somewhat later in the development of Christian ideas, the Church Fathers wrestled with speculations that perhaps the role and purpose of Jesus was to be a teacher of a special wisdom (gnosis) by which one could become "Christ-like" oneself. But this "Gnostic" form of Christianity was rejected. Instead, early Christians—along with secondary founders like Saint Augustine and Martin Luther—insisted that the entire purpose and work of Jesus was to be a savior, that his death and resurrection "paid the price" of all sin, and that the door of heaven was henceforth open to anyone who would accept "salvation by **grace**."

Within the Christian religion, this idea of salvation has been philosophically elaborated rather extensively, and the emerging picture of the holiness of God, the corruption of human sin, and the "atoning sacrifice" of Jesus becomes a cohesive and well-developed system of thought. In this context, the problem for humanity is not just ignorance or some moral lapse that can be overcome with greater submission to the will of God. Instead, the separation between God and humanity is irreparable, except by the self-sacrificing work of God's own forgiving love. In other religions, a similar emphasis on "salvation by grace" can be found in much less elaborate form. In the Pure Land sect of Buddhism, for example, we find depicted the existence of a heavenly realm ruled by a compassionate Buddha, who takes people to his world if they merely call his name: Amida Butsu. In the more devotional forms of polytheistic

Figure 12.2   A statue of Amitabha (or Amida) Buddha, adorning a Pure Land temple.

Hinduism, we find again a sense that by mere devotion to, say, Krishna, one finds salvation based not on one's moral works but on Krishna's acceptance of the follower's devotion. "Whatever actions you do," Krishna tells his devotees, "do as acts of devotion to me, and you will be free from the bondage of action."[8] In these contexts, it is not at all evident that there needs to be any forgiveness of sin, but it seems clear, as in Christianity, that moral action is not the way to liberation. Rather it must be a gift from God.

It should seem evident, of course, that there can be a gift from God only where there is a "God" that can give gifts. We cannot expect grace from the Dao, from Brahman, or from the Buddhist Void. Moreover, we might expect that the most thoroughly developed theory of salvation appears in Christianity, where the doctrines of sin and redemption are linked to ideas of God as moral law-giver and righteous judge. Thus within Christianity, God is both a God of judgment and a God of love, and we see again how the various elements of religious life link themselves back to a concept of Ultimate Being.

As usual, however, we should not make these connections simplistically. We noted in Chapter 8 that there can be some danger in religions of grace in the possibility of moral antinomianism, the possibility that morality can become irrelevant and religious behavior chaotic. The Christian religion responded to this danger by insisting that morality, while it cannot save the sinner, is nonetheless vital to Christian life. "Faith without works is dead," the Apostle James wrote, and even Saint Paul, so emphatic about being saved "by grace alone," insisted that one is given salvation by Jesus so that one may then turn and live a righteous life as a "new creation."[9] We also saw how the Buddha and the Hindu philosopher Sankara would include moral training as a preparation for meditation and enlightenment, even if nirvana cannot be gained merely through moral effort. We might also note that, for a good Muslim, obedient submission to God is of course the primary call of the religion, but Allah is also "gracious and merciful," and forgiveness of one's sins is arguably necessary for us all.

Even in this complexity, however, it should be evident that mercy, like grace, requires a theistic view of Ultimate Being while, at the same time, the achievement of union with the Absolute in a more monistic religion would emphasize enlightenment as the means of liberation. We find this played out, interestingly enough, in the complexity of Hinduism itself, where famously there exist both a *jnana marga* and a *bhakti marga*, liberation through "the way of knowledge" and through "the way of devotion." And while these two *margas* or "pathways" of salvation are both Hindu, the first clearly applies mostly to the ideal of renunciation and meditation as the means of finding union with monistic Brahman; it is gnostic. The latter, in contrast, applies to the ideal of devotion and worship as the means of finding union with a god like Krishna. One can argue that these two make Hinduism itself curiously inconsistent, but we can note that each "way of salvation" has its own consistency with its own focus on Ultimate Being.

THE PROBLEM OF HELL

Perhaps before we finish this discussion of religion's "highest good," it is only fair to consider the lowest bad. Certainly the idea of hell, or a variety of terms that seem similar to that notion, exists in many religions from India and in the Judaic traditions. While many of us in the West might be familiar with images of hell suggested by Dante or, ultimately, by Islamic traditions, the images of hell associated with Buddhism throughout its centuries of development are quite vivid. The *naraka* hells of Buddhist tradition describe in detail the torments of freezing and burning that accompany those unfortunate enough to be reincarnated in these realms, and though rebirth in the hells is technically temporary, the duration of lifetimes of the sufferers is astronomically long. In Buddhist texts from Japan and China and, ultimately, the supposed words of the Buddha himself, there are realms of rebirth in which the denizens are roasted and burned, dismembered slowly by demons, or frozen so horribly that their bodies crack open so the organs, too, can freeze. And if one loses consciousness from the pain, one merely awakens later, whole and healthy, so one can start suffering again.[10]

This latter image is similar to a troubling text from the Quran in which Allah warns that those in hell are tortured by fire until their skin burns away, and then God gives them new skin so it can burn away again. The Quran, indeed, seems replete with such images of torture, images as sensual and horrible as their corresponding heavenly images are sensual and delightful. On the other end of the scale, Judaism, already rather vague about "the world to come," leaves entirely unclear the nature of the afterlife for any kind of damnation. Certainly there is imagery of a burning ground called *gehenna*, but it seems more like a cremation for dead bodies than a place of constant torture. Early Christianity, Jesus himself in fact, used a similar term, though Jesus' own description of this hell was less about fire and instead about an "outer darkness," where people "weep and gnash their teeth." It is in Jesus' parable of "Lazarus and the Rich Man" (see Luke 16:19–31) and in the apocalyptic myth of Revelation (see, e.g., Revelation 21:8) that we find the fire imagery so common in folklore.

As with the images of heaven described before, it is an open question whether we ought to take the hellish images literally. But even as a more benign "outer darkness," some might find all such ideas of damnation haunting and, ultimately, unacceptable.

Figure 12.3 Area of the Wan Saen Suk park outside Bangkok, Thailand, representing the tortures of the *naraka* hells of Buddhism.

That is, some might find such imagery, even if only imagery, more like nasty threats than religious instruction. It is difficult to see how the ten thousand years of Buddhist hell, let alone the eternal hells of Islam or Christianity, can belong to the teachings of a "compassionate Buddha" or a "gracious and merciful" God. Nonetheless, these images are there in the basic literature of these religions, and one cannot escape the difficulty of considering what they mean for the larger picture of religious life. At their best, perhaps, they are mythic encouragements toward a better religious commitment; at their worst they seem perhaps like the vengeful and cruel threats of an angry tyrant.

Perhaps for this reason, some people might prefer a kind of **religious universalism**. This term refers to the belief that ultimately all people achieve the ideal state of being, whether it be a Buddhist nirvana or a Christian heaven. Perhaps if one overlooks the thousands of years of the Buddhist hells, one might more optimistically note that, after a few thousand such lifetimes perhaps everyone learns his or her lesson and seeks enlightenment. In the Mahayana sects of Buddhism, compassionate bodhisattvas are said to be persons who delay their own entry into Final Nirvana so as to be reincarnated, lifetime after lifetime, to help others find nirvana. Thus, these enlightened beings vow that they will not enter Final Nirvana until all sentient beings are ready to enter as well.[11] Or perhaps, as some Christian universalists have argued, God must ultimately finish and perfect His creation, and this implies that finally all persons will see God's mercy and come to that mercy through Jesus, whether in this world or the next.[12]

This text is not the place to debate religious universalism, but on its face, though a hopeful idea defended in a number of different contexts, it is not an obvious position. It is, of course, possible that Allah could eventually grant unlimited mercy to all men and women, but that does not seem to be what the texts and traditions of Islam say. And even if enlightenment is a hope for all sentient beings after however many re-births, it is evident that it is not a promise for all of us in this life. Whatever future awakening and liberation await whatever rebirth, it seems clear that this liberation will not come to me, this current writer, nor probably you, this current reader.

In a different effort to justify the idea of hell, perhaps in the end, as the Christian writer C. S. Lewis has suggested, the gates of hell "are locked from the inside." That is, perhaps God gives people what they want, and if some do not want heaven and the divine presence, then they are not forced to have it. One might argue, as Lewis does, that this is a kind of divine justice, even divine love, however unpleasant its implications. Perhaps, however, hell is only a kind of purgatory, a realm of darkness and horror meant to call the sad and rebellious sinner to repentance, a repentance that is, in the infinity of eternal time, inevitable. Or perhaps all sentient beings do finally come to nirvana, although there are, as the Mahayana vow so paradoxically proclaims, no sentient beings to save. We should note, however, that all of these positions are not mutually reconcilable, nor is it obvious that any particular idea of liberation or any particular hope of universalism is truly what seems most evident in any particular religion's doctrine. Perhaps, then, as we ponder the "problem of hell," we must simply leave it as a problem. Some hope of universalism might be beautiful, but perhaps it is beyond us to declare whether it is good or true.

THE GOODNESS OF THE HIGHEST GOOD

William James, who, as we saw in Chapter 10, had important things to say about the va-rieties of religious experience, noted in his defense of faith, "The Will to Believe," that religion in general says two things. First, religion tells us that there is more to life than life, more to reality than the mundane things for which we struggle, whether for sheer survival or for excess and indulgence. And secondly, religion tells us that we are better off if we believe the first religious claim. That is, not only does religion point us beyond the world—this fact being evident from the outset of this text in the opening definitions—but religion also tells us that a proper relation to the greater, transmundane reality is ultimately good for us. We have seen in this chapter that religions seem to be telling us that this proper relation to the transmundane reality is finally the highest good, our beatitude.

This is not to say that all religions teach that the world we know here, the world of families and loneliness, of pain and sensuality, of philanthropy and war, is intrinsically evil. We have seen at various points in this text that the religions of India have a relatively suspicious view of the physical and sensual world, and we have seen that their images of the highest good are therefore relatively world-denying and the means of salvation world-renouncing. But we have also seen that the Chinese religions are relatively world-affirming, and that even the Judaic religions tell us that God created the world and made it good. Yet it is clear that the Judaic religions, perhaps especially Christianity and Islam, have their noble martyrs, men and women who have been willing literally to die to this world in hopes of a bounty and beauty beyond. And even in Confucianism, a religion so worldly that some would not call it "religion" at all, we see the Master himself making clear and forceful distinctions honoring those who seek the harmony of virtue in contrast to those who seek worldly profit, gain, or comfort.[13] As William James might say, these religions tell us that life is better if we understand that life alone is not enough.

Thus this hint of the highest good, a complete beatitude that religion seems to promise, takes us back to Chapter 6 and the Problem of Evil, as we begin to suspect that there is some dissatisfaction with the world and with merely worldly success. Perhaps it suggests that there indeed ought to be some level of dissatisfaction with ourselves. Perhaps the religious promise of beatitude takes us back to Chapter 8 and the possibility of finding motivation for morality that goes beyond our interests in the world and the apparent injustices that might tempt us to give up principle and virtue for gain and profit. Perhaps the religious hope for some final and perfect fulfillment reminds us of Chapter 10 and the possibility that small foretastes of beatitude can be found here in this life in the tastes and scents of religious experiences. But in the end, this promise and hope of the *summum bonum* might point us back to Chapter 2 and some description of Ultimate Being, for it is the connection to that ultimacy that seems to be the foundation of the promises of religion. Indeed, as we've seen, all the chapters of this book have been pointing back to that center, and when we study the various religions' notions of salvation, we are looking at one more element in the grand nexus of the religious phenomenon.

KEY TERMS IN CHAPTER 12

beatitude   Happiness, or even blessedness, though not as a temporary mood, but as a sense of complete fulfillment, a final and total wholeness of existence, a completeness of who we are.

bhakti marga   In Hinduism, the "way of devotion," a means of salvation through one's devoted relationship to a personal god.

grace (salvation by)   The idea of receiving salvation as a gift of divine love.

jnana marga   In Hinduism, the "way of knowledge," a means of salvation through gnostic realization of one's identity with Brahman.

moksha   Literally, "liberation"; the idea in religions of India of a salvation described as an escape from rebirth in samsara.

religious universalism   The belief that ultimately all people achieve the ideal state of being.

samsara   In religious traditions of India, the realms of life and rebirth, thus all the realms of possible reincarnation, ultimately viewed negatively as the world to be denied and escaped.

summum bonum   Literally, "the highest good," a term used generally as synonymous with beatitude.

EPILOGUE TO PART III:
The Promise and the Problems of Religious Beauty

The promise of religious beauty lies perhaps in a general idea of salvation. If by that term we can imagine a very broad sense of ultimate beatitude, it seems that religions all over the world hold out for us some promise of fullness and completeness, an experience, perhaps, of being all that we are meant to be. Yet we have seen that religions promise very different images of this "highest good," and it just does not seem possible that somehow a heaven of wine and houris can be the same ideal as a dispassionate and impersonal nirvana. And worse, the religions of the world cannot agree on how this ideal state is achieved, such that the hope for universalism, believing all religions give us a God that rewards moral goodness or an enlightened nirvana at the end of meditative practice, just cannot be assumed. The dream that perhaps in some grand culmination of all reality there is a complete and final harmony of all being cannot help but be thwarted by specific religious doctrines that must either contradict the dream or be declared false.

Yet all this is perhaps too dogmatic. I have organized this text to consider doctrine, practice, and, finally, experience, and we have seen since the end of Part I that doctrine, as such, has the tendency to create conflicts of logic. If we think about the ideas of nirvana and heaven, and if we think about salvation by good deeds, by gnosis, and by grace, we cannot help but find cognitive conflicts. But that is if we insist on thinking. Perhaps the solution to all the division and exclusiveness of religion is to escape our attachment to ideas and simply to let experience be experience. After all, we don't need to dispute about whether chocolate ice cream is really better than vanilla; we can just let each person enjoy the flavor he or she wants.

The promise of a kind of religious pluralism focused on the variety and indisputability of religious experience might seem quite hopeful. Indeed, we found in Chapter 10 that some scholars refer to mystical experiences in particular as a way to see all religions coming together, not in their doctrines but in the possibility of feelings that transcend language. Ramakrishna, the important Hindu mystic of the nineteenth century, declared that he had seen the unity of religions inasmuch as he had had visions, not only of Kali and other native Hindu deities, but of Jesus and Muhammad.[14] And even more scholarly approaches, like that of Raimundo Panikkar, have suggested that the experience of wholeness and completeness—our very general sense, perhaps, of *summum bonum*—brings religions together and makes the disputes of doctrine irrelevant.[15]

continued . . .

continued . . .

The problem with all this hopefulness, perhaps, is that we have seen how even re-ligious experiences must be understood in their contexts, and that we cannot easily declare that somehow the *satori* experience of the Zen student is like a Christian being "born again," except perhaps in the most abstract sense. We saw that, in fact, even in the more experientially focused traditions of Zen, there is a kind of orthopathos, a way in which religious experience, too, must have a kind of regularity and rightness, im-plying that it is possible to have the wrong kind of experience. Experiences therefore do not exist in a religious vacuum; they are parts of the larger wholes that are the various, more-or-less cohesive phenomena we call religions.

Thus the corollary problem with a kind of religious pluralism rooted in "beauty" is that it seeks to separate the elements of religion and suggests we can somehow have experiences without doctrine or practice. We might hope, of course, that even if beauty, truth, and goodness are indeed interwoven, somehow the beauty element could be predominant, and what people share in the realm of religious experience can somehow override what divides them in the realm of belief or practice. Perhaps we can say that, as long as people of different religions share, in some sense, a feeling of peace or awakening, they can let their doctrinal disputes rest on the sidelines, like a sports team rivalry between friends who enjoy the same game.

But we saw at the end of Part II a similar hope in the desire to emphasize ortho-praxis over orthodoxy, only to find that, in some way, even an emphasis on praxis over doctrine has to presume some kind of cognitive criteria for judging the right kind of moral ideals that are shared. Similarly, an effort to find unity in religious experience because all feel peace or all feel a transcendence of ego apparently still has to insist that peace and transcendence are somehow more right or general than feelings of moral guilt or the terror the prophets felt in the presence of the Almighty.

So we seem stuck on the problem that not all religions can be true. Can they all be good? We saw at the end of Part II that the answer might be yes, but only if we defend some claim—a truth claim—about what is truly good. Here we ask: Can all religions be beautiful, and again we might answer "yes," but only if we are willing to risk state-ments about what religious experiences are, what they mean, and how they are achieved. Indeed, we see in the discussion of salvation that there are not only truth claims about the highest good, but also important discussions about the means, or the practices of how the ideal experience is achieved. Thus it might be argued that ortho-pathos depends on both orthodoxy and orthopraxis. As important and vital as reli-gious experience must be, it doesn't seem we can make it too prominent without ultimately ignoring the whole context in which we have these experiences.

Interestingly, this complex interweaving of beauty, truth, and goodness might even show us where challenges to religion often fall short. People who might dislike the exclusiveness of some salvation idea could, perhaps, insist that anyone who "is sincere" or who "is a good person" should be accepted into heaven. How unjust, they might say, if God excludes a good person just because he or she doesn't believe. But such an argument can't really be developed without significant assumptions about moral goodness and justice, not to mention ideas of God and heaven. Even when we criticize religion, we make philosophical and moral assumptions.

But let us risk saying, here at the end of this study, that this inevitability of assumptions is not a bad thing. If we, in some way, simply do and must consider truth claims, moral claims, and experiential feelings in a kind of hierarchical unity, then let us do so carefully and thoughtfully, recognizing our assumptions and being willing to rethink them. But we must also be willing to act according to our ideas, and we must, somehow, be open to the feelings, pleasant or unpleasant, that might follow. We can look back on religion in a somewhat holistic fashion, daunted perhaps by the complexity of the religious phenomenon, but not therefore driven to uncritical silence. ☀

EPILOGUE:
RELIGION AS TRINITY

As an epilogue to this entire study, it might seem unnecessary to reiterate the complexity of religion in the three-fold division of Beauty, Truth, and Goodness. This has, after all, been a theme of this text since the middle of Part I. But here I have risked using the term "trinity." This term, clearly a Christian notion, is chosen purposefully to emphasize tri-unity, three-ness that is also oneness. For the separateness of these three general elements is ultimately meant to be a single phenomenon, a unity of life. Sometimes it seems people speak of their own religions in ways that avoid the term "religion" itself, preferring perhaps to call it "a way of life." But we might conclude here that this is simply true of all religions. Taken in their entirety, no religion is merely a religion, as if the word only refers to its rituals, or some isolated and unproductive belief. Religion is always a way of life, one could argue, because it always implies beliefs, behaviors, and feelings interwoven into a single way, a way of life.

Even so, we have seen unavoidably that religions are different. They cannot be easily reconciled logically, as we have noted, but it is also true that they cannot be easily reconciled in practice or even experiences apart from the logic of their beliefs. Perhaps there is a kind of inevitability of disagreement among religions, and we cannot find a simple unity, whatever the absorptive Hindu or the all-inclusive Baha'i religions might say. That is, even if one desires, however open-mindedly, to add Jesus or Allah to the pantheon of Hindu gods, one cannot do so without violating what Christians and Muslims believe. One cannot make Baha'u'llah the prophet of an all-inclusive religion like Baha'ism without denying that Muhammad is the last prophet.

At the same time, neither can we somehow ignore the differences between religions simply by avoiding commitment. That is, one might be tempted to hope for a kind of peace among religions by simply refusing to choose any religious way of life. But this strategy, too, it seems, ultimately denies a significant part of what religion contains, namely the absolute finality of Ultimate Being, on one end, and the promise of a kind of final fullness and completion on the other. There is a kind of seriousness about the religious ways of life that we can't ignore, even in our pursuit of somehow trying to be open-minded. Unfortunately, an open mind will have to consider even the necessity of the kind of religious commitment that demands exclusivity. To refuse to consider commitment to a religion that contains religious exclusivity is, ironically, not to be open-minded. Or it is, just as ironically, a kind of commitment of its own.

But perhaps all this means that we need to stand before the religious phenomena of the world with a kind of fear and trembling that is nonetheless kind of glorious. After all, if we take seriously the struggle to understand religious beliefs, the labor of trying to be as good in our actions as religion directs, and the possibility of the beauty of religious experiences, we are treating both religion and ourselves with the kind of seriousness we deserve. We may think and choose and feel in dramatic ways that, it seems, no other animal on earth can do. And we might even find it possible to unite these three into one way of life, to find that the fullness of religious experience after all includes the value of logic and belief and the significance of our moral, ritual, and social actions. The three are one, and the one is three, even as we ourselves, individuals in the loneliness of an isolated consciousness, are the trinitarian whole of thought, will, and feeling. Religion, then, is us: a kind of fascinating labor and a glorious possibility.

GLOSSARY

Adi Granth The primary holy text of Sikhism, being the poetry of the founder Guru Nanak and successive leaders. It is ultimately itself considered the holy guru.

ahimsa The ideal moral notion of non-violence, especially derived from Jainism and the belief that all living things have an inviolable soul.

Analects The sayings of Confucius, collected to become one of the "Four Books" taken as scripture in Confucianism.

analogical description The effort to describe Ultimate Being in human terms, acknowledging that divine qualities are only like, not equivalent to, human descriptions.

anatman In Buddhist teaching, the claim that there is "no self," denying the Hindu concept of Atman and insisting instead that the self is nothing more than a temporary collection of parts.

aniconic The characteristic of having no images (icons), or rejecting the use of images.

animism Belief in spirits that inhabit nature and interact with people.

anthropomorphic The quality of being like a human, in human shape, thus a potential criticism of theism for having God/gods that seem only like magnified human beings.

antinomianism Literally "against the rules," suggesting a philosophical or religious view that may justify breaking or disregarding common morality.

Atman In Hinduism, the Self, eternal and unchanging essence of the individual, yet different from the finite and limited empirical self. Ultimately, Atman is the same essence as Brahman, the eternal and impersonal Ultimate Being.

avatar The "descending" of a god, especially Vishnu in Hinduism, into physical form.

beatitude Happiness, or even blessedness, though not as a temporary mood but as a sense of complete fulfillment, a final and total wholeness of existence, a completeness of who we are.

bhakti marga In Hinduism, the "way of devotion," a means of salvation through one's devoted relationship to a personal god.

bodhisattva In Buddhism, an enlightened person, still living in this or other worlds, who serves as a teacher and savior figure.

Buddha Nature In some forms of Mahayana Buddhism, the innately pure, enlightened mind or "true self" of all persons, even all things.

caliph In Islam, literally a "successor" to the political authority of Muhammad.

calligraphy Literally "beautiful writing," thus the art of making letters (as in the Quran) or glyphs (as in Chinese) especially decorative or elaborate.

canon A group of writings, especially scriptures, that form a limited and defined group, thus amounting to a list of a religion's authoritative texts.

caste Hindu class structure; organization of levels of religious and social privilege based on birth family, or, religiously, on reincarnation determined by past karma.

closed canon The sense within a religion that the list of authoritative texts, the scriptures, cannot be added to, in contrast to an "open canon" where some possibility of adding new scriptures exists.

commemorative ritual The ritual "remembering" of a religiously significant event, thus the celebration or re-enactment of a legendary or historical event deemed central to a religion.

commissioning experience A supernatural encounter that calls a person to special service to God.

Dao In China, the "Way," the final pattern and order of nature as exemplified (for Confucians) in human relationships like father to son, subject to ruler, or exemplified (for Daoists) by nature itself in the balance of night and day, male and female.

Daodejing The foundational text of Daoism, Daoist scriptures, attributed to the sage Laozi.

deontology A conception of morality primarily in terms of rules, so that the rules as such carry authority, in contrast to stressing the value of the end or result of the action.

dhimmi In Islam, the traditional distinction of non-Muslim people, especially Christians and Jews, under the "protection" of an Islamic state.

ecstatic (religious experience) Literally, to "stand outside oneself"; having an experience of absorption in a sacred power outside oneself.

effective ritual Religious rituals performed in the hopes that the actions actually change reality and do so with a kind of supernatural power.

elements (of religion) The various specifiable contents of religion in general.

empirical self The "I" that one hears in one's thoughts; the person that one recognizes oneself to be through reflection on one's character and beliefs.

enstatic (religious experience) Literally, to "stand inside oneself," having an experience of absorption in a deeper experience inside oneself, absorbed perhaps in one's own contemplations.

epistemology (of religious experience) Generally, an analysis of the relation between experience and truth claims. In religion, the concern may be with the relation between religious experience and claims about Ultimate Being, generally whether religious experiences yield any information about the truth of religious beliefs.

epistle Literally "letter." Particularly in Christianity, one of the letters of the New Testament scriptures written by those "sent" by Jesus to spread His teaching.

exegesis Literally "to draw out," referring to the process of deriving doctrine and truth claims from a religion's authoritative writings.

fallenness From the Christian interpretation of the myth of Adam and Eve, the claim that the perfectly created state of humanity in the Garden of Eden was lost due to human disobedience, and that this sinfulness still corrupts the human will.

Four Noble Truths Fundamental Buddhist teaching about the inevitability of suffering and its ultimate causes in our own desires for the temporary, unsatisfying things of the world.

functional equivalents of religion Ways of life that function for people like a religion function, but which are not religions.

functions (of religion) Specifications of what religions do, the effects they have in human life.

gentile Literally "nations"; the term within Judaism for anyone not born into the people of Israel, thus not ethnically Jewish.

gnostic Relating to a special kind of insight gained through religious experience.

grace (salvation by) The idea of receiving salvation as a gift of divine love.

Hadith A collection of written "traditions" that functions as a secondary scripture in Islam. It contains the words and actions of Muhammad, providing for Islam example and context for understanding proper submission to God.

heretic One who teaches false and pernicious ideas within an established religion, apparently violating that religion's orthodoxy.

hermeneutics The art of interpretation, often involving explicit theories and methods for deriving meaning from a text.

ignorance Specifically in Indian Hindu and Buddhist philosophies, the understanding that an innate purity of self or mind is nonetheless clouded by humanity's tendency to identify with the ego and thus our inability to see and live out the ideal of the deeper self.

Imago Dei Literally the "image of God"; the idea from Judaic creation myth that the human soul, with reason and responsibility, somehow reflects the individual and conscious nature of God Himself.

immanent A description of Ultimate Being emphasizing its quality as being within the world, perhaps diffused into all things or directly active in nature.

incarnation Literally "to enter into flesh," thus the idea that the Ultimate Being may become a human being and reveal Himself or Itself to humanity.

jnana marga In Hinduism, the "way of knowledge," a means of salvation through gnostic realization of one's identity with Brahman.

Just War Theory In Western philosophy, the systematic effort to consider how war should be waged, what are its limits, and what are its proper motivations.

kami A god of Shinto, the native religion of Japan.

karma Literally "action"; the concept that actions done previously in life and, especially, in prior lifetimes, have consequences in later lifetimes, thus explaining suffering and good fortune as the effects of prior acts.

laity The people of a religion who do not take on any role of religious professional, and yet definitely count themselves as full participants in the traditions. Also *layman, laywoman,* and *laypersons.*

lama In Tibetan Buddhism, a teacher and leader, sometimes both with spiritual and secular authority, taken to be a reincarnation of earlier generations of spiritual teachers.

Laws of Manu A Hindu text that reasserts the value of participation in social life by clarifying the duties of persons according to class and gender.

liturgy A relatively formal and structured system of prayers and songs and readings performed in religious ritual, especially worship ritual.

mana Polynesian monistic concept of Ultimate Being, taken to be a pervasive natural force that exists in nature and in powerful persons.

mandala In Tibetan Buddhism, a detailed and colorful representation of, for example, the dwelling of an enlightened being. The artwork itself is meticulously and meditatively produced and then destroyed.

Mandate of Heaven In Confucian thought, the idea that a king has the authority to rule because of his virtue and wisdom, guiding the entire nation into harmony with the Way.

mimetic ritual   Religious ritual that accomplishes its purpose by intentionally imitating some other event, either as desired in the world (e.g., mimetic hunting rituals) or as understood from myth (e.g., creation re-enactment).

Mishnah   The collection of laws from the Torah as understood and explained by the Jewish Rabbis of the first centuries of the Common Era.

moksha   Literally "liberation," the idea in religions of India of a salvation described as an escape from rebirth in samsara.

monism   Belief in an ultimate reality that is single and unique, a final single substance of being or existence, but not personified or relational.

monotheism   Belief in one God.

mysticism, or mystical experience   A powerful religious experience in many faiths that is described as a deep absorption into the Ultimate and a corresponding loss of identity. Generally, a deep sense of "oneness" with Ultimate Being.

myth   A story culturally or religiously used to define the nature of life or of a group of people; the story may be of literally cosmic proportions, telling us something about the origins or meaning of humanity or the world or some specific cultural phenomenon.

Nanak (1469–1539)   The founder of the Sikh religion.

negative theology   The effort to describe Ultimate Being not in terms of what it is but in terms of what it is not, thus in contrast to the finite and worldly.

obligatoriness (of morality)   A kind of force that morality has, such that moral statements are not merely suggestions but have the feel of a demand.

orthodoxy   Literally "straight doctrine," thus some body of ideas or beliefs that function as a standard for what does and does not fit into a particular religion.

orthopathos   Literally "straight feelings," the suggestion that even subjective religious experiences will display a certain consistency with claims of religious truth and directions for religious practice.

orthopraxis   Literally "straight practice," thus a set of prescribed specific practices that are required and proper, defining what does and does not fit into a specific religion.

pantheism   A monistic view of Ultimate Being that places "God" within the substance of nature, rather than as a distinct, relational being.

parable   A story invented to illustrate a moral or ideological point, thus stories not intended to be understood as history.

Perennial Philosophy   An interpretation of religion that views all religions as fundamentally built on the same mystical experience of oneness with higher reality.

performative art   Those artistic practices that are active, like dance or drama.

petitionary prayer   Ritual speech to God or gods that make requests for blessing or protection, etc., acknowledging the prayer's dependence upon Ultimate Being to answer.

phenomenology (as a study of religion)   An approach to studying religion that intentionally avoids discussions of which religion might be true or valuable and, instead, attempts to pursue simply a description of what the phenomenon is.

polytheism   Belief in multiple gods.

proof text   Selected pieces of scripture used to defend a particular doctrinal point.

prophet A man or a woman who hears, in some sense, what God would have people know and then speaks forth the message of God to humanity.

puja In Hinduism, the ritual actions of worship directed at images of various gods.

Quran The scriptures of Islam, literally the "recitation" of God's words to Muhammad.

Ramayana Scripture of popular Hinduism featuring the epic tale of the god Rama.

reductionism The definition or study of a relatively complex concept (like religion) that reduces it to some simpler or secondary quality (such as religion's social functions).

religion (this text's proposed definition) A complex set of beliefs, behaviors, and experiences rooted in some notion of trans-mundane reality thought of as Ultimate Being.

religious experience Feelings, emotions, and the more affective and aesthetic experiences one has particularly in connection with some supernatural reality.

religious universalism The belief that ultimately all people achieve the ideal state of being.

renunciation The religious ideal of leaving the common world of relationships and possession, thus refusing to participate in common duties of social life.

rishis Literally "seers"; in ancient Hinduism, the men and, possibly, women who heard from the gods, or discovered in their own ecstatic states of consciousness the hymns that became the Vedas, the earliest scriptures of Hinduism.

rites of passage Rituals that mark and sanctify changes in the stages of one's life, such as rituals performed at birth or puberty or death.

ritual Any kind of formal, regularized behavior that is performed in accordance with specific occasions or conditions.

sacrament Especially in Christianity, a set of rituals rooted in the authority of Jesus and taken to be especially effective.

sage A human being who has some kind of uncommon insight that reveals to others something of the nature of Ultimate Being.

salat In Islam, the regular, structured prayers that include scriptural declarations and prostration, in order to physically enact submission to God.

samsara In religious traditions of India, the realms of life and rebirth, thus all the realms of possible reincarnation, ultimately viewed negatively as the world to be denied and escaped.

satori In Japanese Zen Buddhism, the sudden, breakthrough experience of enlightenment.

scripture "Holy text," the writings within a religion that carry a special status of authority, often based on the direct relation between the recorded words and the founder, thus finally to Ultimate Being.

seasonal ritual Religious rituals associated with annual seasonal cycles, thus with planting or harvesting or solar cycles.

secondary founders Men and women who do not found a new religion, but who are instrumental in following the teachings of an original religion and developing new or renewed teachings within that religion.

social order The organization of people in a society according to various ranks and privileges.

subjectivity (of religious experience) Experiences characterized as events in a person's inner life rather than in the observable world, i.e., in contrast to objectivity.

summum bonum   Literally "the highest good," a term used generally as synonymous with beatitude.

sutra   A sermon or teaching, especially by the Buddha, remembered and collected by generations of monks who compiled the earliest Buddhist scriptures.

Talmud   In Judaism, the multiple-volume collection of Mishnah and commentary, amounting to a secondary authority for studying divine law as revealed in the Torah. Also called the Oral Torah.

teleology   A conception of morality that primarily justifies moral claims in terms of what they accomplish, the value of the achieved ends.

theism   Generally the belief in God or gods, transmundane power that is personal or personified.

theodicy   Specifically trying to explain suffering in terms of divine justice; more generally, any effort to explain how the apparent injustices of human suffering occur, and why the world is not as perfect as it should be.

too broad   The nature of a definition of "religion" that is so general, specifying so little content, that it includes human behaviors that are not religion.

too narrow   The nature of a definition of "religion" that specifies too much content and so omits some religions.

Torah   The holy scriptures of Judaism attributed to Moses, collected as the first five books of the Bible.

transcendent   A description of Ultimate Being emphasizing its quality as being outside and beyond the world.

transformative ritual   Religious rituals whose effects are primarily on the person performing the ritual, in some way changing that person's spiritual state.

transmundane   Having the quality of being beyond the normal world.

trickster   In some native traditions, a mythic person or animal that, through foolishness or ignorance, brings about problems for humanity.

ultimacy   The quality of a transmundane being suggesting finality, a greatness or power or existence that is the last and final thing that creates or makes sense of everything else.

Veda   The oldest scriptural texts of Hinduism, evolving from approximately 1200 BCE through forms of hymns to ancient gods, ritual formulae, and magical mantras.

virtue theory   A focus of moral thinking on character traits and the cultivation of behavioral habits, rather than on moral rules or achieved ends.

Void/Emptiness   A Buddhist notion of the ultimate reality, arguably a monistic concept considered as the true nature of all things, expressing the interdependence of all things.

wisdom literature   Short statements and aphorisms collected like wise old sayings to give advice or teaching, such as "Proverbs" of the Bible or the sayings from Confucius' Analects.

worship   The ritual act of declaring or acknowledging the greatness, or "worth," of the Ultimate Being in itself, thus like praise or veneration.

wu-wei   Literally "non-action"; in Daoism, the virtue of wise and willing acceptance of things as they are and non-resistance to change.

zakat   In Islam, the moral requirement to give 2.5 percent of one's wealth to the poor; charity or alms-giving that acts to "purify" (the literal meaning of *zakat*) the rest of one's wealth.

NOTES

Chapter 1

1. See Tisa Wenger, *We Have a Religion: The 1920s Pueblo Dance Controversy and American Religious Freedom* (Chapel Hill: University of North Carolina Press, 2009).
2. Sigmund Freud, *The Future of an Illusion*. See the reference and discussion in Daniel Pals, *Seven Theories of Religion* (Oxford: Oxford University Press, 1996), Chapter 2.
3. See Pals, Chapter 4.

Chapter 2

1. See Huston Smith, *Why Religion Matters* (San Francisco: Harper Collins, 2001), 4ff.
2. See Richter et al., *Understanding Religion in a Global Society* (Belmont: Wadsworth/Cengage 2005), 69–71.
3. "Theomorphic" means to be in the form of God. The more common Christian/Judaic phrase comes from the creation myth in which humans are said to be made "in the image of God." For a useful summary of the "image of God" discussion in Christianity, see http://www.religionfacts.com/christianity/beliefs/imago_dei.htm.
4. For a collection of some of Aquinas' ideas on analogical descriptions of God, see Mary T. Warren, *An Aquinas Reader* (New York: Fordham University Press, 2000), 89–93.
5. *Daodejing*, Chapter 37; see also Chapter 34.
6. For a general discussion and some mention of these writers, see the article "Pantheism," in *The Encyclopedia of Philosophy*, Vol. 6 (New York: Macmillan Publishing, 1967), 32–35.

Chapter 3

1. Confucius said, "I transmit, I invent nothing. I trust and love the past" (Analects 7:1).
2. Information on any of these divine persons can be found with a simple Internet search. For example, information about Swami Narayan can be found at official websites of the religion's current sects, such as www.swaminarayan.org and www.baps.org.
3. For the exalted but not incarnational view of Jesus in Islam, see Tarif Khalidi, *The Muslim Jesus* (Cambridge: Harvard University Press, 2001); for the Judaic view, see Peter Schaefer, *Jesus in the Talmud* (Princeton: Princeton University Press, 2007).

Chapter 4

1. "Sri Guru Granth Sahib." *Official Website of Shiromani Gurdwara Parbandhak Committee, Sri Amritsar*. Web. Accessed February 1, 2016. http://sgpc.net/sri-guru-granth-sahib/.

2. Richman, Paula, *Many Ramayanas: Diversity of a Narrative Tradition in South Asia* (Berkeley: University of California Press, 1991).

3. Shree Swaminarayan Temple Bhuj. *Vachanamrut.* Web. Accessed February 1, 2016. http://www.bhujmandir.org/datastore/library/scriptures/pdf/Vachanamrut/Vachnamrut %20English.pdf.

4. It is, however, possible that a new authoritative text, a new scripture, can appear within a religion that essentially has a closed canon. If this occurs, there must almost inevitably be a struggle, it seems, and a great debate about whether the appearance of this new text ultimately makes the new sect "heretical." This is precisely the case with the relation between Mormonism and Christianity.

Chapter 5

1. J. R. R. Tolkien, *The Silmarillion*, 2nd ed. (New York: Houghton Mifflin Company, 2001), 46.

2. Augustine's interpretation can be found in his *The Letter of Genesis*, written between 401 and 415. See "Augustine's Commentary on the Biblical Book of Genesis." Accessed February 2, 2016. http://college.holycross.edu/faculty/alaffey/other_files/ Augustine-Genesis1.pdf

3. Taken from the D. C. Lau translation (London: Penguin Classics, 1963).

4. See the Yampolski translation of *The Platform Sutra of the Sixth Patriarch* (New York: Columbia University Press, 1967), especially Section 16.

Chapter 6

1. Read the basic myth in the Bible, Genesis chapters 1 and 2.

2. From the first question in the Westminster Shorter Catechism. See The Orthodox Presbyterian Church. "Shorter Catechism." Accessed February 3, 2016. opc.org/sc.html

3. See, e.g., the Mundaka Upanishad, 3.1 in the Frederick Manchester translation (New York: Signet Classics, 2002), 46.

4. For the fundamental presentation of the early Buddhist no-self doctrine, see the "Discourse to the First Five Disciples," in John J. Holder, *Early Buddhist Discourses* (Indianapolis: Hackett Publishing, 2006), 83–86. For a later, more cryptic use of "self," see Kazuaki Tanahashi's collection of the teachings of Zen Master Dogen, *Moon in a Dewdrop* (New York: North Point Press, 1985), e.g., 164.

5. Peter L. Berger, *The Sacred Canopy* (Garden City: Doubleday and Company, 1969), 23.

6. *Mengzi* 6A8.

7. Richard Erdoes and Alfonso Ortiz, *American Indian Myths and Legends* (New York: Pantheon Books, 1984), 470–471.

8. See Sengaku Mayeda's translation and commentary on Sankara's *A Thousand Teachings* (Albany: State University of New York Press, 1992), 76–82.

9. See Yoshito S. Hakeda (trans.), *The Awakening of Faith in the Mahayana* (New York: Columbia University Press, 1967), 50.

10. Watson, Burton. *Chuang-tzu, Basic Writings* (New York: Columbia University Press, 1996), 81.

11. For the story, see the Book of Job in the Bible's Old Testament. For its theodicy, the reader learns from the story itself that Job's suffering is really a kind of test, and in

the end God gives Job no explanation, except to emphasize that God is the ruler of all things and cannot be judged by mere humans. And Job agrees.

12. In the Quran, see Sura 56; see also 4:56.
13. Analects 11.12 and 2.5.

Chapter 7

1. See James 2:26 and Luke 6:46 (NLT).
2. Analects 11:12.
3. X, Malcolm and Alex Haley. *The Autobiography of Malcolm X* (New York: Penguin Putnam, 2001), see Chapter 17.
4. The Passover story can be found in Exodus, Chapters 11 and 12; the quoted phrase occurs in Deuteronomy 26:8 and in much ritual Passover liturgy to this day.
5. An introduction to the annual cycle of *katchina*-associated rituals can be found at Carnegie Museum of Natural History website, http://www.carnegiemnh.org/online/indians/hopi/calendar.html.
6. See Leviticus 16.
7. One can find a National Geographic video on this tribal ritual at http://video.nationalgeographic.com/video/newguinea-crocscars-pp.
8. *Bhagavad Gita* 9:26.
9. The Christian ritual recites "creeds" of various lengths. One can find these full creeds at various websites, including http://carm.org/creeds-and-confessions, by the Christian Apologetics and Research Ministry. The content of the Islamic "witness" more simply declares, "I witness that there is no God but Allah, and that Muhammad is his messenger." The "Three Jewels" of the Buddhist confession say, "I take refuge in the Buddha; I take refuge in the Dharma [the Buddha's teaching]; I take refuge in the Sangha [the community of Buddhist monks]."
10. Wing-tsit Chan, in his *A Source Book in Chinese Philosophy* (Princeton: Princeton University Press, 1967), indexes a number of key references to ritual propriety (or "ceremony") on page 18. Also, a basic textbook on world religions will have a section on *li*; see, e.g., Jeffrey Brodd et al., *Invitation to World Religions* (Oxford: Oxford University Press, 2013), 286–287.

Chapter 8

1. The great compendium of the Babylonian Talmud is available online at http://sacred-texts.com/jud/t01/index.htm. One can search various topics and read in different contexts to get a feel for the literature and some sense of its detailed content. For the bit on candle wicks, see Tract Sabbath, Chapter 2.
2. A famous discussion of the virtuous basis of human nature can be found in *Mengzi*, Book 6A; specifically on the "seeds" of virtue, see 6A6. For a good translation, see Van Norden, Bryan W. *Mengzi: With Selections from Traditional Commentaries* (Indianapolis: Hackett Publishing, 2008).
3. The allusion to putting a human face on the constantly changing Dao can also be found in *Zhuangzi*, in the amusing parable of Hun-tun. See Watson, Burton. *Chuang-tzu, Basic Writings* (New York: Columbia University Press, 1996), 95.
4. See Mayeda's notes on Sankara's philosophy in Mayeda, Sengaku. *A Thousand Teachings: The* Upadesasahasri *of Sankara.* (Albany: State University of New York Press, 1992), 93–94.

5. The "quote" is a paraphrase. For the Biblical text, see John 13:12–17.
6. See Paul's Letter to the Romans, specifically Romans 6:1.
7. See Mill's essay, "The Utility of Religion," in *Essential Works of John Stuart Mill* (New York: Bantam Books, 1965), 418f.
8. Deuteronomy 20:16–18; in the Quran, see 4:34.

Chapter 9

1. Richard Niebuhr, *Christ and Culture* (New York: Harper and Row, 1975); see the Table of Contents.
2. See the famous *purusha* myth of creation in Rig Veda x.90. See also a presentation of the history of caste designation in John Keay, *India: A History* (New York: Grove Press, 2000), 52–54.
3. Galatians 3:28 (NLT).
4. See Isaiah 60, verses 5 and 9 (ESV).
5. Max Weber, *The Protestant Ethic and the Spirit of Capitalism* (New York: Charles Scribner's Sons, 1958).
6. On the introductory page of Joel Osteen's church's website, it says his message simply is that God "desires to bless those who are obedient and faithful." See https://www .lakewoodchurch.com/pages/new-here/joel-osteen.aspx.
7. William Clebsch, *From Sacred to Profane America* (Ann Arbor: Scholars Press, 1968), 171–172.
8. *Bhagavad Gita*, 2:19.
9. See the Interfaith Youth Core website at http://www.ifyc.org/.
10. See Knitter's essay, "Toward a Liberation Theology of Religions," in *The Myth of Christian Uniqueness* (Maryknoll, NY: Orbis Books, 1987); see Chapter 11.

Chapter 10

1. Kent E. Richter, Eva M. Räpple, John C. Modschiedler, and R. Dean Peterson, *Understanding Religion in a Global Society* (Belmont: Wadsworth/Cengage, 2005), 64.
2. The Biblical story of the parting of the Red Sea can be found in Exodus 14.
3. William James, *The Varieties of Religious Experience* (New York: Mentor Books, 1958); see Lectures VI and VII.
4. For the source of the concept, see Saint John of the Cross, *Dark Night of the Soul*, e.g., the E. A. Peers translation (London: Burns and Oates, 1953).
5. Hieromonk Gregorios, *The Divine Liturgy: A Commentary in Light of the Fathers* (Columbia, MO: Newrome Press, 2012).
6. D. T. Suzuki, "The Reason of Unreason: The Koan Exercise," in William Barrett, ed., *Zen Buddhism: Selected Writings of D. T. Suzuki* (New York: Anchor Books, 1953), Chapter 6.
7. Confucius, Analects, Chapter 2.
8. See the "Introduction" to Mascaro's translation of *The Upanishads* (London: Penguin Classics, 1965).
9. See Huxley's book, *The Perennial Philosophy* (New York: Harper Collins, 2014).
10. See a brief explanation of the utterance by Al-Hallaj in Martin Lings, *What Is Sufism?* (Berkeley: University of California Press, 1977), 109–110.

11. See Bernard McGinn's "Theological Summary," in Edmund Colledge and Bernard McGinn, *Meister Eckhart* (New York: Paulist Press, 1981), 53f.
12. See Chapter 7 in Houston Smith's *Cleansing the Doors of Perception* (New York: Jeremy P. Tarcher/Putnam, 2000).
13. See Bertrand Russell's essay, "Mysticism," available online at https://scepsis.net/eng/articles/id_4.php.

Chapter 11

1. Trevor Leggett, *A First Zen Reader* (Rutland, VT: Charles E. Tuttle Company, 1960), 222–224.
2. See, e.g., the heading before Psalm 80 or Psalm 88.
3. J. Hill, *What Has Christianity Ever Done For Us?* (Downers Grove: Intervarsity Press, 2005), 42.
4. Saint Augustine, *Confessions*, X.33.

Chapter 12

1. Augustine, *Confessions*, Book I, Chapter 1.
2. See Revelation 21:3 and 22:5.
3. See section of "The Questions of King Malinda" in Edward Conze, *Buddhist Scriptures* (New York: Penguin Classics, 1959), 156–157.
4. In one early "Discourse," the Buddha was explicitly asked about the nature of Final Nirvana and whether the liberated monk continues to exist or ceases to exist. The Buddha simply declared that such questions are not helpful and refused to answer. See the *Malunkyaputta Sutta* in John Holder, *Early Buddhist Discourses* (Indianapolis: Hackett Publishing, 2006), Chapter 6.
5. See in Acts 23 the story of Saint Paul's trial before the Jewish court and the disagreement among the Jewish leaders when he spoke of life after death.
6. Analects 15.28.
7. Sengaku Mayeda interprets Sankara this way: "Action does not contradict nescience but is of the same nature. Therefore, action cannot be the means of final release." Sankara himself says, "Because of the incompatibility [of knowledge with action] a man who knows [the identity of Atman and Brahman] cannot perform action." See Mayeda, *A Thousand Teachings: The Upadesasahasri of Sankara* (Albany: SUNY Press, 1992), 85.
8. Paraphrased from *Bhagavad Gita* 9:27–28.
9. James 2:26 and 2 Corinthians 5:17.
10. A dramatic description of the burning hells can be found in the "Devadatta Sutta" in Bhikku Bodhi, *The Middle-Length Discourses of the Buddha* (Boston: Wisdom Publications, 1995), 1032–1035.
11. A classic form of the Bodhisattva vow is "Though there are innumerable sentient beings, I vow to help enlighten them all," or, as some say, the Bodhisattva will delay Final Nirvana "until the grass itself is enlightened." Even so, as suggested in the Mahayana Buddhist text called *The Diamond Sutra*, the Bodhisattva might rather say, "I vow to liberate all sentient beings, knowing there are no sentient beings to liberate." See the text in *The Diamond Sutra and The Sutra of Hui-Neng* (Boulder: Shambala Press, 1977), 64.

12. One finds this notion of the final perfection of God's creation, especially in the Eastern Orthodox churches, which appeal to the early teachings of Church Fathers like Origen and the concept of *apocatastasis*, a term that refers to the "completion of all things." See a good modern reconsideration of this idea in Hans Urs von Balthasar's book *Dare We Hope That All Men Be Saved?* (San Francisco: Ignatius Press, 1988).

13. See Analects 4:16, 4:11.

14. See the chapter "Ramakrishna's Life" in F. Max Muller, *Ramakrishna, His Life and Sayings* (1898). Accessed February 13, 2016. http://www.sacred-texts.com/hin/rls/rls14.htm

15. "The Jordan, the Tiber and the Ganges," being Chapter 6 in Hick and Knitter, *The Myth of Christian Uniqueness* (Maryknoll, NY: Orbis Books, 1987).

CREDITS

INDEX